PUSHING AT BOUNDARIES

D1136354

GERMAN MONITOR No. 64
General Editor: Ian Wallace

PUSHING AT BOUNDARIES

Edited by

Heike Bartel & Elizabeth Boa

Amsterdam - New York, NY 2006

The paper on which this book is printed meets the requirements of "ISO 9706:1994, Information and documentation - Paper for documents - Requirements for permanence".

ISBN-10: 90-420-2051-2
ISBN-13: 978-90-420-2051-1   *1005161516*
©Editions Rodopi B.V., Amsterdam - New York, NY 2006
Printed in the Netherlands

Acknowledgements

The editors and publisher wish to thank Karen Duve and Eichborn Verlag for their kind permission to publish the chapter 'Die Mummel' from *Die entführte Prinzessin*.

Most of the essays in this volume originated as papers for a symposium on the work of Karen Duve and other recent German women writers held in May 2004 at the University of Nottingham during Karen Duve's stay as DAAD writer-in-residence. The editors would like to thank the DAAD (German Academic Exchange Service) for generous financial assistance in helping to bring Karen Duve to Nottingham and the University of Nottingham for financial help to hold the symposium and prepare this volume.

We wish also to extend our warmest thanks to Karen Duve whose active participation in the symposium and in life in the Department of German Studies made her stay as writer-in-residence a memorable event. Students and staff at Nottingham as well as the contributors and everyone else who attended the symposium immensely enjoyed the discussions with her, her wit, good humour in answering questions, seeing her riding her bicycle, 'Gazelle', around campus and sharing life at university and in Willoughby Hall with her (although it wasn't quite Hogwarts).

Thanks are also due to Anthea Bell, translator of Karen Duve's work into English, who allowed us to be part of the fascinating dialogue between author and translator during the symposium.

We would also like to thank Evelyn Haase-Klein for giving us permission to use her painting, *Medea – A Stranger*, for our cover, Silke Meyer for her initiative to invite Karen Duve to Nottingham, and Manuel Alonso for his help in putting this volume together.

University of Nottingham

Heike Bartel & Elizabeth Boa

Table of Contents

Heike Bartel and Elizabeth Boa

Introduction

Pushing at Boundaries is the title we chose for this volume of approaches to contemporary German women writers which combines essays on the writings of Karen Duve with studies of works by Anne Duden, Jenny Erpenbeck, Julia Franck, Michael Fritz, Kerstin Hensel, Julia Schoch, Malin Schwerdtfeger, and Maike Wetzel, while the closing essay by Franziska Meyer leads us further on a tour through recent Berlin novels by Sibylle Berg, Tanja Dückers, Alexa Hennig von Lange, Judith Hermann, Unda Hörner, Inka Parei, Kathrin Röggla, Anke Stelling, and Antje Rávic Strubel. The many different names already indicate that, although these authors all belong in the literary landscape of the late 20th and early 21st century, their approaches and styles vary greatly. The different works push at boundaries in a multitude of ways: the subversion of gender stereotypes; the breaking with confines traditionally associated with certain literary genres; the merging of 'high' and 'low' culture; the invasion of cultivated spheres such as house and garden by 'wild' nature and the (con)fusion of town and countryside; the contamination of nature through modern industrial life; the political and geographical crossing of borders between East and West Germany after the *Wende* and Berlin as capital city and urban jungle. At the same time, the volume as a whole throws up many fascinating echoes and cross-connections, suggesting the value of comparative reading in highlighting the discursive formations and historical conditions which texts have in common as well as the different voices of individual authors and the contrasting positions they may adopt in today's heterogeneous and often conflictual culture.

The volume opens with an excerpt from Karen Duve's latest novel that will offer readers who know her earlier fictions a surprising taster of the very different manner and matter of *Die entführte Prinzessin. Von Drachen, Liebe und anderen Ungeheuern,* published in 2005. In contrast to the uncanny, subterranean humour of *Regenroman* or the realist mode of *Dies ist kein Liebeslied*, Duve's latest novel offers, as its title suggests, a highly amusing parody of romance literature in the marvelous mode. Crossing generic boundaries proves to be a key feature of many of the works considered. The opening essay by the distinguished literary translator Anthea Bell shows many paths across linguistic boundaries, offering an insight into the tribulations and pleasures of translating and a first appreciative analysis of Duve's literary gifts from someone who has engaged with the texts with the intensity peculiar to the translator. *Rain*, Bell's translation of Duve's *Regenroman*, won the annual Schlegel-Tieck award for the best translation of a book from German in 2002 and she has since translated Duve's *Dies ist kein Liebeslied*, which appeared in English in 2005 as *This is not a Lovesong*. The title is a re-translation back into English of the German title, it in turn a translation from the English of the 1983 post-punk hit by the group Public Image Limited. Such border-crossings between languages and media are emblematic of the cultural interchange which the symposium and this volume of essays aim to promote.

It is a measure of the provocative quality of Duve's work that critical opinions in five subsequent chapters in the volume – those by Peter Graves, Teresa Ludden, Elizabeth Boa, Heike Bartel, Elisa Müller-Adams, and Lucy Macnab – diverge somewhat on the relative success of Duve's novels and stories as measured against each other and on the quality of her work compared with that of other writers. Ludden offers a dissenting critical view in contrast to the other largely positive assessments: compared with Anne Duden's radical experimentation, Duve fails, so Ludden argues, to offer exploration in depth of difference and change. Macnab, by contrast, detects a rebellious potential in Duve's collection of stories, *Keine Ahnung*, which she sees as distorting the binary oppositions of gender ideology. Boa enjoys the grotesque-sinister mood of *Regenroman* as a vessel of oblique cultural criticism and highlights Duve's comic travesty of myth. Müller-Adams locates Duve's monstrous water woman and the satin-black salamander within the pervasive symbolic field of elemental spirits, which Duve's *Lexikon der berühmten Tiere* surveys. Graves finds *Regenroman* too schematic, however, seeing Duve's second novel as in the end more humanly affecting, while Bartel maps the mosaic of low and high cultural citation in *Dies ist kein Liebeslied* which draws on the icons of a consumer society in a witty critique of consumerism. The differences of view may stem in part from differing evaluations of modernist experimental writing as against post-modernist playfulness. Such a tension has long roots. German aesthetic debate has tended to treat avant-garde experiment in contrast to the productions of 'Kulturindustrie' as antithetical categories, an opposition Duve's *Dies ist kein Liebeslied* undermines, so Bartel suggests: the motif of the mixtape, as a key symbol for a multi-media age and signaling active choice rather than passive subjection, also points self-reflexively towards Duve's novel as a mixtext with its mosaic of 'high' and 'low' cultural references.

Along with essays devoted solely to texts by Duve, some compare her with other authors and other contributors explore work by various writers in the broad field of contemporary women's writing. Macnab detects good reasons for comparing the authors she has selected, Karen Duve, Julia Franck and Malin Schwerdtfeger, in the recurring motif in their work of the body and its cultural meanings in the discourse of gender. This proves to be one of the most frequently recurring motifs in several of the texts. The essays on Duve, Ludden's discussion of Anne Duden, Katie Jones on Erpenbeck's *Geschichte vom alten Kind*, and Inka Parei's *Schattenboxerin* in Meyer's contribution all look at the body as an arena in which social power relations are played out metaphorically and sometimes all too literally in depictions of the violation of (female) bodies through murder, rape and physical abuse. The transgressive undoing or parodic exaggeration of the bodily markers of femininity and masculinity, the theme of eating disorders and the physical expansion or shrinking of the human body or the becoming fluid of boundaries, physical and psychic, between self and other, figure in several of the essays. Historically women were defined through their bodies. As Macnab's essay suggests in readings informed by the theories of Judith Butler, women writers continue both to explore yet also to subvert the bodily inscription of gender norms: they disrupt the process of 'becoming woman' through images of bodily change, of 'becoming bodies' which deny fixed meaning.

Other contributors seek out texts exploring the archetypal association of femininity with water imagery that recurs in *Regenroman*. Watery women and other metaphors of fluid or porous boundaries between culture and nature, so prominent at the turn of the 19th to the 20th century, seem to be almost as omnipresent at our *Jahrhundertwende*, as witness the examples Müller-Adams cites. Along with the 'schöne (Wasser)Leiche', referred to by Boa, Ludden and Müller-Adams, one of the most intriguing water women, as Petra Bagley brings out, is the floating grandmother in the titular story of Jenny Erpenbeck's *Tand*, who floats on her back in a hand-knitted bikini, her nose appearing above the water of the lake like the tail fin of a shark. Compared with Romantic or *Jugendstil* Undines and Melusines, this ageing, somewhat frightening water woman, like the fat nymph of the marshland in *Regenroman*, adds a splash of mockery or comic parody to the tradition. Erpenbeck's grandmother confirms Müller-Adams's thesis, however, that the water nymphs – or sharks – had and have a poetological meaning in signifying the poetic text. For the body of the grandmother, whose command of literary language once dominated over her granddaughter, now provides the material of the granddaughter's writing.

The variations on the watery theme exemplify a key feature of many of the texts explored here, namely the wealth of intertextual allusion, games with genres, and exchange between different media. Bell notes the frequency of allusions to fairy tales. The ubiquitous mermaids are joined by other fairytale figures, as Lyn Marven's discussion of motifs drawn from the Grimms' *Märchen* and from Hans Christian Andersen in the work of Kerstin Hensel indicates. Marven explores the parodistic function of such motifs both in the context of gender ideology, but also in Hensel's wry satire of the GDR. Such citation is, as Bartel notes, a key aspect of contemporary post-modern culture, tending often, as Bartel's title 'Von Johnny Rotten bis Werther' signals, to blur traditional distinctions between 'high' and 'low' or popular culture. *Beowulf* and *Der Zauberberg* rub shoulders in Duve's *Die entführte Prinzessin*, as Boa and Graves note, and bananas appear as an ever-welcome gift in a sly asynchronic allusion in a world of dragons to the more ludicrous aspects of German-German relations at the time of the *Wende*. Several essays draw comparisons with films, pop music, or strip cartoons in discussing the representation of violence or of skin-creepingly disgusting motifs in Duve's writing. Boa analyses how Duve challenges the audience pleasure in representations of violence in the entertainment media whilst Jones explores the aesthetics of disgust in Erpenbeck's *Geschichte vom alten Kind*. Violence, horror, and disgust push at the conventional aesthetic boundaries and break cultural taboos, sometimes with shocking force but often too in comic parody. Thus Ludden and Boa outline Duve's parodic reprise of cartoon or television heroics that comically counteract gender stereotypes; Jones, on the other hand, notes the danger that parody may tend to reinforce the very stereotypes it seeks to subvert.

Bodily metaphors, water women and other fairy tale motifs, and the many intertextual allusions to culture high and low convey a great range of themes which are not specifically German, notably gender politics, consumerism, environmental issues, or post-enlightenment critique of the violence endemic to Western Civilization, as Ludden argues of Anne Duden's work. Many of the texts discussed do, of course, touch on specifically German matters. Several essays, Marven on Hensel, for example, Jones on Erpenbeck, or Meyer on Berlin novels, deal with the GDR and unification. Bagley raises the question of a generational shift, proposing the term 'Großmütterliteatur' in echo of the earlier categories of Väter- or Mütterliteratur which grappled with the tensions arising from German history and the Third Reich. She suggests that with the passage of time a literature of memory now transmitted from grandparents may go along with a generation more at ease with itself in the unified Germany of the Berlin Republic. On the other hand, Meyer's highly critical survey of recent prose fiction set in Berlin offers a disturbing panorama of urban alienation. This essay draws out fascinating affinities and contrasts in how the texts evoke the different areas of Berlin, but queries a solipsistic tendency to turn inwards away from the potentially enriching cultural heterogeneity of the city. It is a chance outcome of the offers of papers that our volume lacks contributions on cross-national writing, other than the inclusion of the Austrian author

Kathrin Röggla in Meyer's essay. Meyer does, however, touch on seeing Berlin from an exotic elsewhere as a motif in Judith Hermann's stories and Duve's heroine in *Dies ist kein Liebeslied* travels to London; the fantastical geography of Duve's latest novel is a further opening to another world which may save our volume from seeming too solipsistically inward turning.

The category 'women's writing' was central to the feminist critical project, initiated in the 1970s, to change the overwhelming bias towards male authors in the canon of writing studied by students of modern languages, a bias which was particularly powerful in German literary history. But it might be asked in the first decade of a new millennium whether such a category still makes sense and, indeed, whether feminist reading is still an appropriate approach in supposedly post-feminist times to writers who happen to be women. One possible reason for looking at contemporary women's writing as a category comes up in several of the essays of this volume, namely marketing and the widespread journalistic assertion of the prominence of young women in a perceived shift towards a new generation of authors producing readable, popular fiction: 'das literarische Fräuleinwunder' is a facet of the supposed 'Neue Lesbarkeit' which is apparently saving the German book market from being overwhelmed by literature in translation. (If only the British market saw more of a flood of literature in translation by translators like Bell.) German authors, especially women, are, it appears, writing readable best sellers. There are historical precedents. 'Chick lit', a sister category to the German *Fräuleinwunder*, is a designation continuing a long tradition of condescension towards popular women writers, the Brontes or Marlitts or Vicki Baums, who occasionally get recuperated as great or at least interesting writers in later, more enlightened times. Several of the essays, notably those by Graves, Macnab and Bagley, look sceptically at the marketing labels which have shaped public reception of Duve and some of the other writers under discussion and query the linking together of authors of disparate ages and interests and the condescending tone of such labeling. All this suggests that feminist cultural critique is not yet superfluous. While the authors in this volume cannot be categorised under one simplistic label, one recurring motif in their work is the body as a site of cultural struggle as women seek to negotiate space in our supposedly post-feminist, consumerist society. Deeply implicated in identity formation, gender discourse is an all-pervasive context for the literary texts discussed here which could belong in many different categories, but which can, we would contend, be fruitfully explored under the heading of women's writing.

Karen Duve

Die Mummel[1]

Erstaunlich, wie schnell man sich an die Gesellschaft eines Drachens gewöhnen kann, dachte Ritter Bredur, während er auf Grendel durch ein Kornfeld schaukelte und zusah, wie ein Bauer in haltlosem Entsetzen seine Sense von sich warf und wegrannte. Der Große Gaspajori versuchte, Grendel soviel wie möglich durch die Wälder und unbewohnten Gegenden zu lenken, aber manchmal ließ es sich eben nicht vermeiden, daß sie einem Menschen begegneten.

»Du, Friedlin, hab ich eigentlich schon erzählt, wie Prinzessin Lisvana mir zum ersten Mal auf der Treppe begegnet ist?« fragte Bredur den violetten Rücken, der vor ihm hin und her schwang.

»Ja«, sagte der Zauberer knapp und ohne sich umzudrehen.

Wenn man so lange zusammen reiste, wie die beiden es taten, ließ es sich kaum vermeiden, daß man einander allerlei anvertraute. So kannte der Große Gaspajori sich jetzt bestens mit Prinzessin Lisvanas Stammbaum, ihren Vorzügen und Launen aus, kannte ihr Schicksal, ihre Heimat und ihre unvergleichliche Lieblichkeit, als wäre sie sein Enkelkind. Wäre sie ihm über den Weg gelaufen, er hätte sie zweifellos erkennen müssen. Anfangs hatte Friedlin auch noch interessiert zugehört und gemeinsam mit Bredur spekuliert, wo denn die Prinzessin gefangengehalten werden könnte und ob wohl bereits eine Hochzeit stattgefunden habe. Aber wenn Ritter Bredur sich allzulange in der Beschreibung von Lisvanas Schönheit erging oder zum fünften Mal erzählte, wie er die Hand der Prinzessin im Turm ergriffen hatte, strich sich der Zauberer den Bart und sagte »soso« und wirkte nicht immer, als würde er zuhören. Im Gegenzug dämmerte auch Ritter Bredur manchmal weg, wenn Friedlin Gaspajori einen interessanten Gedankengang aus seinem Drachenbuch zum wiederholten Male variierte oder vertiefte. Denn hieraus bestand vornehmlich der Gesprächsbeitrag des Zauberers, täglich die einzelnen Kapitel über Drachensorten, Drachenzähmung, Drachenkampf und die Herstellung und Auflösung von Sympathieverbindungen zu referieren. Inzwischen wußte Bredur so viel über Drachen, als wäre er selbst von einem geschuppten Ungeheuer mit würziger Drachenmilch großgezogen worden.

»Es kann nicht mehr weit sein«, rief der Große Gaspajori und zeigte nach vorn auf einen Wald. Die Verwüstung war unübersehbar. Zwei breite Schneisen waren in das Gehölz gebrochen, ehemals stolze Eichen standen geknickt, an mehreren Bäumen hingen zusammengerollte und versengte Blätter. Eine halbe Stunde später stießen sie auf den

Abdruck einer Drachentatze im Schlamm, und kurz danach blieb Grendel ruckartig stehen, um an einem riesigen Haufen zu schnuppern.

»Höhlendrachenkot«, sagte der Zauberer, nachdem er einen flüchtigen Blick darauf geworfen hatte.

An diesem Abend erreichten sie den7 Festplatz für die Drachenwettkämpfe jedoch nicht mehr, sondern mußten ihr Lager wieder im Wald aufschlagen.

»Vor etwa zwei Kilometern hat rechts ein Teich gelegen. Dort wirst du Schilf für Grendels Bett finden. Denk daran, daß es ganz trocken sein muß«, sagte der Große Gaspajori, während er seinem Drachen die Packtaschen abnahm. »Und schau bei der Gelegenheit, ob du nicht auch etwas Saftiges für ihn zu futtern findest. Diese vertrockneten kleinen Blätter, die Grendel in letzter Zeit gefressen hat, geben kaum Kraft. Schließlich ist übermorgen sein großer Tag. Ich will ihn in drei Wettkämpfen antreten lassen.«

»Ist gut«, sagte Bredur, sattelte Kelpie und ritt die Strecke, die sie eben erst gekommen waren, wieder zurück. Bei der Schlammpfütze mit dem Abdruck der Drachentatze sah er etwas hinter den Büschen blinken, stieg vom Pferd und schlug sich ins Dickicht. Der Teich war von einem sumpfigen Ufergürtel umgeben, und das trockene Schilf, auf das Bredur es abgesehen hatte, stand auf der gegenüberliegenden Seite. Er mußte entweder über den grünen, glitschigen Baumstamm, der quer über dem Teich lag, balancieren oder außen um das versumpfte Ufer herumlaufen. Bredur entschied sich für den Baumstamm und wäre fast ins Wasser gefallen. Zurück wählte er den Landweg. Ein Rudel Hirsche sprang vorbei, aber er konnte keinen Pfeil nach ihnen schießen, weil er die Arme voller Schilfbündel hatte. Jetzt noch etwas Saftiges für Grendel. So spät im Jahr war etwas Saftiges gar nicht so einfach zu finden, aber als er über den Baumstamm balanciert war, hatte er mitten im Teich eine große Schwimmblattpflanze mit fleischigen grünen Blättern gesehen. Er wagte sich noch einmal auf den glitschigen Stamm, ging auf die Knie hinunter und erntete, was er zu fassen bekam.

Als er mit dem Schilf und den Blättern wieder auf den Weg trat, war Kelpie verschwunden. Bredur pfiff, und kurz danach brach das Pferd aus dem Unterholz. Es trug einen Fasan im Maul. Bredur wollte ihm den Vogel abnehmen, aber Kelpie ließ nicht los, sondern bestand darauf, seine Beute selber zum Lager zurückzutragen.

Als sie ankamen, war es bereits dunkel. Der Große Gaspajori hatte ein Feuer gemacht und hantierte mit dem Kessel. Grendel döste grünlich schimmernd in einem Dornbusch. Nachts glomm sein Schuppenpanzer wie faules Holz. Bredur band die Schilfbündel von Kelpies Rücken, polsterte eine Bodenmulde damit aus und lockte den Drachen herüber. Dann warf er ihm die saftigen Blätter vor.

»Hast du eine Ahnung, wo ich den großen Suppenlöffel hingesteckt habe?« fragte Gaspajori und drehte sich zu Bredur um. Grendel beschnupperte gerade die Blätter und beleuchtete sie dabei mit seiner phosphoreszierenden Nase. Der Zauberer stieß einen gellenden Schrei aus, stürzte zu seinem Drachen und riß ihm das Futter weg.

»Bist du wahnsinnig?« schrie er Bredur an. »Willst du ihn vergiften? Warum fütterst du ich nicht gleich mit Glasscherben?«

»Wieso?« sagte Bredur. »Du hast gesagt: etwas Saftiges. Und da habe ich eben diese Mummelblätter mitgebracht. Die sind doch nicht giftig.«

»Willst du, daß er anfängt zu quaken? Übermorgen soll Grendel in der Feuerspeiprüfung antreten, und der schlaue Herr Ritter füttert den Drachen mit Wasserpflanzen. Als ich etwas Saftiges sagte, habe ich natürlich Fleisch gemeint! Das kann man doch gar nicht mißverstehen.«

Der Feuerschein flackerte unheimlich auf dem Gesicht des Zauberers. Plötzlich trat auch noch ein fiebriges Glitzern in seine Augen.

»Oder machst du das absichtlich? Du machst das absichtlich! Du willst, daß Grendel in den Prüfungen versagt! Wer hat dich geschickt? Der Große Ouspensky? Gib zu, daß du für den großen Ouspensky arbeitest! Was hat er dir bezahlt?«

Der Zauberer hob einen Stein auf und drohte, damit auf den überraschten Bredur loszugehen. Grendel winselte aufgeregt und glomm vor lauter Sorge etwas heller.

»Nichts! Unsinn! Ich kenn deinen Großen Ouspensky überhaupt nicht. Ich habe wirklich gedacht, du wolltest, daß ich saftige Pflanzen hole«, sagte Bredur beschwichtigend.

»Sieh mir in die Augen!« schrie der Zauberer und zeigte mit zwei Fingern auf seine dicken Brillengläser. Sein Gesicht war immer noch von Argwohn und Irrsinn entstellt. »Sieh mir in die Augen, und dann schwöre, daß dich nicht der Große Ouspensky beauftragt hat!«

»Ich schwöre«, sagte Bredur gereizt.

»Das reicht nicht, schwör bei etwas, das dir heilig ist!«

»Ich schwör bei meiner Ritterehre, bei meinem Schwert Greinderach und meinen silbernen Sporen, daß ich deinen Freund Ouspensky noch nie gesehen habe und daß ich Grendel niemals schaden würde. Sonst wäre ich doch nicht so offen mit den Mummelblättern angekommen, sondern hätte sie ihm heimlich in anderes Futter gemischt.«

»Gut«, schnaufte der Zauberer, »diesmal will ich dir noch glauben. Aber tu das nie wieder, hörst du. Nie wieder!«

»Und du drück dich in Zukunft deutlicher aus«, sagte Bredur, nahm seinem Pferd den Fasan aus dem Maul und warf ihn dem Drachen vor. Der Große Gaspajori brummelte versöhnt. Kelpie lagerte sich neben

Grendel. Er war mit dem Untier inzwischen so vertraut, daß er ihm das Moos vom Schuppenpanzer abweidete und nicht einmal den Kopf hob, als Grendel aufstoßen mußte und dabei kleine Flammen aus seinem Maul züngelten.

Anmerkungen

1 Karen Duve, *Die entführte Prinzessin. Von Drachen, Liebe und anderen Ungeheuern*, Eichborn: Frankfurt am Main, 2005, S. 181-85.

Anthea Bell

Translating Karen Duve into English with a few peripheral observations on translation in general

This is an account of my work on the translation of *Regenroman* and *Dies ist kein Liebeslied*, with some general reflections on the process of translation, the way in which foreign books come to be translated and published in the English-speaking world, the research often necessary even in the translation of a work of fiction, and relations between authors, translators and publishers.

I did not, strictly speaking, deliver a paper at the Nottingham University seminar in May 2004 when Karen Duve was writer-in-residence for three weeks, but as the translator of her first novel, and just beginning work on the translation of her second, I was delighted to be invited and to take part in a parallel reading with her. The remarks below are based on my memories of the very interesting seminar and a few notes made at the time, with some reflections arising from the my work on Karen's books.

I had first met Karen Duve in 2002 in Chicago, where she was one of three guest authors invited by the Goethe-Institut to give an evening of readings, and to take part in the day-long seminar at the annual gathering there on the occasion of the award of the Helen and Kurt Wolff Prize. My presence there at the same time was a most fortunate coincidence, since I had just completed the translation of *Regenroman*.[1] The English title is *Rain*, with what I still feel is some weakening of effect, although nothing was ever going to strike quite the same alliterative and atmospheric note as the German original. For this novel is a book where the atmosphere, not just metaphorically but also literally, counts for much, with the chapter headings all drawn from weather forecasts. I had offered the publishers *A Rainy Story*, but I know I am not particularly good at thinking of titles. Indeed, I heave a sigh of relief when a book to be translated has a proper name as its title. That was the case, for instance, with the late W.G. Sebald's *Austerlitz*,[2] the translation of which had taken me to Chicago and my first meeting with Karen Duve in 2002. With a proper name as title, the translator and publisher of the translation have no problem.

Not a proper name but a song title does the same for Karen Duve's *Dies ist kein Liebeslied* (*This Is Not a Love Song*),[3] which I had begun to translate in May 2004, though I had not yet gone further than the rough draft stage, and was therefore unable to give precise answers to the several participants in the seminar who asked me what I was going to do with certain lines from popular songs of the 1970s onwards. All translators have their own favourite methods of approaching a work, and mine is to go right through a book producing a complete first draft as quickly as possible, before revising and re-revising more slowly. This is partly because, quite often, some question or problem arising early in the book will be answered by something else that comes up later on. However, I know translators who fret at the idea that something is not yet as good as they can make it, and prefer to polish everything up as they go along. I even know one who would rather not have read a book at all before she translates it, so that she can enjoy to the full the experience defined by Willis Barnstone in his *The Poetics of Translation*: 'Translation tends to be a certain kind of reading, an "intensive reading" of the original text.'[4] Myself, I am not quite sure how she can be certain that she will *want* to translate a book if she hasn't read it first; perhaps she at least takes a quick look. Not always, but very frequently – and I write not as an academic but as a general, all-purpose practising translator working in several fields, although with a distinct preference for fiction – the translator of a book will already have read it anyway in order to give a publisher a report on its merits and its suitability for that publisher's list.

In a recent and excellent article in *The Author*, the journal of the Society of Authors, of which the Translators' Association is a part, Eric Dickens deplores the comparative dearth of translations into English, and suggests that 'many literary translators themselves could make sound judgements and suggest books with a professional eye.'[5] In my own experience, this at least half-happens much of the time, for it is up to the reader to give a meticulously honest account of a book to a publisher, who more often than not is unable to read it in the original. (Coleridge says somewhere that we tend to overvalue a book read in a foreign language because we are secretly pleased with ourselves for being able to read it at all. Not so, however, if we are reading for publishers. It is incumbent upon a reader to be ultra-cautious in recommending a publishing firm to put its money where his or her mouth is.) If, however, I am asked out of the blue to translate a book that has not come my way already, I always have to read it before agreeing. And every translator knows what a test of a book the actual process of translation is; if you happen to have read and recommended a title, and it then comes back to you to be translated, you will certainly know by the end of your work whether your original assessment was correct.

As a matter of fact I had not read *Regenroman* for its English-language publisher Bloomsbury, which is one of the few publishing houses lucky enough to have an editor who can read German for herself. Rosemary Davidson happened to have been a guest member on the editorial committee of the twice-yearly journal *new books in german*, of which I have for some time been a member myself. The journal, as its name indicates, aims to interest English-language publishers in books just published, or about to be published, in Germany, Austria and Switzerland, and one or two publishers are invited to be on the editorial committee for each issue. When the novel was published by Eichborn in Frankfurt, therefore, it was one of the titles offered to *nbg*. As it happened, our reader of *Regenroman* for *nbg* had not been in sympathy with the novel, and since the journal may be offered up to a hundred books by their German-language publishers for possible inclusion, and can publish reviews recommending only some twenty of them in each issue, it was not included. The editorial committee has to act to a considerable extent on its readers' opinions, for no one can read *all* the books, though the editors to date, most notably Rosemary Smith the first editor, and until mid-2005 Sally-Ann Spencer, have done their best to read as many as possible. Sometimes, therefore, there will be misjudgements, and I realized as soon as I myself read *Regenroman* that this had been one of them. Fortunately, Rosemary Davidson was intrigued by the summary of the book in the reader's report, asked for a copy, read it herself and bought the rights for an English-language edition.

If I soon saw that we ought indeed to have included the novel in *nbg* when I began reading it, I felt even more convinced of its originality and the merits of its style once I was well embarked on the enjoyable process of translating it. For the close work of translation is an acid test. Our *nbg* reader had failed to see such extended set pieces as the bulimic episodes and the scene of murder by flame-thrower in context, and in context they are by no means written purely for the shock-horror factor, but are entirely appropriate to the structure of the novel. While it is difficult to like Karen Duve's protagonist, the pretentious would-be cult writer Leon, whose gradual decline and disintegration the book traces, I became very fond of his unfortunate wife Martina, born Roswitha but rechristened by Leon himself to give himself a wife with a trendier and more modern name. Roswitha/Martina meekly goes along with this decision, in the same way as she generally goes along with what other people say she should do. She is a beauty, but a beauty with very low self-esteem because all her life her teachers and her family, particularly her father, have made her feel that she is useless at anything other than looking decorative. Her bulimia only too obviously stems from her father's lack of interest in her, and although when I sent in the manuscript of the translation to Bloomsbury it was with a warning to any editor reading it not to tackle the passages containing the accounts of her bulimia just before lunch (unless of course the editor actually *wanted* to skip lunch), those pages were by no means gratuitous, but help to build up Martina's character. Only recently at the time of writing (early summer of 2005), I have been reading for a publisher yet another true-life confession of bulimia by, in this case, a young French actress; by comparison with Karen Duve's clever narrative use of the condition in *Regenroman*, it appeared pure self-indulgence. Similarly, the flame-thrower murders are entirely in character with their perpetrator, the quixotic and practical lesbian Kay, hopelessly in love with Martina; she is one of the Schlei sisters who live near the damp and ill-built marshland retreat unwisely bought by Leon, and I became fond of her too, though her sister Isadora, overwhelmingly fat and sexy, is just the kind of seductive nemesis that one cannot help thinking Leon deserves.

I especially enjoyed the black comedy of the novel, for that is what it is: *grand guignol*, very black but very funny. One of my hobbyhorses is a desire to correct the widespread belief in the English-speaking world that the Germans and their literature lack a sense of humour; I cite examples to the contrary whenever I get a chance, and Karen Duve has provided me with excellent ammunition. First published in English in 2002, *Rain* was chosen as the winner of the annual Schlegel-Tieck award for a book translated from the German in that year. It has become usual in recent years for all the translation prizes from various languages to be presented at a joint occasion, preceded by brief readings from all the winning books. When it came to readings from the books at the prize-giving ceremony, I am happy to say that the *only* extracts from any language to raise laughter were from the German. The reinstated biennial Cornelius M. Popescu Prize for European Poetry Translation could have been won by a book of poems from any European language, but went to David Constantine's translation, *Lighter Than Air*, of Hans Magnus Enzensberger's *Leichter als Luft*.[6] He read some of his graceful and highly ingenious versions of lyrics from that volume; I read the passage from *Rain* in which the teenage Roswitha, timid but always desperately over-anxious to please, is led into offering to perform oral sex on the would-be class stud, who proves quite unable to live up to his own self-image by the time the two of them are discovered by Roswitha's furious father. It is a sad but also hilarious and touching scene – I chose it partly because it is almost a little short story in itself, but again, it helps to account for the grown-up Martina's inferiority complex, and like David Constantine's reading it went down well with the audience, although one woman, sounding enjoyably shocked, did ask me afterwards, 'Oh, how could you read that aloud?' I said that if Karen could write the passage and I could translate it, I certainly had no problems about reading it. The other readings, from the same year's prize-winning books from the French, Dutch, Spanish and Swedish, were all from wonderful books in brilliant translations, but it must be said that there wasn't a smile to be raised among them.

In Nottingham Karen and I read what would have been my alternative choice of a comic passage from *Regenroman*: the unfortunate Leon's attempt to get rid of several buckets full of slugs collected from his slug-infested garden without upsetting Martina's tender sensibilities, culminating when he dumps them in a lay-by and attempts to convince the truck driver who runs over them that they are in the middle of a slug migration. Slugs slither their way right through the novel, despite the visual mistranslation of *Schnecken* on the cover of the British edition, showing a couple of handsome snails with decorative shells. In fact there is one solitary *Hausschnecke* mentioned in the book, and it's dead anyway: a delicate snail shell hanging from a blade of grass. All the other species are *Nacktschnecken* or *Wegschnecken*: the gardener's abhorred slugs. The American cover shows just the head and feelers of what could be either a slug or a snail, avoiding the *Schnecke* pitfall.

I translated these and many of the other set pieces in the book with relish, and especially enjoyed the dialogue. The same ability to write snappy, authentic-sounding conversation is evident in *Dies ist kein Liebeslied*, where the protagonist Anne also has a dysfunctional family, not to mention a series of unlikeable boyfriends and a pretentious psychotherapist. Battling with these problems, her over-weight and her struggle with diets, and her unrequited love for the only man she has ever really wanted, Anne is a courageous survivor who, despite indulging in daydreams, faces life as it is and wins the reader's sympathy; she certainly won mine in the course of translation. It also presents a picture of the society in which Anne grows up, from the 1960s through to the end of the story in 1996, when in desperation she visits the man she loves in London at the time of the European Cup football semi-final between England and Germany. Rosemary Davidson, at Bloomsbury, finds it, she says, 'wonderfully evocative of the times all the music, clothes, details, etc.' This title did go into *new books in german*, but was lined up by Bloomsbury very soon for translation anyway.

As to the details of the book's structure, I was amused to see, at the May 2004 seminar, that every Englishman present groaned with remembered horror at the mention of the penalty shoot-out on which England lost the game in 1996; I have to admit that any memory of it I may have retained had to be reinforced by websites found through Google, 'the translator's friend,' as a colleague described the search engine to me recently, and indeed it will almost always find just those scraps of out-of-the-way information needed by the translator's magpie mind. It dredged me up the names of all the bands mentioned in the novel, and many of their songs, often with the full text. At the time of the seminar, I remember that there was a good deal of discussion of *Dies ist kein Liebeslied*. I had then begun on the translation but had not completed it, and do not now remember the specific questions that I was asked: how was I going to deal with such and such a point? They had, however, mainly to do with the songs, and with the mention of such specifically German cartoon-like characters as Wum the dog and the Pillhuhn. In the event, each such mention had to be dealt with in its context as it came up. Names of bands such as the well-known Kraftwerk were of course left in the original German; actual lines from songs were on the whole translated in order to reflect the length and singability of the original. (Intriguingly, one song which particularly takes Anne's fancy, and is heard again at the end of the novel, played by the man who doesn't love her in his London flat, is never identified by band or by title.)

I may add, as an aside, that serendipity often plays a part in the translator's life; when I came to the mention of the *Kohlenklau-Mantel* worn by Diedrich Diederichsen (p. 176 of the German edition of the book) I had already and quite recently done my research on the identity of the *Kohlenklau* wartime propaganda figure in Germany, rather similar in purpose to his contemporary the Squanderbug in wartime Great Britain. I had first met the Coal-Stealer in translating another Eichborn book, Hans-Georg Behr's childhood memoir *Fast eine Kindheit* (published in English by Granta as *Almost a Childhood* in August 2005).[7] I greeted him as an old friend. And just to prove my point about serendipity, when I came to a quotation from Matthias Claudius, the eighteenth century poet and father of popular German journalism, in *Fast eine Kindheit*, I had done my homework on it earlier in yet another book, Cornelia Funke's fantasy novel for young people, forthcoming at the time of writing, and a sequel to her *Tintenherz*.[8] In this sequel, *Tintenblut*,[9] published in both German and English in the autumn of 2005 (in English as *Inkspell*, because the British publisher didn't want any blood in the title), the author had used the identical quotation from Claudius as one of her chapter epigraphs, so that I not only recognized it instantly but had already translated it into English verse. Meanwhile, back with *Dies ist kein Liebeslied*, another of my problems – how to translate the game of *Völkerball*, for neither Nations-Ball nor National Ball sounded right – was solved for me as, in pursuit of an English equivalent for *Gummitwist* as a kind of skipping mentioned in a short German children's book (it turns out to be French Skipping in British school playgrounds), I turned up playground games on the Internet and discovered that something rather less contentiously called Dodge-Ball is played in exactly the same way as *Völkerball*.

I believe – and certainly hope, since Karen was kind enough to say I could get in touch with any questions – that one way and another I found out all the references in the text of *Dies ist kein Liebeslied*, closely bound as it is to the aura of its period and setting, without having to pester her. Again, this is a matter of personal preference among translators. I have heard some translators say that their first move is to read the book through, either for the first time or if they have already read and reported on it for the second, listing everything that they want to ask the author. That is an option, of course, only when the author is alive. I translated E.T.A. Hoffmann's *Kater Murr*[10] for Penguin Classics a few years ago, and found several points which ought to have had endnotes, as indeed Penguin's excellent copy editor pointed out, but I could find no one who knew for certain what Hoffmann was referring to. I consulted half a dozen scholarly editions; every one of them simply ignored those points. And authors are usually kind enough to be very willing to answer questions. Indeed, on occasion it would be remiss *not* to ask. In translating Uwe Timm's *Am Beispiel meines Bruders*, published by Bloomsbury in the UK and Farrar, Straus & Giraux in the USA as *In My Brother's Shadow*,[11] I found what I suspected was a neologism coined by the author, or as he recounts it recollected by him in a dream of his long-dead brother, the word 'Doldenhilfe'. It was indeed a neologism, a kind of composite nonsense word, and Dr. Timm told me that every single translator of his memoir of his family had asked about that one; clearly it would have been a very bad mark not to. I eventually translated it as 'Floweraid', on the analogy of such words for charities as Band-Aid, and feeling that the more technically botanical 'umbel' for the first half of the compound was a little difficult for non-botanists in English. In most cases, however, it is a principle and a point of pride with me – and with many other translators of my acquaintance – to solve all the problems and find out all the references we can on our own before turning to the author.

And a further aside: when your author is not only dead but deliberately wrote nonsense, you are on your own in facing an English-language publisher's questions. I translated, for North-South in New York, a selection of Christian Morgenstern's verses, twelve chosen and beautifully illustrated by the Austrian artist Lisbeth Zwerger.[12] Baffled comments came back from the editorial office: 'This doesn't make sense.' Well, no, I replied: Morgenstern was a nonsense poet, think Lewis Carroll, think Edward Lear. After a five-page single-spaced letter, containing far more wordage than there was in the translations of the poems themselves, I carried my point, but still received anxious questions: 'There's no such word as this in English.' No, well, it was a rendition of a word which doesn't really exist in German either. I'd have given much to be able to appeal for support to Morgenstern, by all accounts a delightful character, and can only hope that he would have approved of my versions.

In the afternoon of the seminar at Nottingham discussion moved from Karen Duve's work to that of other young German writers, and in particular to those of them who play around with, or refer back to, the tradition of the German folk and fairy tale, as exemplified in the collections of the Grimms and other 19th-century folklorists. In retrospect, these papers were particularly interesting and relevant, since Karen Duve's next book, published in the spring of 2005, *Die entführte Prinzessin*,[13] also plays with such subjects, although (interestingly) in what I would myself regard as more of an English than a Teutonic way. Our *nbg* reader – Lyn Marven, who herself was at the Nottingham seminar and delivered a fascinating paper – recommended it for inclusion in the journal, and like its predecessor it went straight in. It is a new departure for Karen Duve: a tale of dragons, princes and princesses, knights and court dwarves, written in what is now described as the crossover genre – but the author's engaging manner suggests that her tongue is in her cheek now and then. It would be very tempting to translate that title as 'How Not to Abduct a Princess', since all concerned make a terrible job of it. On reading the book with great enjoyment, I was reminded not so much of the tradition emanating from what Emer O'Sullivan, in her magisterial work on *Kinderliteratur Komparatistik,* in my English translation *Comparative Children's Literature*,[14] describes as the German fairy-tale forest, a tradition used to excellent effect by Cornelia Funke, as of the somewhat more sophisticated literary *Kunstmärchen* of English-language writers from the nineteenth century to the present day. Anyone who has read *The Oxford Book of Modern Fairy Tales,*[15] Alison Lurie's fine anthology of such works – although described as 'modern', they begin with works from as far back as Ruskin's 'The King of the Golden Mountain' – will know the genre that I mean. It is a tradition perfectly suited to Karen Duve's wry, dry style of humour. I particularly enjoyed an account of a dragon show, something between a gymkhana and a dog show (we know already, from her two earlier novels, how fond she is of dogs and how perceptively she writes about them). As I write this, I hope very much that *Die entführte Prinzessin* will be translated into English, and shall be surprised if it is not, particularly given the present vogue for crossover writing – and the very considerable variation between the literary merits of the would-be emulators of J.K. Rowling's Harry Potter that I see written in languages other than English and offered to British and American publishers. Some of them are only too obviously constructed on purpose to contain what look like the sure-fire ingredients for a best-seller. It seems to be inevitable that those which proclaim on the jacket, 'Better than Harry Potter!' are not. Cornelia Funke, for instance, has no need to make any such claim, and nor very certainly, in a slightly different genre, does Karen Duve

It has been a privilege and a pleasure, then, to translate Karen's work, and it was also a pleasure to be invited to the Nottingham seminar to meet her again, and to discuss her books with so many other interested people. I greatly enjoyed it all.

Notes

1 Karen Duve, *Regenroman*, Eichborn: Frankfurt am Main, 1999. English translation: *Rain*, tr. Anthea Bell, Bloomsbury Publishing: London, 2002.

2 W.G. Sebald, *Austerlitz*, Carl Hanser Verlag: München & Wien, 2001. English translation: *Austerlitz*, tr. Anthea Bell, Hamish Hamilton: London, 2001; Modern Library (Random House): New York, 2001.

3 Karen Duve, *Dies ist kein Liebeslied*, Eichborn: Frankfurt am Main, 2002. English translation: *This Is Not A Love Song*, tr. Anthea Bell,Bloomsbury: London, 2005.

4 Willis Barnstone, *The Poetics of Translation*, Yale University Press: New Haven and London, 1993, p. 7.

5 Eric Dickens, 'Offshore and aloof', *The Author*, vol. cxvi, 2, summer 2005, p. 75.

6 Hans Magnus Enzensberger, *Leichter als Luft*, Suhrkamp: Frankfurt am Main, 1999. English translation: *Lighter Than Air*, tr. David Constantine, Bloodaxe Books: Tarset, 2002.

7 Hans-Georg Behr, *Fast eine Kindheit*, Eichborn: Frankfurt am Main, 2002. English translation: *Almost a Childhood*, tr. Anthea Bell, Granta: London, 2005.

8 Cornelia Funke, *Tintenherz*, Cecilie Dressler Verlag: Hamburg, 2003. English translation: *Inkheart*, tr. Anthea Bell, Scholastic: New York, 2003; The Chicken House: Frome, 2003.

9 Cornelia Funke, *Tintenblut*, tr. Anthea Bell, Cecilie Dressler Verlag: Hamburg, 2005. English translation: *Inkspell*, tr. Anthea Bell, Scholastic: New York, 2005; The Chicken House: Frome, 2005.

10 E.T.A. Hoffmann, *Lebensansichten des Kater Murr*, Ferdinand Dümmler: Berlin, 1820 (vol. i) and 1822 (vol. ii). English translation: *The Life and Opinions of the Tomcat Murr*, tr. Anthea Bell, Penguin Books: London, 1999.

11 Uwe Timm, *Am Beispiel meines Bruders*, Verlag Kiepenheuer & Witsch: Köln, 2003, p. 104. English translation: *In My Brother's Shadow*, tr. Anthea Bell, Bloomsbury: London, 2005, p. 128; Farrar, Straus & Giroux: New York, 2005, p. 130.

12 Christian Morgenstern, *Kindergedichte und Galgenlieder*, ausgewählt und illustriert von Lisbeth Zwerger, Michael Neugebauer: Gossau-Zürich, 1992. English translation, *Lullabies, Lyrics and Gallows Songs*, tr. Anthea Bell, North-South Books: New York, 1995.

13 Karen Duve, *Die entführte Prinzessin*, Eichborn: Frankfurt am Main, 2005.

14 Emer O'Sullivan, *Kinderliteratur Komparatistik*, Universitätsverlag C. Winter: Heidelberg, 2000. English translation, *Comparative Children's Literature*, tr. Anthea Bell, Routledge: London & New York, 2005.

15 Alison Lurie, ed., *The Oxford Book of Modern Fairy Tales*, Oxford University Press: Oxford and New York, 1994.

Peter J. Graves

The Novels of Karen Duve: just 'chick lit with [...] grime' (and dragons)?

This article focuses on Karen Duve's second and third novels, *Dies ist kein Liebeslied* (2002) and *Die entführte Prinzessin* (2005). Rejecting the well-meaning but unhelpful commendation of her work as 'chick lit [...] with grime', it examines different stylistic features of her writing, particularly the perspective and tone of the narrative voice, the manner of characterisation, and the blending of sources. It identifies as a common theme in these otherwise very different novels the depiction of problematical relationships between the sexes and generations, highlighting the emotional depths that are uncovered in the process. At the same time it questions the suggestion that Duve is evidently working to a feminist agenda, and it locates her work within some of the continuing debates in Germany concerning the function of the novel.

Through no evident fault of her own Karen Duve seems to attract what might be called the backhanded compliment, an observation intended as an accolade but carrying a certain ambiguous edge to it. The most obvious in this context is the notion of the 'literarische Fräuleinwunder', that term coined in 1999 by Volker Hage in the *Spiegel* to salute the new wave of women writers breaking onto the German literary scene, of whom Karen Duve was probably the most notable.[1] Although clearly meant as a gently humorous tribute, it rapidly became wearisome not just through over-use but above all for its homogenizing effect and its condescending undertone. As a serious literary designation it proved no more useful than Hage's similarly affirmative but equally reductive summary of Duve herself as the 'Neue Wilde der Erzählkunst'.[2]

A similar point could be made about another comment on Karen Duve, one referring this time to her second novel, *Dies ist kein Liebeslied* (2002), which sought to capture the book's essence in the catchy but questionable phrase, 'chick lit with [...] grime'. The description appeared in a review published by *new books in german*, the anonymous reviewer, having sketched in the novel's content, concluding with these words:

> This tale is a piece of *grand guignol* with a difference. Duve's sense of the ridiculous undercuts the pathos of Anne's lonely obesity and reflects the events of her earlier life through the lens of her adult disappointment and cynicism. Swapping a female for the male of her first novel *Rain*, she also engages a wider context, from wars and ecological disasters to passing fashions. The result: chick lit with a thick coating of grime and fat.[3]

Since the purpose of the periodical is to interest British publishers in recent or forthcoming works from Germany, it would be harsh to chide the writer for indulging in some enticing spin, but much of the summary is also misleading. Although the presence of fat in *Dies ist kein Liebeslied* is undeniable, since the plot revolves around the body-weight of the central character, there is rather less of what might be called grime, and

the term 'chick lit' is, at the least, problematic. If, in the words of one of
that genre's practitioners, 'most chick-lit fiction is about a single girl
trying to meet Mr Right',[4] then Duve's novel would seem to fit the bill,
but so would countless other works of literature, from the Old Testament
book of Ruth onwards. The term itself is said to have started life at
Princeton in the early 1990s as an undergraduate nickname for a module
on the female literary tradition, but it has since moved emphatically
downmarket to denote young women's romantic fiction of the fun kind,
probably frivolous, certainly undemanding. Jenny Colgan, the author of
one such novel, has called it 'a deliberately condescending term they use
to rubbish us all. If they called it slut lit it couldn't be more insulting'.[5]
Since abuse was in no-one's mind here, it would seem prudent simply to
discard the term as an inappropriate piece of media-speak out of the same
drawer as the 'Fräuleinwunder'. Beryl Bainbridge has referred to chick lit
as 'froth'.[6] None of Duve's novels, whatever else may be said about
them, is froth.

    That does not mean, however, that they are not extremely readable:
virtually every review of her work, whatever the final judgment,
acknowledges the vigour and flair that sustain her writing. Of
Regenroman one critic noted the 'enorme Stilsicherheit',[7] another the
'drastischen Beschreibungen',[8] a third the way the novel 'hält Tempo,
ohne abzustürzen'.[9] The comments on *Dies ist kein Liebeslied* were
scarcely different: 'Es wird erzählt […] mit Tempo und kraftvollem
Rhythmus',[10] wrote one critic, another referred to the 'Leichtigkeit des
Erzähltons',[11] another discovered no fewer than 'tausend sophistische,
wahnsinnig komische Sätze',[12] and a fourth summed up the reaction of
many when she declared, 'die Liebes-Biografie von Anne ist
unterhaltsam und bringt ein großes Lesevergnügen'.[13] The pace that will
drive the narrative is apparent in each case right from the opening words.
Regenroman lands the reader *in medias res* with Martina's question,
'"Was sagst du? Was …?"',[14] followed by a single paragraph into which
are compressed details of her location, her status as a newly-wed, the
reason for the current expedition with her husband, her bewilderment at
his momentary non-reappearance, her clothes, her appearance, her
contrasting effect on men and women, and – of course – the weather.
Dies ist kein Liebeslied opens with the laconic but intriguing antithesis of
the first two sentences, 'Mit sieben Jahren schwor ich, niemals zu lieben.
Mit achtzehn tat ich es trotzdem',[15] followed by a breathless *tour
d'horizon* not just of the central character's love-life from late teens to
mid-thirties but also two decades' worth of international confrontations,
political events, technological advances and changing fashions.

    In neither novel, then, does the narrative voice waste any time in
getting down to business, and in that respect both works amply reflect the

slogan set out prominently on the internet homepage of the Eichborn Verlag, Karen Duve's publisher: 'Das Leben ist zu kurz für langweilige Bücher'.[16] Although the sentiment may seem a populist commonplace, its particular significance to contemporary German literature is perhaps best illustrated by a telling phrase in one of the reviews of *Dies ist kein Liebeslied*, where 'die junge deutsche Literatur' is credited with having brought to modern German fiction, among other benefits, 'Erlösung vom Terror des Tiefschürfenden'.[17] The view is by no means untypical, but if the profound is regarded as holding a terror from which one has to be delivered, it reveals a great deal about the way in which, over recent years, the contemporary German novel has undergone a crisis of identity. Still fresh in the memory are the agonized debates in Germany during the 1990s over the direction in which contemporary writers should be moving, especially in the light of the dominance of the German literary scene by Anglo-Saxon authors in translation, with their vibrant depictions of reality as against what was perceived as the ponderous 'Innerlichkeit' of much home-grown fiction. Hence the delight at the emergence of the radically new tone embodied in the so-called 'neue deutsche Dichter', five of whom, including Karen Duve, were celebrated on the famous *Spiegel* cover in October 1999.

Regenroman is, without doubt, one of the most striking examples of this new German literary exuberance, but although it continues to be treated as Duve's defining work, it seems appropriate now to give attention to the novels that have followed. It is well known that the burden of expectation after a commercially successful novel can itself hamper a repetition. Some nine years after the publication of *Captain Corelli's Mandolin* Louis de Bernières, asked how he was progressing with his next novel, is said to have replied, 'Writing today is like being stood stark naked in Trafalgar Square and being told to get an erection'.[18] The analogy may be indelicate but in our present context not inappropriate, for the male problem which Martina in *Regenroman* first encountered with Thomas Marx in the back seat of the yellow Audi also seems to dog Anne Strelau in her dealings with pubescent men in *Dies ist kein Liebeslied*. And there are many other similarities between the two books, most obviously their fundamental configuration: at the heart of each is a deeply problematical relationship between the sexes with, alongside strings of often dysfunctional men, a central female character who is carrying into adulthood the scars of emotional mistreatment as a child. Despite the passions on display, however, there is in both novels a constant lightening of the mood through some often deliciously mischievous narrative asides, exercises of that acerbic wit which has become a hallmark of Karen Duve's style and has undoubtedly contributed to her popularity. To suggest that *Dies ist kein Liebeslied* contains one thousand 'wahnsinnig komische Sätze' is, of course, wild hyperbole, but it is still instructive to compare the novel in this regard with one of Duve's earlier short stories. Published in 1999 in a collection of the same name, 'Keine Ahnung' contains a virtually identical plot, even down to some of the peripheral detail, and reads in effect like a compressed dry run for the later novel. The crucial distinction is that it almost entirely lacks that remarkable humour which constantly breaks through Anne's narrative and gives it its particular flavour. *Dies ist kein Liebeslied* may at base be the story of a deeply unfulfilled individual, but the tragic potential is regularly deflected by Anne's gift for the deflating observation and her eye for absurdity, not least her own.

And this last point highlights a significant difference from *Regenroman*, one that arguably marks an advance on that first novel (although critical opinion in Germany was more divided). If the earlier *grand guignol* reference applies to anything in Duve's work, then to such scenes in *Regenroman* as the brutal rape of Martina or the immolation of Harry and Pfitzner. In *Dies ist kein Liebeslied* there is (discounting a few dismembered frogs patched up by well-meaning children) nothing remotely similar, for the tone of this work is far removed from that of its predecessor: where *Regenroman* is radical and unrestrained, at times almost gratuitously aggressive, *Dies ist kein Liebeslied* is wistful, melancholy and ambiguous. As example one could cite the way in which Martina and Anne, in their respective final scenes, seek to break with their past through an act of self-affirmation: Martina does so by the drastic expedient of setting fire to the symbol of her father's humiliation of her, the yellow Audi, and it is evident that we are intended to see her own feelings of inadequacy and personal 'Verdorbenheit' (R62) also going up in the flames; Anne, by contrast, enjoys a brief moment of union with the one man she has ever loved, but although it too is a very conscious attempt to overcome what she describes to him at the time as her 'unbewältigte[…] Kindheit' (L275), any catharsis is far more subtle. Indeed, whether it could ever be sufficient to counter the persistent 'Gefühl der Minderwertigkeit in mir' (L169) remains deeply uncertain.

The obvious formal explanation for this difference between the two works is the shift from a third- to a first-person narrator, a move from distance to empathy. The narrative voice in *Regenroman* has a brutal, callous edge to it, not just in some of the events depicted but in the deployment and eventual dispatch of the characters. The humour often borders on the cynical, and even Martina is portrayed with little real warmth. *Dies ist kein Liebeslied* by contrast presents Anne's own story, the personal confession, the unfolding of a life from the inside. The image she projects of herself, in particular of her physical bulk, may at times be scarcely less grotesque than that of some of the characters in

Regenroman, but it is she who does the projecting, the criticism of her is self-criticism, the mockery self-mockery, and all emerges from a far more complex set of drives and emotions that are candidly laid out in her narrative and with which she wrestles before us in full consciousness of what she is doing. In that respect she is rather like an inverse Claudia, the protagonist of Christoph Hein's *Der fremde Freund* (1982): also a middle-aged woman unsuccessful in relationships as the result of a troubled childhood, also narrating her own life, she steadfastly refuses even to acknowledge her emotional deformities, let alone deal with them. The upshot is a tale of personal repression and self-deceit. Anne may be faced by a similar temptation, the impulse to deny an unpleasant reality and replace it by the 'völlig neue Identität' (L49) she had longed to create for herself as a child. At times indeed she succumbs to it through the device of what she calls her 'Kopfkino' (L124), the fantasy world which allows her brief moments of imaginary fulfilment, whether as the best class representative her school has ever seen, or as a stunningly successful sportswoman, or as the owner of a romantic beach-bar who is suddenly discovered by a record-company. The reality in every case is cruelly different, even her ludicrously inept suicide attempt failing to match the spectacular drama of its imagined precursor. Christoph Hein's Claudia, as a practising doctor, can maintain the façade of a well-adjusted citizen. For Anne, by the very obvious nature of the feature that sets her apart from others, her ballooning weight, that option is not open, and she is therefore forced into daily confrontation with an external truth that seems wholly at odds with what she feels is her genuine essence.

It is this familiar conflict between being and appearance which generates the tension sustaining the novel, and it receives its most obvious outworking, and its most poignant expression, in the relationship between Anne and Peter Hemstedt, her would-be lover. '"Du denkst wahrscheinlich,"' she says to him at the end of the novel, '"daß ich wahnsinnig fett geworden bin, aber das sieht bloß so aus. Innen drin bin ich dünn und verletzlich und begehrenswert. Man kann es bloß nicht sehen"' (L276). Conscious that her love for him is unreciprocated, she had tried to decry it as 'widerlich', 'aufdringlich' (L169), 'minderwertig' (L177), 'ekelerregend' (L198), even declaring its non-existence: 'Liebte ich ihn überhaupt noch? Nein, da war nichts. Gar nichts. Da war auch nie wirklich etwas gewesen' (L203). But Anne is no Claudia, and whilst Hemstedt could take the 1983 track by the band Public Image Limited, 'This is not a love song', and casually give it to Anne on a taped compilation, her own attempt to associate herself with the sentiment was always going to be shallow and half-hearted. This realisation had dawned at the latest during her writing of an unsent letter to Hemstedt when she was in school and supposed to be composing an essay on *Werther*. Just as another literary predecessor, Edgar Wibeau in Plenzdorf's *Die neuen Leiden des jungen W.*, had found in *Werther*, to his great surprise, an echo of his own love-struck feelings, dismissing it first as 'Reiner Mist' written in an impenetrable 'Althochdeutsch' but concluding, 'Ich hatte nie im Leben gedacht, daß ich diesen Werther mal so begreifen würde',[19] so Anne is equally scathing of Werther's 'empfindsames Gewinsel' and calls him 'ein zickiger, eingebildeter Sack', but 'als er anfing, von seiner Liebe und seinem Unglück zu sprechen, da war mir, als sähe ich in mein eigenes Herz. Es spricht so klar und wahr und traurig. Ich verstehe vollkommen, was Goethe meint' (L163). That song from Hemstedt which gives the novel its title may reflect his own position, but as a declaration of Anne's feelings it is manifestly false.

The central male character in *Regenroman* is incompetent, weak and ineffective, a wimp par excellence for whom his wife comes to feel nothing but contempt. His successor in *Dies ist kein Liebeslied* is of a very different breed. Though not necessarily any more likable or sensitive to the needs of others (Anne calls him at one point 'widerlich und gemein' [L199]), he seems to possess the kind of self-assurance and naïve poise that will carry him through all life's trials unflustered and unfazed. To Anne he clearly embodies an image of balance and personal integration, the harmony of inner and outer which she longs for but can never attain, or only fleetingly when in his presence: 'Nur wenn ich bei Hemstedt war, spürte ich Kontur und wurde zu etwas Eigenständigem. Vielleicht war gar nicht er es, der mir fehlte. Vielleicht fehlte ich mir bloß selbst' (L199). If one may detect in Anne's personal rivenness an echo of the Kleistian clash between 'Sein und Schein', then in her connection with Hemstedt there is perhaps a related note. In his essay *Über das Marionettentheater* Kleist examined the conflict between innocence and knowledge, between the spontaneous, unconscious, natural movement of the puppet with a single centre of gravity, and the youth who looks at himself in the mirror and through his self-consciousness destroys his natural harmony for ever. In Duve's novel the contrast is reflected in the gulf between Hemstedt, unknowing and untroubled, his life on a seemingly effortless upward curve, and Anne, made cruelly conscious at an early age of the fracture between body and self that would, in every sense, weigh her down for the rest of her life. Hence the irony of the curse she utters against Hemstedt when they meet as adults in London:

> 'Du wirst glücklich sein! Dieses Leben wird dich glücklich machen. Du wirst überhaupt nicht merken, was für ein Drecksleben du führst! Noch auf dem Sterbebett wirst du denken: Das war ja alles richtig prima, hätte gar nicht besser laufen können.' (L211)

Yet if Hemstedt's blissful ignorance is a curse, far worse is the curse of Anne's own self-awareness. The two of them belong in different lives, which is why at the end of the novel she steals silently away.

All this takes place against the background of the 1980s and 1990s, with numerous cultural reference points along the way. But unlike a novel such as Matthias Politycki's *Weiberroman* (1997), which reads like a veritable catalogue of cultural ephemera almost for their own sake, in *Dies ist kein Liebeslied* they are included only in so far as they illuminate or reflect, as does the title song, Anne's personal dilemmas. Even one of the most resonant episodes, the penalty shoot-out between England and Germany during the Euro 96 football tournament when Anne is in London in the novel's final chapter, is wittily integrated into this configuration. Pondering the fateful abortive kick by the England defender Gareth Southgate, Anne offers the following analysis:

> Southgate[...] fängt an zu denken. Er denkt, weil bisher alle Tore nach rechts gingen, wird der Torwart sich diesmal nach rechts schmeißen. Southgate schießt anders, als er es eigentlich vorgehabt hat. Southgate schießt links. (L270)

If only the hapless Southgate had acted with the unconscious innocence of the puppet, the result would have been different. But he had obviously not read his Kleist: knowledge, reflection and thought entered, and England was banished from Paradise.

The presentation of a footballer's anguish as merely a variation of Anne's own reflects (*pace* the review cited earlier) the novel's close focus. Direct social criticism, let alone the moralizing of a Böll or a Christa Wolf, is wholly foreign to the younger generation of German writers, and even social comment is less than pointed. Anne's condition is too extreme, for instance, for her to be seen simply as victim of some artificial, culturally determined norm of female beauty, and although, as in *Regenroman*, the issue of gender stereotyping is constantly hovering, especially in male behaviour, it is handled more with gentle affection than any crusading feminist zeal. So fun is poked at the tribal instincts of men in their allegiance to bands and football teams, or at the primitive antics of football supporters and goal-scorers. Yet whilst Anne professes herself moved when she learns that Hemstedt wept at a scene from *E.T.*, she is far less at ease with any more fundamental change in masculine behaviour. When one of her friends explains how his therapist disabused him of the need to pretend to a false machismo image, she is less than enthusiastic about 'diese neue Form männlichen Selbstbewußtseins', reflecting that men's failings are offset by precisely their stereotypical strengths, for instance that 'meine Kfz-Mechanikerfreunde immer meine jeweiligen Autos [...] tipptopp in Schuß gehalten und mir die schwersten Kisten hochgetragen hatten'. And yet, she continues to muse:

'Andererseits: War ich denn auch nur für fünf Pfennig glücklich gewesen mit meinen Kfz-Mechanikern?' (L221). This vacillation exemplifies not just Anne's own confusion but also the essence of this novel as a study in individual character, accessible certainly and often amusing, but with a lightness that is never more than skin-deep. Even as Anne's 'Kopfkino' projects its images of her popularity and success, there are constant intrusions from what she calls 'der ägyptische Hinrichtungsfilm' (L180) showing a gruesome scene of her own beheading, which is why in London she is so drawn to the picture of the Execution of Lady Jane Grey (not identified in the text, but obviously the Delaroche in the National Gallery). As she observes the interplay of light and dark on the canvas, it confirms her fundamental pessimism that 'das Leuchtende und Helle nicht die allergeringste Chance hat gegen all das Dunkel um es herum' (L263). *Dies ist kein Liebeslied* is a moving but also bleak tale of failure and disappointment. As Karen Duve said in an interview on the work, '[u]ngelebtes Leben ist doch kein Witz'.[20]

And writing the novel, we now learn, was at times so personally distressing for the author herself ('Mir ging's da richtig dreckig') that she felt compelled to break off and write something 'was ganz und gar nett war und wo ich davon ausging, das würde auch nur ein gutes Ende haben'.[21] Thus the genesis of *Die entführte Prinzessin* (2005). If the skill of a writer may be judged in part by an ability to surprise, then Karen Duve must be reckoned particularly adroit, for after the fierce realism of *Regenroman* and *Dies ist kein Liebeslied* comes nothing less than a full-blown fairy-tale, beginning with 'Es war einmal', concluding with a marriage, and peopled in-between by princes and princesses, fairies, dwarves, magicians, monsters and dragons.[22] It tells the story of the beautiful princess Lisvana wooed by the handsome prince Diego, of his precipitate abduction of her following a dispute between their two kingdoms, of her rejection of his suit for this perceived insult to her family and her subsequent humiliation as a washerwoman, and of the intervention of the noble knight Bredur also seeking Lisvana's hand. After numerous adventures involving perilous sea-voyages, dangerous forests, exotic islands, mysterious encounters, mistaken identities, further kidnapping and imprisonment, and much else besides, it all ends with a happy resolution.

There is, of course, rather more to this than meets the eye, not least the exuberant plundering of familiar literary models. The basic pattern of prince seizing foreign princess who then refuses his advances and is condemned to menial work comes straight from the Gudrun saga. Grendel, the principal dragon in the story, is a namesake of the creature slain by Beowulf, and there are due references to the dragon's blood of the Siegfried legend. The sea-monsters smack of the biblical leviathan or the Ketea of Greek mythology, an extended episode within a harem evokes the Arabian atmosphere of *1001 Nights*, Lisvana's loss of a shoe and its later restoration by her suitor repeats the Cinderella motif, the three wishes attached to a magic bell recall Aladdin and his lamp. But many of these come with an impish twist. Lisvana's degrading labour in captivity is less punishment than self-imposed sulk from wounded pride, and the royal houses finally join, not in battle but in an inflated celebration of friendship. Grendel, far from the evil creature of tradition, is an incorrigible coward, less Beowulf in other words and more Ogden Nash; and rather than making the skin of others impervious, he himself needs gentle caressing, like some touchy-feely Californian hippie, to restore his battered self-confidence. In the harem scene the sultan's favourite daughter is replaced by a knight in drag, the sea-monsters just want to frolic, the bell is dented and the wishes it grants are correspondingly askew, and so on. And all this is seasoned with a liberal sprinkling of modern allusions – Diego's rich kingdom, for instance, boasts, like contemporary Hamburg, 'mehr Brücken als Venedig' (P45),[23] and its visitors to Lisvana's impoverished homeland take gifts of bananas, 'ein Geschenk, das […] immer gut ankam' (P54) – together with a thoroughly cavalier approach to linguistic consistency: in this ancient world a meagre dowry can be described as 'popelig' (P 5), a foolish act as 'komplett plemplem' (P37), an unworthy gift as 'Ramsch' (P41), an unwanted wedding as a 'Scheißhochzeit' (P289), a faithless lover as 'diese verdammte Schlampe'. (P366)

Whilst this cheerful asynchronicity may be testimony to the novel's origin as 'therapeutisches Schreiben', there is a similar modernity in the much more significant area of characterisation, lending the work a depth it would otherwise lack.[24] For although in their outward conduct the characters operate wholly within the conventions of a traditional fairy-tale, they are no mere ciphers to be manipulated, the third-person narrator offering sympathetic insights into the roots of their behaviour and allowing them through indirect interior monologue ample opportunity to reveal themselves as they battle with their own emotions. The centrality of this theme is already hinted at in the novel's subtitle, 'Von Drachen, Liebe und anderen Ungeheuern', and although the humorous juxtapositioning indicates the general tone of what is to come, human relationships can still be sufficiently painful, even in fairy-tales, to allow Bredur to conclude that love is 'überhaupt etwas Fürchterliches, etwas, das nur schief gehen konnte' (P300).

In his case the turmoil stems not least from a continuous need to justify himself in the eyes of his father, the doughty Fredur Wackertun who, like name like nature, has excelled himself in deeds of valour (and of drinking) and resents his son both for causing the death of his mother in childbirth and for his alleged feebleness: Bredur as a result 'hatte es schwer, seinem Vater etwas recht zu machen' (P19). We are here in familiar Duve territory, that of baleful cross-generational influences, the child as victim of the parent. Martina's bulimia in *Regenroman* is directly attributed to her father's ostracisation of her after the teenage incident with Thomas Marx referred to earlier, and although Anne Strelau's condition in *Dies ist kein Liebeslied* has a variety of causes, prime among them is the shock of her father's cruel rebuff when, as a child, she sought his love and was accused of nursing an Oedipus complex: 'In diesem Moment', she writes, 'explodierte meine Welt' (L72). *Die entführte Prinzessin* contains nothing of such intensity, but the Bredur experience is not an isolated one, nor indeed is emotional cruelty restricted to the male of the species. The all-consuming obsession of Diego's mother is with her garden, and as a result she gives her son 'so viel Aufmerksamkeit […] wie einem Stein' (P50). Although a humorous explanation is immediately adduced, in that at the time of the prince's birth a new fashion for vast skirts made all physical proximity impossible, a later confrontation between the two lacks nothing in bitterness from the son and wounding condescension from the mother: '"Du hast mich nie geliebt", brüllte der Prinz, […] "Weißt du überhaupt, was das heißt – lieben?" […] "Aber gewiß doch, mein lieber Sohn, ich habe dich sehr gern"' (P290).

The object of the two men's affections meanwhile, princess Lisvana, wrestles between desire and duty like some Schillerian heroine, between Diego, whom she has 'von Anfang an geliebt' (P335), and the 'Ehre ihres Vaters' (P373), which requires that she reject him. Although a friendly companion advises her to abandon such patriarchal constraints and instead, in language lifted straight from *Der Zauberberg*, enjoy 'die bodenlosen Vorteile der Schande, ein Weib zu sein' (P122), mixed into her temperament is a strong dose of personal vanity, and she continues to play 'die Stolze' (P231), allowing room for some psychological jousting unthinkable in a traditional fairy-tale. '"Du denkst"', Diego accuses her, '"bloß weil meine Mutter mich nie geliebt hat, suche ich mir jetzt eine Frau, die mich auch nicht liebt"', to which Lisvana replies, '"Ich denke, Ihr seid verwöhnt und habt immer alles gekriegt, was Ihr wollt, und jetzt könnt Ihr es nicht akzeptieren, wenn jemand nein sagt"' (P220). Not least of the merits of this engaging novel is that such self-analytical exchanges do not protrude awkwardly amongst the paraphernalia of myth and magic. At the same time the intricacies of the plot, and the emotional twists and turns within the characters, hold the reader absorbed until the traditional happy end restores (more or less) the integrity of the genre with which the story opened. The conventions of the fairy-tale may have been treated throughout with irony, but it has invariably been gentle and dispensed with never less than affection.

Critics in Germany, more used to fantasy literature from a Tolkien or a J.K. Rowling than from one of their own, were in general rather bemused by this seemingly innocuous offering from a writer previously known for her astringency. Whilst some praised the work's 'souveräne[...] Heiterkeit'[25] and the skill with which the disparate elements were held together, others also found it 'ein bißchen dünn und fadenscheinig',[26] lacking 'den Biss und die Zumutungen ihrer anderen Bücher',[27] whilst the novel itself, so the charge went, failed to make clear 'wohin man eigentlich unterwegs ist und warum'[28] and did not appear 'von etwas wirklich Wesentlichem zu handeln'.[29] The debates of the 1990s may have petered out inconclusively, but as this last comment indicates, the issue at their heart, the nature and function of the novel, continues to exercise the German literary world. So much so indeed that, in mid-2005, *Die Zeit* could publish a feature entitled, 'Was soll der Roman?', in which four authors of the so-called middle generation, born between 1955 and 1964, put forward a 'Manifest für einen Relevanten Realismus', arguing that 'dem Roman heute eine gesellschaftliche Aufgabe zukommt'.[30] Although they were immediately challenged by four of their contemporaries, the re-emergence of familiar arguments, and the prominence given to the exchange, seem to confirm a remark made by Uwe Wittstock at the start of the earlier debate: 'Die Idee, die Arbeit eines Schriftstellers müsse, um auf Interesse zu stoßen, jederzeit irgendeine sozialtheoretische Relevanz nachweisen, scheint mir eine sehr deutsche zu sein'.[31]

In *Dies ist kein Liebeslied* there is a brief but significant allusion to this controversy. As Anne Strelau composes that unsent letter to Peter Hemstedt referred to earlier, she speculates mockingly as to what her dutiful classmates were doubtless at that moment writing in their essays on *Werther*: 'Vermutlich schreiben sie, daß der Autor Gesellschaftskritik übt, das ist ja immer schon die halbe Miete' (L162). She herself, however, is far more interested in the depiction of Werther himself, and although she allows that one could 'vielleicht [...] daraus eine Gesellschaftskritik drechseln' (L162-3), in her view this is at best secondary to the exploration of character. Duve's own novels, particularly the two under examination here, reflect this position. In the works of an author who has said of herself, 'Wie jede vernünftige Frau verstehe ich mich als Feministin',[32] it is unsurprising to find a particular focus on power relations between the sexes, a part of whose expression is the power of one generation to shape (or blight) the life of the next. In neither of these relationships, however, is the distribution of vice and virtue clear-cut or the outcome necessarily predictable. It has been suggested that such ambiguity is simply a 'strategisches Vorgehen' on the part of an author who knows 'wie schwer es ist, feministische Themen bei einem breiten Publikum durchzusetzen'.[33] Duve herself, however, whilst acknowledging that her views on feminism may be discerned 'gelegentlich' in what she writes, sets the priority elsewhere: 'Literarische Maßstäbe haben aber immer Vorrang'.[34]

What marks out her writing, then, are the energy of its narrative style, its inventive and often witty use of language, the lively creation of character and mood, and the skill with which different forms and perspectives are melded together. Despite their outwardly very dissimilar nature there is at the heart of her three novels to date a common theme: the battle of the sexes played out in various forms and contexts. But it would be mistaken to assume, as that earlier suggestion implies, that her literary activity is therefore fuelled by some didactic intent, for although one can undoubtedly, if one wishes, 'daraus eine Gesellschaftskritik drechseln' (L162-3), her writing convinces precisely because it does not, in the words of Keats's dictum, have a palpable design on us. It is for a different reason that *Regenroman* fails to satisfy: the characters in that novel, for all their outlandish appeal, remain essentially pawns in a narrator's plan and are never allowed to come fully alive. But where we witness, as in *Dies ist kein Liebeslied*, the unpeeling of an individual consciousness as it responds not just to outward pressures but in particular to its own drives and urges, Duve's writing can be genuinely affecting. Even in *Die entführte Prinzessin*, where the constraints of the genre itself might have been expected to stifle the life out of the characters, they emerge with a vitality and depth that belie the trappings surrounding them. This last novel, audacious in its formal break with its predecessors, has further underlined the versatility of a writer who had already shown her ability to attract both a popular readership and academic interest. Together with the qualities of her artistry discussed here, this would suggest that there is indeed rather more to Karen Duve than that dubious compliment which was our starting-point.

Notes

1 Volker Hage, 'Literarisches Fräuleinwunder,' *Der Spiegel*, 12, 22 March 1999, p. 7.

2 Volker Hage, 'Ganz schön abgedreht,' *Der Spiegel*, 12, 22 March 1999, pp. 244-46 (here: p. 244).

3 *new books in german*, Autumn 2002, 17. (Also available at: http://www.new-books-in-german.com/backlist.html)

4 Sinead Moriarty, quoted in Henry McDonald, 'Chick-lit flourishes in singletons' Dublin,' *The Observer*, 29 February 2004 (available at: http://www.chicklit.us/News.htm)

5 Quoted in Anjula Razdan, 'The Chick Lit Challenge,' *Utne Magazine*, 22 April 2004 (available at: http://www.chicklit.us/News.htm)

6 *The Guardian*, 23 August 2001 (also available at: http://books.guardian.co.uk/bookerprize2001/story/0,1090,541335,00.html).

7 Helmut Zuegler, 'Heftiger Schauer,' *Die Woche*, 19 February 1999, p. 35.

8 Thomas Bollwerk, 'Die Frau, das Moor, der Tod,' *literaturkritik*, 6 (June 2000): http://www.literaturkritik.de/public/rezension.php?rez_id=1158&ausgabe=200006

9 Jörg Albrecht, 'Gurgeln in Priesnitz,' *Die Zeit*, 11 March 1999, p. 48. In my own review of *Regenroman* I was happy, despite other criticisms, to acknowledge the 'uninhibited energy' of Duve's writing and her 'descriptive pyrotechnics': 'Replanting the garden of the North,' *Times Literary Supplement*, 8 October 1999, pp. 7-8 (here: p. 8).

10 Mathias Schreiber, 'Die neue Heftigkeit', *Der Spiegel*, 7 October 2002, p. 180.

11 Susanne Tank, untitled review: http://www.literatur-fast-pur.de/2liebeslied.html

12 Evelyn Finger, 'Exzesse der Trostlosigkeit,' *Die Zeit*, 22 November 2002. (Also available at: http://www.zeit.de/2002/47/L-Duve).

13 Mechthilde Vahsen, 'Wenn eine Sehnsucht zu Ende geht,' *literaturkritik*, 1 (January 2003): http://www.literaturkritik.de/public/rezension.php?rez_id=5609

14 Karen Duve, *Regenroman*, Eichborn: Frankfurt am Main, 1999, p. 7. Future references in the text are abbreviated to 'R'.

15 Karen Duve, *Dies ist kein Liebeslied*, Eichborn: Frankfurt am Main, 2002, p. 7. Future references in the text are abbreviated to 'L'.

16 http://www.eichborn-verlag.de/s2/

17 Jochen Förster, 'Kein Plan, keine Liebe, keine Idee,' *Die Welt*, 31 August 2002. (Also available at: http://www.welt.de/data/2002/08/31/441981.html)

18 Quoted in Andrew Billen, '"I'm so sick of the corrections",' *The Times*, 23 March 2004, T2, p. 4.

19 Ulrich Plenzdorf, *Die neuen Leiden des jungen W.*, Suhrkamp: Frankfurt am Main 1973, pp. 37, 99, 124.

20 Susanne Messmer, 'Es ist eine erbärmliche Sucht,' *taz*, 25 September 2002. (Also available at: http://www.taz.de/pt/2002/09/25/a0172.nf/text)

21 Deutschlandradio, 'Spinnert, aber hart am Leben':
http://www.dradio.de/dlf/sendungen/buechermarkt/350210/

22 Karen Duve, *Die entführte Prinzessin*, Eichborn: Frankfurt am Main, 2005, p. 5.
Future references in the text are abbreviated to 'P'.

23 See also pp. P104, P206, P227, P347.

24 Deutschlandradio, 'Spinnert, aber hart am Leben'.

25 Wolfgang Schneider, 'Das Schöne und Fürchterliche an der Liebe,' *Neue Zürcher
Zeitung*, 12 April 2005.

26 Martin Halter, 'Nun komm schon, Mädel,' *Frankfurter Allgemeine Zeitung*, 24
March 2005, p. 38.

27 Katrin Müller, 'Dem Krötigen treu geblieben,' *Die Tageszeitung*, 1 March 2005, p.
16. (Also available at: http://www.taz.de/pt/2005/03/01/a0238.nf/text).

28 Petra Kohse, 'Die Prinzessinnenrolle,' *Frankfurter Rundschau*, 16 March 2005
(also available at:
http://www.fr-aktuell.de/uebersicht/alle_dossiers/kultur/literatur_rundschau/?sid=40e
cdfef90103324f3c8238d5b096831&cnt=647420).

29 Deutschlandradio, 'Spinnert, aber hart am Leben'.

30 'Was soll der Roman? Eine Debatte unter Schriftstellern über die moralischen und
ästhetischen Aufgaben der Literatur,' *Die Zeit*, 23 June 2005, pp. 49-50 (here: p. 49).

31 Uwe Wittstock, 'Ab in die Nische?,' *Neue Rundschau*, 104, no.3 (1993), pp. 45-58
(here: p. 57).

32 Volker Hage and Mathias Schreiber, 'Ich stehe gern im Regen,' *Der Spiegel*, 11
October 1999, pp. 255-58 (here: p. 258)

33 Heidelinde Müller, *Das 'literarische Fräuleinwunder'*, Peter Lang: Frankfurt am
Main, 2004, p. 77.

34 Hage and Schreiber, 'Ich stehe gern im Regen,' p. 258.

Teresa Ludden

Nature, Bodies and Breakdown in Anne Duden's 'Das Landhaus' and Karen Duve's *Regenroman*

This essay examines the gendered representation of human relations with the natural environment in two texts by contemporary German women writers, 'Das Landhaus' by Anne Duden from her first book, *Übergang* (1982), and Karen Duve's literary debut *Regenroman* (1999). Whereas 'Das Landhaus' explores new patterns of relations between mind and body, nature and culture, I shall argue that *Regenroman*, despite elements of criticism, does not seriously re-evaluate the treatment in our culture of nature, female bodies and death.

This essay examines the gendered representations of human relations with the natural environment in 'Das Landhaus' by Anne Duden from her first book, *Übergang* (1982), and in Karen Duve's literary debut *Regenroman* (1999). Stylistically and formally the texts are very different. *Übergang* has clear avant-garde properties: the plot is undermined and language is foregrounded, the images becoming opaque at several points, not least because the first-person narration does not provide firm ground for the reader. Although the narrator is anonymous and her gender is not immediately explicit, the narrator's mental life remains the focus throughout, the text becoming a mirror of her consciousness. Duve's third-person narrative, on the other hand, is propelled by a page-turner, thriller plot, the text following the trend of 'Neue Lesbarkeit' in German fiction of the late-1990s. It features several characters, but the central focus is the decline and final demise of a male writer, Leon Ulbricht.

Despite these differences, both texts centre on human relations with the environment and implicitly question oppositional relations between culture and nature and mind and body. Both deploy the central metaphor of the house, situated in an isolated rural setting, into which a writer/urban intellectual moves, far away from their usual place of residence. As Juliet Wigmore notes, the word 'Landhaus' mixes notions of nature (Land) and culture (Haus),[1] the 'house in the country' thus serves as a metaphor for exploring boundaries between culture and nature, mind and body. In both texts the protagonists suffer breakdowns precipitated by growing proximity to the natural world. In Duden's text the narrator's hyper-awareness of nature culminates in a becoming fluid of boundaries between inside and outside in metaphors which suggest physical and mental collapse. This is presented as real, not just imagined experience, and as not wholly negative. The text ends abruptly, however, with the arrival of a nameless man (the narrator's lover) seemingly calling her to her senses. The text has been read as a depiction of the 'return of the repressed' or the 'return of the body and nature'.[2] The 'return to nature' is more humorous but also more violent in Duve's text. *Regenroman* is structured around the decline and demise of the male protagonist. The ten chapters plot Leon's collapse: his alienation from, and violence towards, the natural environment; the onset of disabling lumbago and partial paralysis; the descent into an animal-like existence after his wife leaves him. The narrative culminates in a violent storm, the collapse of the house, weakened from months of rain which the foundations and walls have soaked up, and Leon's death by suffocation when he is swallowed up by a muddy pool in the marshland surrounding the ruined house.

One crucial difference is the gender of the protagonists. While the seemingly irresistible decline of the male protagonist in Duve's text suggests cultural pessimism as to the possibility of changing masculinity or dominant antagonistic culture-nature relations, Duden's text is more ambiguous. I read it as suggesting potential re-arrangements which are, however, only possible in marginal spaces such as the artwork itself. The lack of hope of such possibilities in Duve's text could flow not only from the concentration on masculinity, but also the time of the text's production. Between 1982 and 1999, there was the Chernobyl disaster in 1986, increased knowledge of global warming and the effects of pollution, and the failure in 1997 to get the Kyoto protocol on the reduction of greenhouse gases ratified, all of which might lead to pessimism concerning our ability to affect social and cultural change. But part of the problem with Duve's text is that the work of art, while diagnosing a violent and sick culture, has itself become contaminated by repeating the violence it questions.

Nature, the body and the question of gender
Feminist philosophy has been a valuable source of critical thinking about oppositional culture/nature relations, dominant masculinity and the problematic alignment of woman with nature and the body.[3] In an earlier German context, the Frankfurt School also provides interesting insights. In the fragment 'Interesse am Körper' in *Dialektik der Aufklärung*, Adorno and Horkheimer link the antagonism between man and nature to objectification or repression of the body in favour of active 'Geist', a division they see as originating in the slave economy of Ancient Greece.[4] Work and the body were aligned with the slave and stigmatised, a structure replicated in Western class societies. Thus the human becomes defined by distance from nature and the body, resulting in a 'Haßliebe' which posits the body as an object to be possessed. This separation of 'Geist' and objects, of mind and matter, also has implications for the

treatment of others' bodies, resulting in a violence which appears endemic to dominant modes of consciousness.

Luce Irigaray too sees violence as endemic to Western culture. For her, however, the male sex is the site where nature turns against itself. In 'Une Chance de vivre' (1986) she argues that the fundamental destructiveness of Western culture originates in men's relation to the maternal. A symbolic murder of the mother occurs, she suggests, because of the objectifying tendencies men/boys develop when they cannot make sense of the mother's sex because they cannot relate it to their own. Woman's subjective identity, however, is based on another dynamic because she shares the same sex as the mother and thus cannot reduce her mother to an object without so reducing herself. Thus Irigaray puts sexual difference at the forefront of identity and subject-object relations in a way which is useful for our interpretation of Leon in *Regenroman* and in 'Das Landhaus' for our reading of the development of what Irigaray calls an inter-subject economy.[5]

Alison Stone engages with Irigaray's theories of sexual differentiation and the turn against nature in discussing the legacy of German Romanticism.[6] Stone examines Irigaray's dialogue with Hölderlin's essay 'Being, Judgement Possibility' of 1795. For Hölderlin consciousness presupposes both an originary unity with, yet necessary separation from nature. The lost unity between subject and object Hölderlin terms Being which is also Nature of which we can, however, never be truly conscious. Yet as Stone puts it:

> Despite the fact that nature is unknowable for us, […] we retain some sense of it as our basis and origin, for which we are always nostalgic. Consciousness, separation and reflection presuppose an original unity of which we necessarily retain some vestigial awareness. This awareness impels us to strive to reunite with nature.[7]

Stone also notes Irigaray's argument that such a view should not be universalised. Rather it offers a fitting description of male consciousness: '[m]ale nature generated a culture which opposes itself to nature, including female bodies and to male bodies *qua* natural. There is a part of nature – the male sex – which turns against itself.'[8] We will see such hatred of female bodies and of the maternal yet a nostalgia for unity with nature manifested in the character of Leon in *Regenroman* but first a reading of nature-culture relations in Duden's 'Das Landhaus'.

Crisis and Re-patterning in 'Das Landhaus'

'Das Landhaus' questions boundaries and explores different types of consciousness and relations with nature.[9] The text tells of the increasing terror of a person, who, it gradually emerges, is a woman, left on her own in a country house belonging to two scientists who are off on a field trip. The narrator's prolonged isolation and an excess of acute perception lead to fluid relations with the sounds and sights of nature which she cannot ignore and which precipitate the breakdown and re-patterning of relations between inside and outside the house and the narrator's body. The breakdown appears terrifying but also creative in expressing other possible selves with different boundaries and alternative relations with the environment. This is not so much a collapse of the self, as a dis- or re-ordering of relations to a world no longer standing under the domination of reason. Indeed judgement appears to finally become impossible when the narrative focuses on a description of a flower opening, and the narrator's body becomes a membrane for the flow of sounds, birds' songs and the colours of the vegetation. These passages suggest a breakdown of differentiation between subject and object, and the opaque language and images suggest that nature cannot be translated into categories of the mind. The experience does not just express nostalgia for unity with nature and Being; instead nature retains its otherness, which the narrator does not wish to master.

The narrator's breakdown is complicated by her positioning within Western culture whose dominants are expressed through the scientists, their mode of living in 'echte[r] wissenschaftliche[r] Autonomie' (Ü27) and their 'Karteikasten' which fascinate yet repel the narrator. She senses that their relation to the filecardbox replaces energy and passion. The scientists are both male and female, so that the type of consciousness they represent is not related to one sex alone. The 'Karteikasten' evokes the reason which separates and categorises. They control an influx of data by dividing it into ordered units; the index cards appear as their *raison d'être*, their existence secured by continual judgement through separation and division. They do not explore alternative modes of thinking the subject-object relation; chaotic or extreme passions are blocked by the mode of relating to themselves and their environment. The narrator is gently mocking the female scientist's use of language which suggests a judgemental distance from even the most trivial experience.

The narrator assumes that the scientists can easily forget the surrounding environment, the breath of nature and the darkness of night, whereas at night she perceives the darkness as too dark and the light inside as too bright and suddenly feels as if her actions were being watched from outside. She cannot think of herself as on her own, but feels like an object under invisible watching eyes. Whereas the scientists clearly did not feel troubled by night and nature surrounding the house because they have not hung any curtains up, she becomes anxiously over-aware of her body and its movements. Thus the text implies that the scientists are not aware of perspectives *outside* themselves: 'Nichtmal auf dem Klo schien ihnen der Gedanke zu kommen, daß es auch noch eine Außenwelt gab.' (Ü27) The reference to the scientists' mode of living 'ohne Seitenblick' indicates the certainty of the Enlightenment subject which establishes itself as a type of God by seeing itself as the creative centre of the knowable world.

A contrast is implied, then, between the narrator and the scientists. They do not turn to nature outside to discern an imaginary gaze, whereas the narrator is acutely aware of different points of view from outside. Her connections with nature precipitate the breakdown of the subject conceived as a separate, autonomous entity, but not as a sudden change: from the beginning the narrator's uncertainty places the autonomy and reason associated with the scientists in question as she 'reads' their house differently. The 'Landhaus' stands in a hollow, not an elevated position, its lack of privileged perspective being stressed by the narrator. The house's many openings cause anxiety; its exits are a reminder of the house as itself a passage – from inside to outside – rather than a static structure with an impermeable boundary. Nature is also not located in a separate space out there but encroaches on the house:

> Sie [die Fenster: TL] beharrten, gleich zu welcher Tageszeit und trotz unterschiedlicher Licht- und Wetterverhältnisse, auf dem diffusen Dunkel und spiegelten, von einem bestimmten Punkt aus gesehen, zu allem Überfluß auch noch die fast schwarzen Lebensbäume und andere Büsche wider, als wüchsen diese sehr wohl und selbstverständlich drinnen wie draußen. (Ü14)

The windows do not offer transparent access to knowledge; their opaque surface offers only a reflection of dark nature. The distinction between nature and culture starts to break down, so undoing the inside/outside and light/dark dichotomy. The text suggests an allegory of culture-nature relations. Mind and culture do not transcend, but appear as part of nature, or even as produced by nature. The woman's attention (and her self) is described as coming from outside. Thus the spatial model of the ego as located inside the seamless container of the body and opposed to objects outside is questioned. Her mind is not contained within the boundaries of her head but is outside in the dark nooks and crannies of the house and corners of the garden. It becomes impossible to think of the narrator as occupying a series of stable places as the boundaries between narrator, room, house, garden and nature become fluid.

This becoming fluid of boundaries constitutes the narrator's breakdown. The crisis is conveyed through a succession of images of distortions to the mind and body, to time and to instable, moving space. When the narrator begins to merge with the unfathomable sounds of the night, the images suggest a fragmented body, flooding between spaces. Such intense connection with the invisible noises of the night alters the narrator's daytime sight. Clear sight and ordered thought break down because of an *excess* of seeing and the seer can no longer separate herself from what is seen (Ü34). This is not simply a return to nature (which would imply nature was absent in the first place), but a new attentiveness;

it is not just a collapse of culture into nature, but an attempt to highlight nature's agency and difference – there is no anthropomorphizing, nature is not made to symbolise anything. The tenor is of an encounter with something real but beyond the full grasp of the mind.

The narrator's final collapse appears to suggest paralysis as she has to lie down on the carpet, but in fact her state is extremely active. Metaphors highlight the movement of the senses which collapse space and distance. Sounds surrounding the narrator are allowed inside her body until there is pure movement between her, the house, and the outside world. At first the house symbolises a categorising consciousness – books and CDs in alphabetical order, a freezer full of pre-cooked meals –, but by the end the house resembles the narrator's disorganised body as distinctions between the rooms break down when the inside/outside boundary becomes radically fluid: 'Küche, Toilette, Schlafzimmer – brauchte ich alle nicht mehr für die Zwecke, für die sie gebaut und eingerichtet waren.' (Ü38) I read the becoming fluid of boundaries between house and nature, mind and body as a symbolic re-configuration of oppositional mind-body relations, and the narrator's breakdown not as a collapse of self but as expressive of a different self. Towards the end fragmentation and mutating relations with the environment attain a voice. Lack of mastery, coupled with an awareness of nature's agency, signals a movement towards what Irigaray calls an inter-subject economy transformative of the subject-object split.[10] The narrator becomes too aware (compared with a cultural norm) of her surroundings (the sounds of nature) and of the body. But the close does not amount to a 'return of the body' or 'collapse into body'. Rather the fragmentation expresses the dynamism of mind/body moving in new patterns and thus the experience of an embodied mind or mindful body.

Some critics see the narrator in *Übergang* as helpless, a view the return at the end of the narrator's male lover might seem to back up.[11] His words – 'Das ist ja wahnsinnig. Komm sofort hier raus.' (Ü40) – reveal that he operates with a division between inside and outside which has become meaningless for the narrator. This scenario might suggest a male stability which the unstable female subject needs to 'bring her to her senses'. However, an alternative reading is possible: given the dominant violent modes of oppositional subject-object relations, re-arrangements that suggest movements beyond this split appear mad and may only be explored in marginal spaces like the avant-garde work of art. The narrator's reply are the final words: 'Ich höre mich noch fragen: Wohin denn.' (Ü40) which leave the direction of movement uncertain.

Masculinity, *Untergang* and Death in *Regenroman*

Such moments suggesting openness to changing relations to the natural environment are harder to locate in *Regenroman*.[12] Published 17 years later, the novel evokes a pervasive violence, especially male violence towards women, animals and the environment. Commonplace violence is embodied in menacing characters, such as Pfitzner, from the seedy Hamburg underworld of strip clubs, pimps and boxing, who has commissioned Leon to write his biography. Pfitzner's side-kick is Harry, Leon's 'best friend', who brutally rapes Leon's wife, Martina, on Pfitzner's orders. Cruelty and antagonism seemingly underpin the whole social order, including human treatment of nature. Leon's flat in Hamburg is opposite an abattoir which means that the smell of 'Blut und Tod' (R20) is always in the atmosphere and description hints at practices of force feeding, genetic modification and mass transportation of animals driven demented by their confinement. In one episode Leon encounters a truck driver transporting rusty containers, hinting at environmental pollution. Antagonism and violence between man and nature is mirrored by the violence humans inflict on each other. A world of murder lurks under the surface, hinted at through Leon's discovery of a female corpse in the river in the first chapter. Later in the penultimate chapter the police show Leon a whole selection of photos of murdered women.

The natural environment appears from early on as contaminated and controlled. The stream in Priesnitz, is controlled by concrete pipes through which it is threaded above and below the ground (R33); there is 'rostigtrübes Wasser' (R28) in the canal, and the first descriptions of the landscape with the shivering animals are far from uplifting. Leon and Martina's first encounter with nature is in the form of a grassy slope, overgrown with bushes and weeds, at the side of a busy main road. When Martina falls down the slope she smells 'verfaulte[s] Holz und Pilze[...]' and falls 'zwischen Fanta-Dosen, grauen Papierklumpen, leeren Haribo-Tüten und halbverwesten Kothaufen' (R9-10). Nature too seems to be drawn into the cycle of destruction and has started to destroy itself: animals are trained to inflict injury on humans and other animals (as in the dog fight between Harry's bullterrier and Leon and Martina's stray dog, Noah); the prevailing damp or rainy weather produces treacherous mud pools on the moor, flooding and storms. Fruit rots before it has had a chance to ripen. Leon reads about widespread crop failures and slug infestations in the newspaper. But Irigaray's worry that nature might not have the resources to fight back against a male-dominated culture appears unfounded. The stability of Leon's house is in doubt from the start; firm land and stable foundations are constantly being reclaimed by water, and Leon, pitted against the forces of nature, is engaged in a futile battle against his environment.

Natural entities often appear in Leon's imagination to be violent, but the text hints at the projection of human ideas onto nature. At several points the narrative suggests that the violent state of human affairs may reflect violence inherent in nature. This idea appears in a typically laconic exchange between Leon and Martina. Leon wants the starving dog, Noah, to fight for his food: 'Das ist Natur. In der Natur gibt es auch nichts geschenkt', he says. Martina replies, 'Nein das ist nicht Natur, das ist gemein.' (R77) Leon's idea of nature stresses harsh competition and survival of the fittest, but in fact he is glorifying the aggressive competition which characterises his own society and personality. To him nature appears as amoral, cruel and violent, whereas Martina's contradiction suggests an awareness of humans as the source of the violence and cruelty. She does not anthropomorphise, but evokes nature without projecting meaning or ethical concepts upon it. Another more unsettling example of the anthropomorphisation of nature is the depiction of the nature programme about giant lizards that Harry and Leon watch on TV. Here the apparent violence and cruelty of the animal world is fetishised and glamorised, the lizards' disgusting feasting turned into a half-pleasurable spectacle. Shortly after comes a description of Hamburg's red light district as lawless and beyond the civilising influence of the state. The two seem linked; the underbelly of the city appears as having reverted to an older, more natural state, the human reverting to supposedly natural dog-eat-dog behaviour, which civilisation attempts but fails to tame. *Regenroman* thus implies that society valorises violence as natural and as an excuse for not having to think critically about human behaviour.

In *Dialektik der Aufklärung* Adorno and Horkheimer argued that social relations in modern society are made to appear natural and nature is presented as anticipating the hierarchical character of society. Thus people are brought to experience nature as having intrinsic meaning – as prefiguring social phenomena. This process of re-enchantment covers over the effects of human reason and control and contradicts the original goal of the demythologising process of the Enlightenment, which was to disenchant nature. *Regenroman* conveys a mixture of disenchanted and re-enchanted nature: the weather forecasts that precede every chapter allude to the desire to predict and control nature, but the sense of superiority over nature is undermined by the content of the chapters. If the weather forecasts suggest a disenchanted nature ordered through science and no longer through mythology or religion, other aspects of the text, such as the references to the biblical Great Flood, allude to residual enchanted views of nature. Given the centrality of Leon and his gradual demise, the focus is not, however, on modernity or society, but masculinity. Irigaray's point about the male sex being the site at which nature turns against itself is most pertinent. Leon's character, sexuality and his treatment of women and nature will now be examined in more depth.

Leon is differentiated from the criminal Pfitzner and Harry. He is a 'moderner Mensch mit Abitur' (R274) and has Rilke and Schopenhauer on his bookshelves. His gruesome battles with, and mass murder of, slugs that are decimating his garden and his efforts to tame the stray dog that appears on the doorstep seem light-hearted in comparison with Harry's rape of Martina. However, his behaviour towards women, the moor and bodies implicates him and his sex in the whole spectrum of violence. He finds the strength and physicality of Harry and Pfitzner's world attractive, and further details align him with macho values: he is reading a book about bull-fighting. Moreover, his admiration of macho values combined with his cowardice, his patronising attitude towards Martina and the local people in Prieznitz, and his failure to defend Martina all cause him to appear in a negative light.

The narrative often comically diminishes Leon's self-importance. He is first seen as a small, insignificant spot against the broad sweep of the landscape: 'Er wirkte vor der Landschaft wie ein Tintenfleck auf einem Foto.' (R11) He has just discovered the bloated corpse of a young woman in a river at the side of the motorway. Fascinated and disgusted at the same time, he pokes the 'Wasserleiche' with a stick, dunking it down into the river in an experiment to see if the skin will tear. This reveals an extreme objectifying attitude of mastery over the body, nature and death. The narrative voice often represents the natural environment with a dead-pan neutrality, using down-to-earth images which suggest both nature's uncanny beauty and the alienation of the human viewer, as in descriptions of Leon's first sight of the moor, which he fondly thinks will inspire his writing. Leon immediately desires unity with the landscape, an idea, which the narrative quietly debunks:

> Der Anblick des Moores erfüllte Leon mit hilfloser Sehnsucht. Der Schönheit einer Frau konnte man beikommen, indem man mit ihr schlief. Und ein schönes Tier konnte man erschießen oder kaufen oder essen. Aber was konnte man schon mit einer Landschaft anfangen. (R42)

Leon's thoughts, which point towards a pantheistic, nostalgic desire for unity with the landscape, might recall the subject-object split theorised in German Romantic thought. Leon's longing for nature is produced, it seems, because he cannot objectify the landscape. In producing a desire that can never be fulfilled, the landscape represents Leon's undoing: because it cannot be turned into an object to be mastered, it undermines an identity constituted by a dominating subject-object split and Leon is unable to develop any other kind of identity.

moving there, working in garden etc.

Despite his longing for unity, Leon does not respect nature. In an early episode he loses his way in the moor and falls into the quickmud. The first of many falls symbolising his gradual demise, it is described as a terrifying, near-death experience. He is submerged in mud and is able to pull himself free only at the last minute. This experience does not lead to a new awareness of the power of nature. Rather, his immediate concern is the loss of his Nike trainer, which 'blieb verschluckt. Er war zu einem Bestandteil von etwas Unermeßlichem geworden' (R88).[13] Leon's relation to nature is one of 'Haßliebe' rather than simple longing. Chapter 4 features the battle with the slugs and what disturbs him most is the constant procreation: the sight of a slug filled with eggs fills him with disgust, suggesting an underlying fear of birth and of nature as the source of its own generation which is not subject to human control. His inability to control the slugs leads him to conclude that nature is fundamentally antagonistic towards the human world.

Leon thus has a dual view of nature – as something to be longed for but also a cruel force which undermines all his striving. Leon's sexual relationship with Isadora, from the neighbouring house, highlights this duality. Isadora is an absurd character, a cliché of the earth-mother, who functions as a foil against which Leon's mode of relating to nature, the body and the maternal, can be highlighted. She is first glimpsed by Leon bathing naked in the mud outside his kitchen window, with what appears to be a skull between her knees, a sight recalling the 'Wasserleiche' from the first chapter. Subsequent descriptions reinforce her connection to nature and the maternal, but also to death. Hers is an extremely fat, fleshy body, she has intimate knowledge of the mud and the moor, her bed is made out of a tree, and she eats slugs. Her return of Leon's trainer to him even though it has been lost in the depths of the mud hints at the supernatural.

Leon finds Isadora repulsive, but is also attracted: 'Ihre Fettleibigkeit und elementare Schlampigkeit reizten ihn.' (R147) In their first sexual encounter, Leon is split into a more 'rational' side (attracted to his thin wife) and a more 'primitive' side, which is attracted, despite himself, to Isadora. Isadora becomes aligned with a mother figure as her body offers 'ein großes, warmes Kissen voller Trost und Liebe' (R150) and is also likened to cake dough, evoking childhood pleasures for Leon. Childhood desires are also evoked in the description of climax which is likened to falling off a fairground ride. Thus Leon's sexual relations with Isadora appear to have the force of breaking taboos, the descriptions stress a return to the primitive and animalistic. In one of the longest sentences of the book Isadora is aligned in Leon's imagination with nature as he fantasises a union with the moor:

> Es war gut. Es war so … – so weich. So viel. Als würde er mit dem ganzen Moor schlafen. Als wäre der Morast und der Torf und die verfaulten Blätter, die Pustelpilze und die vollgesogene Rinde und all das kleine Gekriech, das darauf lebte, die Moor- und Wasserfrösche, die Kröten, Unken, Molche und Olme und was da sonst noch herumkroch und schiß und sich fortpflanzte, all das Kaulquappenzeug und der Laich und nicht zuletzt der Regen, der endlose alles auflösende Regen, der sich im Moor fing – als wäre das alles zu einer einzigen Frau geworden. (R152-3)

In the sexual encounter with Isadora Leon experiences a dissolving of self as he imagines mingling with the shitting, procreating animals and with nature as a whole through the suggestion that he feels part of the whole water cycle. But fear and disgust are evoked at the same time as pleasure. The whole experience is linked to a loss of a boundary between self and other, where the male ego is positioned as self, and the earth-woman as other. This produces in Leon not an acceptance of the body and nature, but violent rejection. Karen Duve has stated that, while writing *Regenroman*, she was reading Klaus Theweleit's *Male Fantasies* in which the sexual act from a male perspective is often described as an animalistic reduction of the self, which then needs to be distinguished from the 'real' self; giving in to sexual emotions is figured as a sickness, and lovemaking appears 'as being overcome by nature or falling victim to something that has nothing to do with oneself; as with animals, it is in their blood.'[14]

After his encounter with Isadora, Leon experiences an extreme hatred for female bodies: he rejects fleshy softness of the body as other and not part of his idea of his own body. He compares the 'proper' hard male bodies of boxers to this soft female flesh as a wrong type of body:

> Ein Körper ohne Muskeln – wie eine weiße Schnecke. Isadora war besonders schlimm, aber eigentlich waren alle Frauen so, jedenfalls nicht viel besser, nicht einmal Martina. Diese schlaffen Extremitäten – nicht zu vergleichen mit Männerbeinen, Männerarmern. Diese duftlosen Körper – bis auf den Gestank zwischen ihren Beinen. Überhaupt das weibliche Geschlechtsteil – Haare. Schrumpeliges und ein tiefes rotes Loch – und hinterher fühlte es sich an wie zerkochte Nudeln. (R155)

Duve evokes here the classic horror of castration in this description of female genitalia. Reminiscent of Irigaray's account of the male child, Leon violently rejects a body that is different from his and evinces an unwillingness to think of his origins in the maternal body.

Leon's ideas about his body, 'eine gut funktionierende Maschine' (R74), are dealt a blow, however, when he is afflicted with lumbago (the German 'Hexenschuß' implies an attack by a malign female nature). He is unable to move, make love, or work; images of his physical decline suggest that he is turning into a slug. He cannot read or think and becomes enormously fat, even developing breasts (which, he thinks, still aren't as bad as women's as no milk can be secreted from them!). He is now pitted against his body as a new kind of enemy. Despite the body's constant reminder of its presence – his size and weight and the constant pain – there is still a sense of alienation as he rejects his slug-like body as separate from his 'real' self. This rejection of the corporeal is stressed in a further sexual encounter with Isadora, while he is lying semi-paralysed on the floor. When Isadora takes an active role, 'merkte [Leon], wie sein Wille sich aus seinem Körper davonstahl' (R219). Here he thinks there is a radical separation between himself and his penis.

The closing chapters concentrate on Leon's decline and final demise after Martina leaves him. Several experiences lead ineluctably towards death. Leon gets lost in the drowned wood wearing only a dressing gown. Like the forest in fairytales, the wood is a symbol for the unknown, the uncanny, and a loss of self. Leon's childhood fears, of the dark and of creepy sounds – '[ü]berall kroch und raschelte, schlüpfte und glitt es' (R273) – resurface and he comes to doubt his knowledge of the natural world. The damp moisture does not respect the boundary between the human body and the environment: it gets into every pore and the saturated air on Leon's sweaty skin becomes an image of breakdown between the body and the external environment, the body's secretions merging with the water in the air and the soaking trees. The experience brings no new awareness, however, but rather confirms Leon's earlier ideas of an inimical nature. Leon is spared from being crushed by his house when it collapses in the final chapter as he is rescued by Isadora's sister, Kay. Instead he meets his death in the marshy moor. Violence is down-played as the experience contains elements of pleasure, alluding perhaps to a death-drive; giving in to the desire to fill himself with mud and nothingness appears as a final, Schopenhauerian, release. The images suggest that the body finds its true home, as the tubes of the lungs are likened to plant tendrils: 'Leon schmatzte und schluckte, füllte seinen Magen mit Schlamm und Dunkelheit. Wie gut es war, Moder unter Moder zu sein. Leon sank zurück in den Schoß seiner wahren Mutter.' (R297) But this is a death-dealing mother. The life-giving properties of nature lose out to the perspective that links nature to death. Thus Leon does not find unity or Being; instead there is a simple loss of consciousness. In the 'return to nature' Leon's alienation from his body is highlighted as his thoughts (and the narrative voice) reinforce a notion of a split between 'real' self or spirit which is separate from the body.

Duve has stated that, while there is no hope for the male sex in *Regenroman*, there are signs of change on the female side.[15] The female characters, as we have seen through the example of Isadora, are not realistic portrayals, but clichés. The most likely candidate for 'heroine', Kay, the lesbian or 'Mannweib' as Leon terms her, mixes reason and emotions in the right quantities, but appears more as a Ripley/ Sigourney

Weaver character from the *Alien* films when she kills Harry and Pfitzner with a giant blow-torch. Martina, we are led to believe, has by the end attained some self-knowledge. She again is represented as a 'type' – beautiful, thin, with deer-like eyes. Her bulimia stems from extreme self-hatred: 'am liebsten hätte sie sich selbst mit ausgekotzt und dann hinuntergespült' (R71). During another episode, she asks forgiveness for sinning, having internalised what she sees as her father's disgusted dislike of her. But the other side of her bulimia is an extreme selfishness. Her vomiting is linked to an obsessive desire to control her body. Thus her relation to herself and her body is not fundamentally different from Leon's. In the final chapter she returns home and sets fire to the second-hand car which was the scene of her first disgrace. Her father had caught her with a boy in the back seat when she was a teenager and it has remained *in situ* outside the house ever since. Hence the car symbolises the father's power and her alienation from her body and from sexuality. The car going up in flames might be meant to symbolise a new beginning for Martina, but the gesture is unconvincing and superficial, reminiscent of the solutions offered by the self-help books that Martina is depicted reading throughout the text.

Thus the text does not provide serious avenues for exploration of difference and change: the final pages, where an anonymous family come across an animal corpse on the beach (Harry's dog, according to Duve, though readers do not always get this), repeat the pattern of violence. The father and his two young sons are drawn to the corpse and, despite the mother's wish to move away, the father pokes it with a stick to see if the skin will tear, recalling Leon and the 'Wasserleiche'. Thus male behaviour is represented pessimistically as not open to change and women's protests prove ineffectual. And so *Regenroman* itself appears trapped in a cycle of repetition: compulsively drawn to representing violence, it diagnoses dominant cultural relations yet repeats the problems associated with that culture. In particular, the repeated association of the female, the feminine and the maternal with nature conceived as inimical and death-like is problematic. Such associations repeat the misogynistic association of the womb/woman with death and not life. A reading of the 'Wasserleiche' in Chapter 1 will clarify the point. The becoming visible of death and the female body functions as a warning sign that all is not well; the repressed elements in culture are returning to the surface. The trope of the female corpse has come to stand in literature for the otherness which masculinity must reject in order to maintain stability. Femininity and death are brought together in the figure. According to Elisabeth Bronfen the 'dead woman is a pleonasm used to confirm the social structure of gender and efface the reality of death.'[16] That is, the figure merely confirms a separation of the genders and effaces the reality of death because death and women are located together in a space that can be evoked as horrifying but also, in the artwork, as enjoyable, which leads to a perceived confinement and mastering of them. *Regenroman* might appear to question the boundary between the genders through, for instance, Leon's feminised body and his inability to transcend his environment. However, there is no real re-thinking or re-evaluation of the 'feminine', which is predominantly aligned with the disgusting, horrific and animal throughout. Moreover, while Leon's decline and death are represented as a failure to master his body and nature, the reader, who derives elements of pleasure from the representation of Leon's decline, is able to 'master' death and transcend the experiences that Leon undergoes.

Consideration of humour and elements of pastiche might produce a different reading. Teresa de Lauretis suggests that texts in the Western tradition frequently tell 'the story of male desire by performing the absence of woman and by producing woman as text, as pure representation.'[17] The cartoon nature of the female characters in *Regenroman* does indeed highlight their status as 'pure representation', but *Regenroman* does not seriously re-evaluate the treatment of nature, female bodies and death in our culture. The repetition of the trope of the 'Wasserleiche' confirms our culture through repetition of its dominant symbols. Unlike 'Das Landhaus', movement beyond these dominant symbols appears unthinkable.

Notes

1 Juliet Wigmore, 'Visions of Nature in Texts by Anne Duden. Metaphor, Metonym, Morphology,' in: Heike Bartel and Elizabeth Boa, eds., *Anne Duden: A Revolution of Words. Approaches to her Fiction, Poetry and Essays*, Rodopi: Amsterdam, 2003, pp. 88-101 (here: p. 89).

2 See Margaret Littler, 'Diverging Trends in Feminine Aesthetics: Anne Duden and Brigitte Kronauer,' in: Arthur Williams, ed., *Contemporary German Writers, their Aesthetics and their Language*, Lang: Bern, 1996, pp. 161-180.

3 See, for instance, Val Plumwood, *Feminism and the Mastery of Nature*, Routledge: London, New York, 1993; Mary Mellor, *Feminism and Ecology*, Polity Press: Cambridge, 1997; Moira Gatens, *Feminism and Philosophy: Perspectives on Difference and Equality*, Polity Press: Cambridge, 1991.

4 Max Horkheimer and Theodor W. Adorno, *Dialektik der Aufklärung*, S. Fischer Verlag: Frankfurt am Main, 1969, pp. 246-250.

5 See Luce Irigaray's work on this aspect in, 'A Chance to Live,' in: *Thinking the Difference. For a Peaceful Revolution*, trans. Karin Montin, Athlone: London, 1994; and Luce Irigaray, *I Love to You. Sketch of a Possible Felicity in History*, trans. Alison Martin, Routledge: London, New York, 1996.

6 See Alison Stone, 'Irigaray and Hölderlin on the Relation Between Nature and Culture,' *Continental Philosophy Review*, 36/4 (2003), 415-432.

7 Stone, 'Irigaray and Hölderlin', p. 423.

8 Stone, 'Irigaray and Hölderlin', p. 421.

9 Anne Duden, 'Das Landhaus' in: *Übergang*, Rotbuch: Hamburg, 1996, pp. 11-40. Further page references preceded by 'Ü' will be given in the text.

10 See Luce Irigaray, 'A Chance to Live' and Luce Irigaray, *I Love to You*.

11 Ricarda Schmidt, for instance, sees the narrator of *Übergang* simplistically as impotent victim. See 'Arbeit an weiblicher Subjektivität. Erzählende Prosa der siebziger und achtziger Jahre,' in: Gisela Brinkler-Gabler, ed., *Deutsche Literatur von Frauen*, vol. ii, 19. und 20. Jahrhundert, Beck: München, 1988, pp. 459-477.

12 Karen Duve, *Regenroman*, List: München, 1999. Subsequent page references preceded by 'R' will appear in the text.

13 'Nature' apparently enjoys swallowing up symbols of the consumer society – later Leon's mobile phone is consumed by a bucket of slugs.

14 Klaus Theweleit, *Male Fantasies, Women, Floods, Bodies, History*, vol. i, trans. by Stephen Conway, Erica Carter and Chris Turner, Polity Press: Cambridge, 1987, p. 82.

15 Her response to questions at the Karen Duve Symposium, University of Nottingham, 1 May 2004.

16 Elisabeth Bronfen, *Over Her Dead Body. Death, femininity and the aesthetic*, Manchester University Press: Manchester, 1992, p. 208.

17 Teresa de Lauretis, *Alice Doesn't: Feminism, Semiotics, Cinema*, Indiana University Press: Bloomington, 1984, p. 13.

Elizabeth Boa

Lust or Disgust? The Blurring of Boundaries in Karen Duve's
Regenroman

In Karen Duve's *Regenroman* blurring of modal and generic boundaries in the representation of the environment, the body, and violence lends the novel cultural-political significance in the fields of aesthetics and gender. Comic travesty of myth is a key weapon in conveying a feminist-inflected green agenda. A decisive intervention by a woman author in the history of male-authored representations of dead female bodies and of violence upon women, *Regenroman* also offers a provocative reflection upon the pleasure in violence pervading contemporary popular culture.

> Halb zog sie ihn, halb sank er hin,
> Und ward nicht mehr gesehn. (Goethe, 'Der Fischer')[1]

The encounter between Goethe's fisherman with his 'Menschenlist und Menschensinn', and the 'feuchtes Weib' occurs on the border between two worlds which are uncannily alike yet different. In watery reflection, the blue of the sky is 'feuchtverklärt', the moon is 'wellenatmend', and it is his own face which the fisherman sees reflected in the water, suggesting a hitherto unrecognised other self. Goethe was writing in 1778, the meeting point of late Enlightenment and early Romantic stirrings. At such a moment, the water world perhaps symbolises the enchanted realm of poesy in contrast to dry rationalism. It is a metaphor for poetic metaphor which reflects yet transforms the real world and uncovers hidden truths and unacknowledged desires below the prosaic surface. The poem contains the metaphoric other world within a regular metric order, however, and frames the uncanny encounter within folk tradition. No Romantic, Goethe seems to be warning both against Enlightenment instrumental reason in the phallic shape of a fishing rod, but also against a deadly return of repressed desires in the shape of an engulfing 'feuchtes Weib'. In this essay, I want to consider what a 'feuchtes Weib' and a waterlogged other world might symbolise in 1999 in Karen Duve's *Regenroman*.

Regenroman too draws us into a metaphorical other world, like the real world, but a bit off the edge and down the muddy track to somewhere else. But unlike the clear dividing line of a riverbank in 'Der Fischer', here water and earth interpenetrate in a deceptively soggy morass, exemplifying a general blurring of distinctions. The reader of Goethe's poem can safely watch from *terra firma* as the fisherman disappears and the ending allows us to imagine the fisherman 'wellenatmend' in some sub-aqueous world. But at the end of *Regenroman*, squelchy mud penetrates bodily orifices, glugging down into throat and lungs. Like 'Der Fischer', *Regenroman* has alluringly erotic moments but they are generally shot through with disgust in a blurring of boundaries between enchantment and horror, lust and disgust. Three main techniques feed into the heightened realism which makes *Regenroman* so intriguing: extended metaphor intertwines with precise detail of contemporary life, while, conversely, metaphoric motifs, slugs for instance, are rendered with naturalistic precision; the ostensibly impersonal narration is full of perspectival shifts so that we see the world at one point or another through the eyes of most of the characters including the dog Noah; mood and mode shift ambiguously between the comic and the horrific, the parodic and the straight, between realism and traces of the fantastic, of fairy tales, of myth, or of comic-book violence. This kaleidoscopic perceptual field is disorientating, but enlivening, for the blurring of boundaries between the literal and the metaphoric and between literary moods and modes contributes to the import of *Regenroman* as an intervention in contemporary cultural politics, especially in the fields of gender and aesthetics.

Cultural Geography: Disappearing Borders

There has been much talk recently of 'neue Lesbarkeit'.[2] I want to suggest points of connection with 'alte Lesbarkeit', not to reduce *Regenroman* to an imitation, but because affinities with older forms generate fascinating contrasts with contemporary genres as strip-cartoon violence mixes with echoes of poetic realism or modernist appropriations of myth.[3] The novel opens with a journey from Hamburg through provincial east Germany to the dreary small town of Freyenow, the even drearier village of Priesnitz, then the field-track to a house on the edge of a marsh with another mysterious house just visible past the skeletal trees of a dead forest. These locations have a retro flavour: they reprise the contrast between the city and the countryside in *Heimat* literature around 1900, but with a contemporary twist in that the city is west German whereas the countryside is east German. The topography is reminiscent too of Kafka's village tale, *Das Schloß*, with its metaphorical other world to be reached by turning off the highway and crossing a bridge, like the bridge just after Freyenow across the canal to a minor road without a signpost. Key motifs persisting through poetic realism, *Heimat* writing and some canonical modernist texts include liminal locations on the threshold between nature and culture and potentially deadly encounters when the human protagonist, generally a man, strays too far out, whether into the high moor lands, as in Clara Viebig's Eifel tales, or snowy paths that lead nowhere in *Das Schloß*.[4] Here Leon strays too far into the marsh, then wanders in circles like Hans Castorp in *Der Zauberberg*. Hans survives the snow, though he may later drown in the mud of the trenches, but Leon gets definitively lost in the east German mud. The mountain films of the 1920s too show such uncanny encounters, sometimes with female spirits of nature: to stray too far out or climb too far up is also to sink too far down into the psyche towards such alluring but deadly embodiments of the repressed.

The hero who strays too far out is often an intellectual, who hopes through contact with nature to stimulate his creative gifts. The prototype is Goethe's Werther. But nature can crush instead of inspiring and the landscapes generally bear human traces. In *Regenroman* the muddy path to the house in the moor land has 'Treckerspuren'.[5] In Priesnitz, concrete pipes, red plastic strips across a window, a motorcycle, car tyres, ads for video cassettes signify late modernity alongside an up-dated Kafkaesque castle: 'ein hundert Jahre altes, schloßähnliches Gebäude, dessen rechte Hälfte verfallen mit Efeu und Druckwurz überwachsen und dessen linke Hälfte mit sieben Satellitenschüsseln bestuckt war.' (R33) Kafka's broken-down 'Schloßturm' was 'zum Teil gnädig von Epheu verdeckt' and the windows shone in the sun, 'etwas Irrsinniges hatte das'.[6] In *Regenroman* ivy and seven satellite dishes offer an up-to-date maniacal image. Kafka's tower looked as if it were drawn by a child's hand. In *Regenroman*, the dead trees in the marsh look 'als hätte ein Choleriker in seiner Malgruppe sie gezeichnet und dabei den Bleistift verschiedene Male abgebrochen' (R37). The comic-sinister motifs prompt reflection upon what sort of civilisation is leaving its ugly traces in the east German landscape and draw attention self-reflexively to the aesthetics of a novel by a writer who may, like the choleric artist, be angry about something. Inside the story, the would-be writer is Leon. Leon wants to return to nature, which you can do more easily in the east where property is cheap, while parading a Mercedes, an emblematic symbol of western capitalism. The representation of locations in *Regenroman* thus bundles together environmentalist critique with wry sideways swipes at west German post-*Wende* arrogance and east German lust for consumer goods. Two borders are crumbling in this dreary scenario: the rubbish-strewn countryside is turning into a dumping ground no longer distinct from the city; the once iron curtain dividing different world views has vanished. Such juxtaposition of disappearing environmental and vanished political borders obliquely conveys the longing for an alternative to the seemingly inexorable advance of environmental depredation, and while *Regenroman* does not mourn the passing of state socialism, the canine dramatis personae associated with East and West respectively (Noah v. Rocky) suggest sympathy for Ossi underdogs over Wessi triumphalism.

If Rocky's name recalls today's muscular Hollywood heroes, Noah evokes the Biblical flood which threatened to undo Jehovah's separation of the elements. Leon is a hero engaged in a miniature repeat of the great project to conquer nature, draining his land, drying out his house, protecting his woman. The post-diluvian hero strives to re-establish Jehovah's clear division between land and water, hence the scandal of creatures such as slugs or the fire-spitting amphibian salamander. The salamander evokes primordial times before the species specialised between land and water; the lizard shape of a line of nodules repeated in Martina's backbone suggests that woman too transgresses clear boundaries and elemental distinctions. Noah, a carpenter and builder, is a culture hero in the mould of *homo faber*. Underlying their political differences, socialism did share with the liberal ideology of capitalism a common purpose: the scientific understanding and technological exploitation of nature to human ends. Leon's love of the Mercedes signals his attachment to capitalist values. But although he asserts western intellectual superiority over an eastern rude mechanical in a run-in with a garage attendant, as a worker by brain, Leon is also conscious of the intellectual's alienation from handwork. Marx and Engels envisaged a utopia of hunting in the morning, fishing in the afternoon, farming in the evening and writing criticism after dinner.[7] But Leon fails to humanise nature or to write a book, fails to overcome alienation. The historical subject of the Marxist grand narrative is male. Here the real technologist is Kay who dries out rising damp and harnesses the salamander's element of fire in an ultra-modern flame-throwing gadget to defend Martina. Promethean Woman displaces failed male technics. All this is a comic appropriation of historical agency for women in the manner of a cartoon. (Lola rennt nicht, sie schlägt zurück.) *Regenroman* thus offers a twist to post-Enlightenment cultural criticism of Western Civilisation. In Horkheimer and Adorno's *Dialektik der Aufklärung*, cunning Odysseus outwits the Sirens and sails on out of myth into history at the start of civilisation, leaving the female monsters behind on their rocky island washed by the watery element. The episode conveys the repression upon which Western Civilisation is supposedly built and warns of the return of the repressed in the guise of irrational myth. In *Regenroman* myth returns with a vengeance when the hero falls victim to a female monster who like the Sirens is still half sunk in the watery element.[8] *Regenroman* thus travesties elements of both Biblical and Classical foundational myths of the origins of civilisation. It revalues slimy things that creep upon the earth and regenders key players or awards victory to the female: Promethean Woman triumphs; Siren outwits Odysseus. Even Noah, human master over the animals, is replaced by a dog who comes across as the most sensible character in the novel.

Bodily Topographies
Regenroman not surprisingly follows a critical programme rather different from that of Horkheimer and Adorno in the 1940s. It is a

feminist-inflected green agenda deploying comic travesty of myth as a key weapon. The house and garden provide a small-scale model of the borderland arena of struggle between man and nature conveying, if not a programmatic assertion of animal rights, then at the least a plea for change in the prevailing relations between human beings and other animals. The novel also promotes an aesthetic shift from predominant notions of clear-cut elemental distinctions and proper body shapes in an intervention in cultural politics which may not be wholly successful for all readers (especially if they are gardeners). If Noah defends Martina, though he also has the sense to surrender or flee when necessary, the most heroic figures in the novel are the slugs who resist the human coloniser and suffer a terrible massacre, yet keep returning to claim their right to life and a habitat. The slugs, slimily wettish creatures in alliance with the ground water which creeps up the walls, transgress the division between liquid and solid. Slugs commonly induce disgust because of their soft, squelchy dampness, but when, out of their element in a motorway lay-by, they are squashed into a spurting mash by the wheels of a lorry, pity mixes with horror and laughter. The passage is blackly comic: 'Die wenigen Überlebenden entfernten sich unendlich langsam und mit den Fühlern nach allen Richtungen sichernd vom Unglücksort. Sie sahen aus, als stünden sie unter Schock.' (R116) In grotesquely echoing human responses to earthquakes or bombing, the language comically perforates the boundary between human and animal. In *Ekel*, a study of the cultural history and aesthetics of disgust, published in 1999, the same year as *Regenroman*, Winfried Menninghaus links laughter and disgust: 'Die plötzliche Entladung einer Spannung leistet im Lachen wie im Erbrechen eine Verwindung des Ekels, einen Kontakt mit dem "Abjekten", der nicht zu dauerhafter Beschmutzung und Kontamination führt.'[9] By the 'abject', Menninghaus means the disgusting or unclean which resists cultural integration.[10] Leon, disgustingly dripping and bloodied with bits of slug clinging to his eyebrows, offers the reader a butt of laughter. Like Kafka's Gregor Samsa, he becomes the grotesque point of contact between the human and the abject. Rather than looking away with a shudder from the slimily animalesque, we are forced to see and admit the difference but also the secret likeness to our own slimier surfaces. The slugs thus serve a double function. Literally, they may extend human sympathy with animals beyond noble hairy beasts such as dogs or horses; metaphorically they belong in a motivic field concerned with the elements, with primitive sensations of touch, and with bodily boundaries between inside and outside, which challenges dominant aesthetic norms concerning body shape and sexual difference.

Belonging slimily between dryness and wetness, slugs blur a seemingly elemental distinction, as do the mucous membranes lining the passages into and out of the body, which are ambiguously neither clearly inside nor outside. When Isadora swallows a slug, as one might slurp down an oyster, she provides another example of contact with the disgusting which is liable to induce horrified laughter. In contrast to Leon's inadvertent bespattering, however, Isadora chooses to flout good taste and so is not a butt of laughter, but acts as a transgressive agent breaking a cultural taboo. (Note too, swallowing one slug signals a quite different relation to the creature than a mass slaughter.) According to Sister Mary Olivia, cited on the frontis page of *Regenroman*, 'Das Böse gedeiht an feuchten Stellen', a comment of sinister theological import. Yet bodily border-crossings through slimy passageways, whether by gases, fluids or more solid items enveloped in mucous, are essential to life: exiting the womb; breathing; eating, drinking and expelling body waste; copulating. From antiquity on, however, gender ideology has tended to allocate dampness unequally between the sexes in a discourse of bodily difference. The clear shape of the phallus signifies identity, control, power and difference between self and other; the soggy morass of woman's body signifies nothingness, loss of identity, boundlessness or excess, it sucks in and it harbours the embryo of another. Man actively penetrates, woman passively gets penetrated, an opposition echoing man's conquest of nature in the narrative of civilisation. Woman's curvy body changes and swells, man's flat body does not change. Lust threatens the simple oppositions, however, inducing uncontrollable tumescence, then satiety and detumescence. Leon feels post-coital disgust of the sticky, clammy, smelly female body yet it is his fluids that most make moist. This is what Isadora teaches him in a striking lesson in erotics. But Leon fails to remember the magical best climax of his life. Instead, he suffers a neurotic feminisation, greedily over-eating and swelling up to rival Isadora's size.

As a cultural intervention *Regenroman* works through subversion of the subliminal aesthetics of sexual difference, which are all the more powerful for being scarcely conscious, and it launches an attack on a body culture which promotes muscular hardness in men – Rocky the bulldog is emblematic – and boyish slimness yet curving sinuosity for women, so stigmatising unmuscular weediness or 'effeminate' fleshy excess in men as well as the manifold shapes of the adult female body – Kay's angularity or Isadora's billowing flesh signify two extremes. The meanings attributed to sexual difference, it is implied, generate a co-mingling of lust and disgust which is largely impervious to rational argument. A proper man should be a technologist of sex who retains control over the body he skilfully works upon as well as over his own body as implement. Disgust masks lust incompatible with proper muscular manhood: Leon offers a dire case study of masculinity in collapse following the breakthrough of desire he cannot admit for moist oblivion in bountiful flesh. Horror of the female body is not limited to men, however. Secretly bulimic Martina is beautiful by the standards of contemporary body culture. To achieve her slim beauty and punish any incipient over-swelling, Martina eats then purges herself; like a plumber cleaning out a blocked pipe, she uses her finger as a tool to induce a flow in bursts of saliva and vomit. A gruesome metaphoric equivalence links the gobbets of stuff and brownish liquid Martina convulsively sicks up with the balls of waste and rusty water gurgling out of the plumbing. Like car maintenance or clearing drains, the normative aesthetics of female beauty require a technology of beauty maintenance which divides the smooth visible surface of the body from its innards and taboos bodily functions which our culture renders even more shamefully secret for women than for men.

The shameful secrets of the body which conventional aesthetics mask leak out most disgustingly in death. The long tradition of the *memento mori* uncovers the scandal, gruesomely celebrating the consuming worms and displaying the skeleton beneath the flesh: the reflection of a skull in beauty's mirror punishes female vanity. A related though contrasting figure is that of the 'schöne Leiche', on which Elisabeth Bronfen comments.[11] This recurrent motif often has poetological import, signifying the transformation of life into art and the relation between male artist and female Muse. For a dead woman can inspire without distracting interruptions as no live person can. Drowned Ophelia is such a recurrent motif in post-Romantic painting and poetry. In one of Georg Heym's two Ophelia poems (1910) an underwater forest suggests a deadly other world like the 'skelettierten Bäume eines ertrunkenen Wäldchens' (R36) in *Regenroman* and dead Ophelia's hair shelters innocent little water rats, like the scuttling marsh creatures Leon senses in his wanderings:

> Im Haar ein Nest von jungen Wasserratten,
> Und die beringten Hände auf der Flut
> Wie Flossen, also treibt sie durch den Schatten
> Des großen Urwalds, der im Wasser ruht.[12]

But less innocently, the female corpse also serves the male poet as a metaphor for the poet's transformative power. In Gottfried Benn's 'Schöne Jugend' (1912) the water rats nest and give birth inside the drowned girl's body and crabs have eaten away her mouth; no woman's answer to the male poet's creation of new poems in celebration of new life is expected; women, like rats, give birth and moulder, men write poems that will live for ever. So too in Brecht's 'Vom ertrunkenen Mädchen' (1919) the poet's pen is licensed not to wander before, behind,

between, above, below the secret places of a living body, but to track a
post-mortem dissolution:

> Als ihr bleicher Leib im Wasser verfaulet war
> Geschah es (sehr langsam), daß Gott sie allmählich vergaß
> Erst ihr Gesicht, dann die Hände und ganz zuletzt ihr Haar.
> Dann ward sie Aas in Flüssen mit vielem Aas.[13]

As Bronfen puts it when writing of Elizabeth Siddal, Rosetti's wife and
Muse and model for Millais's Ophelia:

> The construction of masculinity and of the masculine artist is made not only in
> opposition and in precedence to a feminine body caught in the process of
> fading, but also in opposition and in precedence to absent femininity, because
> the feminine figure functions as a sign whose signified is masculine
> creativity.[14]

That Leon, a male writer who at the beginning of the novel displayed an
obscene curiosity about a female *Wasserleiche*, should at the end become
a *Schlammleiche* marks a decisive intervention by a woman author in the
long history of male-authored representations of dead female bodies.

Representing Violence

A primary borderland between self and other is the surface of the body. A
dead body is helplessly open to curious probing whereas a live person
generally is not, unless by mutual agreement or through violence. Poking
a corpse with a stick to see how easily the skin tears is not the same as
knifing or raping someone. But as the memorable first episode of
Regenroman signals, Leon stands on a line which leads in the direction of
readiness to do violence against the bodily integrity of another. Leon
refuses to think of the corpse as the mortal remains of a person, but is
moved by a mix of impersonal scientific curiosity and perverse pleasure,
like a schoolboy doing a lab experiment on a female human body rather
than just a frog. ('Just a frog' is a questionable expression, of course, as
the splendid cover of *Regenroman* indicates.) Without simply equating
them, the episode subliminally associates scientific curiosity, lust and
violence. Drawing on the tradition of post-Enlightenment critique of the
violent potential within technological and scientific culture, these
suggested affinities also signal a critical exploration of pleasure in
violence as a pervasive aspect of contemporary popular culture. A glance
at the bestseller lists or the week's offerings on television suffices to
reveal a feast of bodies chopped up or opened up by serial killers or
forensic pathologists.

Quasi-scientific discourse first appears with the weather forecasts.
The authoritative tone and specialist jargon suggest scientific objectivity,
but from the start science is overlaid with the pathetic fallacy. The
increasingly awful forecasts are funny, sinister and prophetic. The
prospect of catastrophe provides a real page-turning impetus. Like the

popular genres of the detective story or thriller, *Regenroman* constructs an expectant reader drawn into complicit pleasure in violence. The issue comes up early on with the television programme about the 'Komodowarane'. Harry and Leon do not look away as the giant lizards tear lumps of flesh from the deer's living body; on the contrary, they enjoy the slaughter and are more disgusted by the woman kissing the lizard. So when Leon thinks of Martina as having 'Augen wie ein angefahrenes Reh' (R31), we just know something awful is going to happen to her. Her suede clothes and impractical shoes at the beginning contrast with Leon's black gear and clumpy boots and set the woman up as a deer for the slaughter and Leon, if not himself as a *Waran*, then as attracted to violence. Of course the men are not watching the real thing but a representation. Yet television animal programmes deploy the medium of film – the deer really did get torn apart. *Regenroman* does not directly address the contentious issue as to whether representation of violence for entertainment and the prevalence of violent crime are causally linked. Rather it draws the complicit reader through a sequence of blackly comic representations pushed to a point, however, where pleasure may falter. For some moments of violence threaten to break through the controlling metaphors and conventions, provoking shock, in some readers perhaps rejection, but judging by the reviews, prompting many readers to at least reflect upon the nature of the violence and the manner of its representation. Rather like Quentin Tarantino's *Pulp Fiction*, the intervention in cultural politics comes self-reflexively at the level of representation.

The comic travesty of myth already commented on goes along with pointed deviations from the standard plotting of popular fiction: the female victim finds allies and fights back; personal revenge is not punished in turn to signal a restoration of order; the prime suspect is not guilty and the murder mystery is not solved; the ending is not happily reassuring; and so on. Feminists have long argued that representations of women as victims of male violence reinforce the powerful effects of gender stereotypes in shaping differing behavioural propensities in men and women, if not directly causing specific actions. Martina's rape comes as no surprise, for she is from the start set up as a victim. But the women fight back. Commenting on recent depictions of rape including *Regenroman*, Beth Linklater notes that 'it is not simply a case of reversing patterns. The violence is not gratuitous, it is about women attempting to wrest back a form of control.'[15] Moreover as Linklater rightly suggests, the rape of Martina is not reduced to a symbol but comes across as important in itself. But it is tied into the text as a whole through metaphors which link up with earlier motifs. How, or whether, such textual integration of the rape and the subsequent revenge by blowtorch works to render the representation of violence acceptable is crucial in evaluating *Regenroman* as an intervention in cultural politics.

   Regenroman is a good read yet it provocatively challenges readerly pleasure in fictional violence which the popular genres cater to. Representations of violence in fiction aimed at a wide reading public must steer between Scylla and Charybdis if they are to keep an ethically minded yet pleasure-seeking readership on board. As the phrase 'obscene violence' suggests, too vivid a picture may be held to overstep the border between the graphic and the pornographic. But too sanitised or too aestheticised a representation may be judged to trivialise or to glorify violence. Tarantino's films furnish examples of work provoking controversy over such issues. The double effect of pleasure yet provocation which *Regenroman* induces depends on combining readability with transgression of the conventional aesthetic boundaries at key points when blackly comic narration modulates into a still darker mode and the reader's pleasure is interrupted. Popular work treading such a tightrope will always be controversial, since different readers have different thresholds at which pleasure gives way to distress, rejection or critical reflection. Surveying the reviews, Peter Graves notes that some readers could read the account of Martina's rape with uninterrupted enjoyment, easily assimilating it to the genre of Anglo-American thrillers, as others could not.[16] Linklater cites a letter from the author contrasting an account of rape she had read, which invoked the horror but did not make clear what the rapists actually did, with her own approach: 'Ich habe diese Methode in meinem Buch nur genau umgedreht, indem ich fast alles detailliert beschrieb.'[17] The devil, it is said, lies in the detail. It is not violence as such, but the disgustingly graphic details of vaginal and anal rape and enforced fellatio which make *Regenroman* provocative as an intervention in a contested cultural field and so liable to divide readers.

   Menninghaus locates the origins of modern thinking about disgust in Kant's aesthetics. Kant posits the disgusting as the defining limit to representation: the border between artistic representation and the object itself becomes blurred so that the receiver cannot distinguish between 'die künstliche Vorstellung des Gegenstandes' and 'die Natur dieses Gegenstandes selbst'.[18] The crucial point, so Menninghaus argues, is Kant's implication that the disgusting object induces in the observer the impulse to consumption ('Genuß') rather than contemplation, so producing the immediate counter-response of rejection (vomiting, spitting out). Kant does not explain further this ambiguous double response of lust (impulse to consume) and disgust (impulse to reject). The analysis comes close to the common view that pornography similarly breaks through disinterested contemplation to stimulate sexual arousal. In context, as Menninghaus notes, 'Genuß' means simply consumption not pleasure, but the proposed initial impulse might suggest that disgust conceals unacknowledged or repressed desire, satisfaction of which would be pleasurable, were it not for social taboos. Hence pornography may offer an umbrella category covering representations stimulating either lust or disgust. Anxiety about pornography, whether arousing lust directly or indirectly via disgust, turns on the fear that just as soft porn may induce arousal followed by sexual activity, so hard porn might, if not induce directly imitative behaviour, then at least weaken inhibition. In considering representations of violence, then, the category of the disgusting becomes problematic. Rather than serving critical ends, it may covertly pander to forbidden desires. Leon and Harry's pleasure as they watch the lizards tearing the deer apart and their disgust when the woman kisses the lizard imply a hidden continuity between blood lust and disgust masking lust aroused by imagining perverse congress between human and animal. '"Die ist doch pervers", sagte Harry.' (R24) Watching the lizard's instinctual behaviour and the woman's transgressive act activates repressed desires which might break out. But the woman's act is a staged performance for the camera, further framed by the television screen, so that the reader of Duve's text is highly unlikely to identify with the internal audience of Leon and Harry. In effect, the passage comically deflates any tendency to indulge polymorphously perverse desires and it promotes understanding of animal behaviour, not just deer but even giant lizards, a theme developed in the different reactions of Martina and Leon to the salamander. Comic deflation is here the key device in representing violence to critical rather than pornographic effect.

The episode of the rape, however, moves out of the prevailing comic mode. But it does continue the through-running technological metaphors. Like Martina sticking her finger down her throat to provoke vomiting, an earlier passage where laughter may stick in the reader's throat, Harry goes to work like an expert plumber testing tubes and outlets, especially in the account of anal rape. The plumbing metaphor is thoroughly de-eroticising. One radical tradition in modernist writing celebrates violent breakthroughs from conventional aesthetic control as the post-Kantian sublime, the hyper-real thing in itself, the ultimate breaking asunder of the repressive order which generates the discontents of civilisation. Such breakthroughs range from anarchic anti-authoritarianism, as in the surrealist films of Buñuel and Dali with their unforgettably disgusting images, through to a proto-fascist tradition celebrating male power unleashed from patriarchal control. Women were marginal, whether as maternal guardians of repressive order or a distraction from male bonding, or else their tabooed bodies served as the field of breakthrough. Heym's story 'Der Irre', and the monstrous figures of Brecht's Baal or of Musil's Moosbrugger in *Der Mann ohne*

Eigenschaften belong here. Duve's representation of rape is like a bucket of cold water after such imaginings. Harry is not in the throes of wild transgressive pleasure; he is obeying Pfitzner, as a plumber might follow the master builder's instructions. This is no breakthrough, but just an exercise in power more demeaning to the obedient agent than the hapless victim. During the rape, Martina too feels a saving distance from her body, as if it were a machine, not her essence as a woman. When Harry condescendingly strokes her head, as if she were a dog, and congratulates her on being a truly beautiful woman, Martina does not care whether she is beautiful; this marks a shift from feminine subordination to an internalised, controlling male gaze. Mirror, mirror on the wall, who is the fairest of us all? Martina no longer cares. If Martina/Roswitha throws off her female status as victim, Leon by contrast almost turns into a woman, with his eating disorders and alienation from his fleshy body. Normally nymphs flee the pursuit of the god Pan or his goaty minions. Leon ends up as an overweight nymph in flight who falls victim to the female deity of the marshland. Martina's machine body, a masculine trope, and Leon's feminised swelling are not of course a happy ending. Both are alienated conditions. The cross-overs do, however, subvert the imaginary power of age-old misogyny and the polarised meanings attributed to sexual difference under which men and women both suffer.

Whether the readership divides along gender lines in finding different bits of *Regenroman* unassimilable – rape, blowtorching, drowning in mud – would be an interesting question. The effects of texts depend heavily on the contexts different readers bring to bear; animal rights activists might find the bludgeoning, then drowning of Rocky hardest to take. The gendered reading proposed here suggests that *Regenroman* cools down or comically deflates the representation of violence performed by men upon women. The representation of violence performed by women upon men can likewise be seen as counteracting female victimhood, though some readers may see merely a reinscription: a vigilante with a flame thrower is not the answer even if she is female. The sheer preposterousness of the revenge by blowtorch is, however, in my view grounds for defence.[19] In the context of post-modern pop, the episode offers a parodic reprise of cartoon, film, or television heroics by such figures as Buffy the Vampire Slayer, which are obviously not designed to promote imitative action, but which do counteract gender stereotypes. The *femme fatale* is another figure with a long history. Steamily sexy, her transgressive violence is always finally punished in a restoration of patriarchy, often by the police; *The Postman Always Rings Twice* or *Double Indemnity* are classic examples. That the women here get away with murder counteracts such a tradition. Again the devil is in the detail: there is nothing steamily sexy about Kay, or the clumsy apparatus she wields, or Pfitzner's plastic tie (a horror of bad taste) melting into his face, or Noah's doggy interventions, which echo children's adventure stories – all this is indeed preposterous and blackly funny. The only *femme fatale* is Isadora whose energetic love biting briefly lends her the bloody aspect of a fat vampire. That she looks so different from the Hollywood vamp, however, comically subverts a powerful tradition.

Leon's project to ghost a biography of the gangster, Pfitzner, in return for a fat fee and a black Mercedes exemplifies *Geist* in the service of *Macht* and Mammon. It is therefore satisfying that he gets his comeuppance. He serves too as a token male author done down by the female author of *Regenroman*, to the satisfaction of an implied female readership. On the other hand, readers, male and female, may be curious to seek out any mirroring between the writer within the story and the author of the story, which might blur the boundaries of heterosexual either/or identities. The novel does not pander to stigmatisation of sexually ambiguous 'weirdoes'. (Thomas Harris's *Red Dragon* might be accused on such grounds.) Transvestite Kerbel turns out not to be a serial killer but nor is he much of a draw to experimentation with alternative lifestyles. Kay, a sympathetic but unsexy figure, does not do much for a lesbian continuum. Christa Reinig's *Entmannung* (1976), dating from the height of 1970s feminism, makes an interesting comparison. More technically experimental, *Entmannung* does share some points of comparison with *Regenroman*, notably wholesale subversion of sexist culture, the theme of female violence, and a drastic representation of rape which unsettles the prevailing comic mode. As the title suggests, Reinig's novel conveys the author's struggle to break with an internalised male gaze dramatised in Otto Kyra, the male protagonist and an authorial alter ego, as his name Kyra in echo of Christa indicates. Reinig achieves such a break more radically than Duve, in an intervention in cultural politics with a lesbian tendency.[20] If we think of the author as having put something of herself into both main characters, then *Regenroman* does suggest a degree of 'Entmannung' in that Martina shakes off her subjection to Leon's way of seeing her. But the primary focus on matters erotic remains heterosexual. There is no real blurring of that boundary.

Postscript: Princesses and Dragons

As its title suggests, erotic orientation in Duve's last work to date, *Die entführte Prinzessin* (2005), remains heterosexual, though sexiness is extended to a physically challenged dwarf. The novel offers a comic parody of chivalric romance. If uncanny marshland encounters placed *Regenroman* on the borders of the fantastic, *Die entführte Prinzessin* belongs as a *Ritterroman* squarely within the marvellous mode.[21] And where *Regenroman* combines comedy and provocation, *Die entführte Prinzessin* offers little room for female agency, but is deliciously funny throughout. In both novels much of the comedy comes from the witty use of contemporary popular idiom both in dialogue and in the narration which is constantly coloured by the characters' perspectives (even Noah's) to ironic effect. In *Die entführte Prinzessin* romance is filtered through the language of here and now to mock heroic effect. Throughout, the reader has a shimmering sense of two worlds, the imaginary world of high romance and a prosaic world of today. A fantastical cultural geography proffers occasional familiar glimpses, which disappear again. Fleeting intertextual echoes and myriad moments of mockery of romance and the chivalric code of honour intertwine. The cynical *Gräfin* urges the idealistic princess to enjoy 'die bodenlose Vorteile der Schande' which Hans Castorp imagines would result 'wenn man endgültig des Druckes der Ehre ledig ist'.[22] As the passive objects of dispute, women do at least escape the injunction which drives men to violence and warfare. The perpetrator of the nastiest violence is not a man, however, but a queen. Like the Red Queen in *Alice in Wonderland*, she is a mistress of the garden who ruthlessly pursues horticultural wonders, though the best practical gardener is the dwarf Pedsi. A *Gärtnerzwerg* rather than a *Gartenzwerg*, Pedsi is also sexily elegant, not a Disney but a courtly dwarf. Some traditionally nasty figures also get thoroughly revalued. The most lovable characters in the novel are a horse and a dragon. The saintly or heroic dragon-slayer generally sits aloft on a horse, his complicit ally in man's victory over nature. Here the horse, Kelpie, and Grendel, the dragon, are best of friends. (In Scottish folklore a kelpie is a demonic water-horse and Grendel is the slobbering, man-eating monster in *Beowulf*.) Feminist cultural criticism has deconstructed the threat dragons pose to virgins, seeing in the killing of the dragon by a phallic spear jabbed down into the open mouth or nostril a mythic conquest of nature and a taming of female sexuality.[23] Duve's dragons have to do a spell of duty protecting a virgin as part of their training. But virgin and dragon briefly begin to coalesce, rather as Martina has a lizard backbone. Patriarchy divides the female into wild monster and tamed virgin. If menfolk go on imprisoning princesses under dragon guard, the princesses will turn into dragons and the dragons will turn against Man. Thus Duve continues the good work of revaluing lizards, dragons and maidens in *Regenroman* and *Die entführte Prinzessin*. Both novels belong in the field of highly readable popular fiction, the first as a provocative intervention in cultural politics, the latter as a witty parody.

Notes

1 Johann Wolfgang von Goethe, 'Der Fischer', *Goethes Werke. Hamburger Ausgabe*, vol. i, Christian Wegner: Hamburg, 1964, pp. 153-4.

2 Matthias Politycki, 'Das Medium ist die Massage', *Literaturkritik*, 9 (2000), www.literaturkritik.de; see also Frank Finlay and Stuart Taberner, 'Emerging Writers: Introduction,' *German Life and Letters*, 55 (2002), 131-6 and Petra Bagley's contribution to this volume.

3 On intertextual appropriations of myth in post-modern pop culture see Heike Bartel, *Mythos in der Literatur*, Aschendorff: Münster, 2004, pp. 33-36.

4 See Elizabeth Boa and Rachel Palfreyman, *Heimat – A German Dream: Regional Loyalties and National Identity in German Culture 1890-1990*, Oxford University Press: Oxford, 2000, pp. 26-27; 49-57.

5 Karen Duve, *Regenroman*, List: München (3. Auflage), 2001, p. 34. Subsequent references preceded by 'R' will be given in the text.

6 Franz Kafka, *Das Schloß*, Fischer Taschenbuch: Frankfurt am Main, 1992, p. 14.

7 Karl Marx/Friedrich Engels, 'Die deutsche Ideologie', *Werke*, iii, Dietz: Berlin, 1962, p. 33.

8 On water women see Irmgard Roebling, ed., *Sehnsucht und Sirene. Vierzehn Abhandlungen zu Wasserphantasien*, Centaurus: Pfaffenweiler, 1992; see also Elisa Müller-Adams's contribution to this volume.

9 Winfried Menninghaus, *Ekel. Theorie und Geschichte einer starken Empfindung*, suhrkamp taschenbuch: Frankfurt am Main, 2002, p. 20.

10 A key text in Ekel is Julia Kristeva's *Pouvoirs de l'horreur. Essai sur l'Abjection*, Seuil: Paris, 1980.

11 Elisabeth Bronfen, 'Die schöne Leiche. Weiblicher Tod als motivische Konstante von der Mitte des 18. Jahrhunderts bis in die Moderne,' in: Renate Berger and Inge Stephan, eds., *Weiblichkeit und Tod in der Literatur*, Böhlau: Köln, Wien, 1987, pp. 87-116.

12 'Ophelia I', *Georg Heym*. Ausgewählt von Karl Ludwig Schneider und Günter Martens, Nymphenburg: München, 1971, p. 40.

13 Bertolt Brecht, *Große kommentierte Berliner und Frankfurter Ausgabe*, xi, Gedichte i, Jan Knopf and Gabriele Knopf, eds., p. 109.

14 Elisabeth Bronfen, *Over Her Dead Body: Death, femininity and the aesthetic*, Manchester University Press: Manchester, 1992, p. 174.

15 Beth Linklater, '"Philomela's Revenge": Challenges to Rape in Recent Writing in German', *German Life and Letters*, 54, (2001), 253-71 (here: 267).

16 Peter J. Graves, 'Karen Duve, Kathrin Schmidt, Judith Hermann: "Ein literarisches Fräuleinwunder"?,' *German Life and Letters*, 55 (2002), 196-207 (here: 199-200).

17 Linklater, '"Philomela's Revenge",' p. 261.

18 Menninghaus, *Ekel*, p. 162.

19 For a more critical view of Duve's text as compulsively repeating the cycle of violence see Teresa Ludden's article in this volume. See also Graves, 'Karen Duve', p. 200, who finds it all too outlandish, but cites Martin Kane who despite the preposterous plot finds the pace attractive.

20 See Georgina Paul, 'Inarticulacy: Lesbianism and Language in Post-1945 German Literature,' in: David Jackson, ed., *Taboos in German Literature*, Berghahn: Providence, Oxford, 1996, pp. 165-84.

21 On the generic terms see Tzvetan Todorov, *The Fantastic: A Structural Approach*, Cornell: Ithaca, 1975.

22 Karen Duve, *Die entführte Prinzessin. Von Drachen, Liebe und anderen Ungeheuern*, Eichborn: Berlin, 2005, p. 122; Thomas Mann, *Der Zauberberg*, Fischer Taschenbuch: Frankfurt am Main, 1991, p. 115.

23 See, for example, Teresa Ludden, 'Allegories of Cultural Relations: An Examination of Anne Duden's Mode of Reading Representations of St George and the Dragon', *German Life and Letters*, 57 (2004), 69-90.

Elisa Müller-Adams

,De nymphis, sylphis, pygmaeis et salamandris' – zur Verwendung eines Motivkreises in Texten von Michael Fritz, Julia Schoch und Karen Duve

Elemental spirits have always inspired the literary imagination. Recent German literature seems increasingly drawn again to stories about mermaids, salamanders and other mythical beings. This article investigates the motif of the elemental spirit in three texts published between 1999 and 2002: Michael Fritz's *Rosa oder die Liebe zu den Fischen*, Julia Schoch's *Der Körper des Salamanders* and Karen Duve's *Regenroman*. While these texts use the motif in various ways, the renewed interest seems always to be characterized by poetological self-reflection.

Elementargeister sind spätestens seit dem Ende des 18. Jahrhunderts ein immer wiederkehrendes Motiv der Literatur, wobei bestimmte Epochen eine besondere Vorliebe für Salamander,[1] Gnome, Sylphen und Nixen zu haben scheinen – und nun, am Ende des 20. und Beginn des 21. Jahrhunderts, scheinen sie in der deutschen Literatur ebenfalls wieder in Mode gekommen zu sein. Dieses Interesse am Elementaren in der Literatur spiegelt sich auch wieder in einem vermehrten Interesse in der literaturwissenschaftlichen Forschung: 2003 erschienen mit Beate Ottos *Unterwasserliteratur* und Monika Schmitz-Emanns *Seetiefen und Seelentiefen* gleich zwei umfangreiche komparatistisch angelegte Studien zu Wasserwesen in der Literatur.[2]

Das Wiederauftauchen des Elementaren in der deutschen Literatur der letzten Jahre soll Gegenstand dieses Beitrags sein, dessen Titel von Paracelsus' Elementargeisterlehre geborgt ist. Genauer gesagt geht es um die Verwendung des Elementargeister- und Wasserfrauenmotivs in drei Texten der Gegenwartsliteratur, nämlich Michael Fritz' Roman *Rosa oder die Liebe zu den Fischen*, Julia Schochs Erzählung *Der Körper des Salamanders* und Karen Duves *Regenroman*.[3] Was diese drei Texte bei aller Unterschiedlichkeit verbindet, ist zum einen der Zeitraum, in dem sie veröffentlicht wurden, (der *Regenroman* erschien 1999, Schochs Erzählband 2001 und *Rosa* 2002), sie sind alle im Osten Deutschlands angesiedelt, spielen kurz vor oder in den Jahren nach der deutschen Wiedervereinigung und sie alle stammen von Schriftstellern, die zu den neuen jungen Autoren gezählt werden. Was sie aber außerdem vergleichbar macht, ist die Beziehung zum Motivkreis der Elementargeister, insbesondere zu den Wasserwesen.

Unter den Elementargeistern sind es nämlich vor allem die Wasserwesen, insbesondere die weiblichen, die die Phantasie der Dichter anregen. Wasserfrauen in ihren vielfältigen Erscheinungsformen scheinen mehr als ihre Verwandten in den anderen Elementen zu künstlerischen und literarischen Darstellung geeignet.[4] Literarische Wasserwesen haben nicht nur eine weitverzweigte Verwandtschaft in der antiken und keltischen Mythenwelt, sondern sie begegnen uns auch in vielfältigen literarischen Metamorphosen z.B. als Sirenen, Melusinen, als Undine, Loreley oder Ophelia. Letztere ist keine eigentliche Wasserfrau, aber mit Shakespeares dramatischer Figur wird, angeregt durch den Nekrolog der Königin in *Hamlet,* der Motivkreis der sich im Wasser (und zeitweilig auch auf dem Land) tummelnden Nixen ergänzt um das Bild der im Wasser aufgebahrten bzw. treibenden weiblichen Wasserleiche.[5] So verschmelzen im Laufe der Kulturgeschichte die verschiedenen literarischen Erscheinungsformen und Mutationen des Motivs stofflich und werden allmählich austauschbar,[6] wie sich die Wassergeister überhaupt auch nicht streng trennen lassen von den Bewohnern der anderen Elemente, mit denen sie eine Reihe von Eigenschaften teilen.[7] Sich eindeutigen Kategorisierungen zu entziehen, erweist sich geradezu als ein Wesenszug der Wasser- und Naturwesen. Es scheint daher legitim, die Analyse der Texte im Folgenden nicht auf einen bestimmten Typus einzugrenzen, sondern den Motivkreis der Elementarwesen insgesamt einzubeziehen.

Was aber macht die Naturwesen so fruchtbar für die literarische Bearbeitung? Schmitz-Emanns macht in ihrer Untersuchung des Motivkreises die Faszination, die die Literatur für das Elementare empfindet, vor allem an einem Moment fest: der Begegnung mit dem Fremden, die als Grundimpuls literarischer Produktivität erscheint.[8] Die Reaktionen auf diese Begegnung mit dem Fremden sind dabei so vielfältig wie dessen Erscheinungsformen. Das Elementare, insbesondere das Wasserreich als Sphäre des Ursprungs, aber auch der Zerstörung, als grenzenloses und unkontrollierbares Element bietet eine Vielzahl von Bildern und Metaphern für das Fremde.[9] Und Ähnliches gilt für die Bewohner des Wasserreichs:

> Als dem Menschen fremde und in ihrer Fremdartigkeit latent bedrohliche Wesen erscheinen die Wasserwesen des Volksglaubens insgesamt, wobei die Grade ihrer Fremdheit wechseln können, je nach ihrem Erscheinungsbild und den Kräften, die ihnen zu Gebote stehen. [...] Sie spielen bezogen auf die menschliche Lebenswelt die Rolle des Eindringlings oder – öfter noch – die Rolle dessen, der den Menschen in seine Sphäre hinüber ziehen will. Ihr Ruf ist ein Ruf in die Fremde.[10]

Dem Ruf in die Fremde folgt auch der namenlose Ich-Erzähler in Michael Fritz' Roman *Rosa oder Die Liebe zu den Fischen,* als er die junge Rosa Lehmert, benannt nach Rosa Luxemburg,[11] kennen lernt. Sie ist die Tochter eines ehemaligen SED-Funktionärs und lebt mit ihrem Vater in einer großen, alten Villa am Rande einer Großstadt, arbeitet erfolgreich als Börsenspekulantin – und sie ist eine Wasserfrau mit den für Nixen fast obligatorischen langen blonden Haaren und „katzenhaft grünen Augen".

Sie ist eine „Loreley des Wendegewinnlertums",[12] obwohl sie weniger
mit der singenden Zauberin und Nixe auf dem Rheinfelsen und mehr mit
der anderen berühmten Wasserfrau der Romantik, mit Fouqués Undine
nämlich, gemein hat. Mit Letzterer teilt Rosa vor allem das Kindhafte, sie
ist, wie Peter von Matt über Undine sagt, „eine Frau, die ganz Kind, ein
Kind, das ganz Frau ist",[13] und eben das macht sie so attraktiv für den
Ich-Erzähler des Romans, dem sie mal als „kleines Mädchen" (Ro154),
mal als verführerische Frau erscheint.

Wie Undine hat auch Rosa ein Element des Wilden, Ungezähmten.
Die Börsenfrau Rosa ist nämlich ein Naturkind, das mit bloßen Füßen
und flatternden Haaren durch den Garten läuft und davon träumt, auf
Wolken davon zu reiten. Neben diesen Charakteristika ist es vor allem
das Mysteriöse und Fremdartige, was den Ich-Erzähler in Rosas Bann
zieht. Denn Rosa, die „Wassermannfrau" (Ro83), wie sich selber nennt,
ist anders als die anderen Frauen, die der Erzähler kannte, vieles an ihr
scheint merkwürdig und geheimnisvoll. Da ist z.B. Rosas Liebe zu den
Fischen im riesigen Aquarium: „Sie sind so wichtig, was wäre ich ohne
Fische" (Ro13), erklärt Rosa ihrem Liebhaber. In ihrer Kindheit spendete
das Licht, das vom Aquarium ausging, der kleinen Rosa nachts Trost.
Auch für die erwachsene Rosa sind die Fische von zentraler Bedeutung,
da ihr beruflicher Erfolg untrennbar mit ihnen verbunden ist: Es sind
nämlich die Schwimmbewegungen der Fische, mit deren Hilfe sie die
Entwicklungen des Dax vorhersagen kann.

> Rosa verfolgte die ausrechenbaren Wege der Fische, die durch das helle Grün
> des Wassers zogen, breiblättrige Pflanzen umrundeten, in der Strömung
> standen, sich spielerisch, so hatte es den Anschein, abtreiben ließen und in der
> vielarmigen Wasserpest verloren [...]. Es gab einen Zusammenhang, wie sie
> herausgefunden hatte, zwischen den Wegen der Fische und den Bewegungen
> ihres Mauls. Wenn die Wege, dieses verschlungene, unvorhersehbare Zick-
> Zack, Zick-Zack an jene Kurven erinnerte, die Aktienkurse beschrieben, so
> mochten die Bewegungen des Fischmauls, das unablässige Öffnen und
> Schließen, das Stoßen gegen die Glaswand Rosa Antwort geben auf die
> dringenden Fragen nach Verkaufen, Halten oder Kaufen von Aktien. (Ro46)

Wenn Rosa ihre Fische studiert, dann taucht sie ab in eine blaue, wässrige
Welt, in der sie für den Erzähler nicht erreichbar ist. Auch das Thema der
Verlockung, dem Wasserfrauen-Motiv inhärent, spielt eine zentrale Rolle.
Rosa lockt den Erzähler nicht auf die Sireneninsel oder in einen stillen
Grund, sondern in die Lehmertsche Villa. Sie überredet den Erzähler die
Stelle als Hausverwalter zu übernehmen, und er gibt daraufhin auch
bereitwillig nicht nur seine bisherige Wohnung, sondern auch seine
bisherige Existenz auf und zieht in das luxuriöse Haus, das sich bald als
eine Art Spukschloss mit labyrinthischen Gängen, verborgenen Zimmern,
verschlossenen Türen und verwunschenem Garten entpuppt. Merkwürdig
ist auch, dass der Erzähler als Hausverwalter eigentlich gar keine

Aufgabe hat, was ihm umso mehr Zeit lässt, den Geheimnissen der Villa und ihrer Bewohner auf den Grund zu gehen. Nach und nach öffnen sich die verschlossenen Türen und langsam kommt der Erzähler der Wahrheit auf die Spur. Die Villa der Lehmerts erweist sich als „Zonen-Biotop",14 als Ort, an dem die Zeit stehen geblieben zu sein scheint. Die verbotenen Zimmer sind der DDR gewidmet und beinhalten Sammlungen von DDR Memorabilia, so dass sich der Ich-Erzähler zurückversetzt fühlt:

> Ich sah Symbole, die ich noch nie gesehen hatte, und kam mir vor wie auf einer vormaligen Demonstration am Ersten Mai oder an jenem Tag, an dem dieser Staat vom Volk seinen Geburtstag feiern ließ. Die Klänge der Marschmusik konnten aus dem ersten Raum herüberschallen, wodurch von sämtlichen Exponaten die Patina der Zeit abfiel, Mitschnitte von den Übertragungen aus dem Radio und vom Fernsehen, stellte ich mir weiter vor, waren zu hören, bei denen die Stimme des Reporters vor Pathos zitterte […]. Hier wusste das Land nichts von seinem Untergang. (Ro91)

Vor allem aber kommt der Erzähler im Laufe des Romans ganz in der Tradition der *Gothic Novel*, deren Elemente von Fritz immer wieder zitiert werden, dem Verbrechen auf die Spur, das sich hinter all dem Rätselhaften in der Villa verbirgt. Rosas Vater Harry, der hochrangige SED-Funktionär, hat nämlich seine alkoholabhängige Frau getötet, ein als Unfall getarnter Mord, da sie drohte seine Nazi-Vergangenheit ans Licht zu bringen. Und während der Vater sich in die düsteren Räume mit DDR-Devotionalien zurückzieht, um dort Marschmusik hörend und Zigarren rauchend in Erinnerungen zu schwelgen und von der DDR zu träumen, kann Rosa das Schweigen im Lehmertschen Anwesen nicht mehr ertragen und beginnt zu erzählen, „wie jemand, der, einem nicht zu bändigenden Drang gehorchend, seine Worte beharrlich nach außen treibt." (Ro9) Damit wird auch die eigentliche Aufgabe des Erzählers deutlich: „Hör mir bitte zu. Du musst nichts weiter tun, als mir zuhören, sagte sie." (Ro14) Mit dem Erzähler als Zuhörer kann Rosa nun endlich ihre Geschichte erzählen, die aber bald über ihre eigene Geschichte hinausgeht und auch die Geschichte ihrer Eltern und damit die DDR-Vergangenheit umfasst.

Rosa, die Wasserfrau, ist also eine Erzählerin, ihre Stimme bestimmt mehr und mehr den Roman und verdrängt damit die Stimme des ohnehin recht blassen Ich-Erzählers. Der Sog, der von Rosas Erzählung ausgeht, ist unwiderstehlich: „Wenn Rosa zu erzählen begann, sprach ihr ganzes Gesicht und fesselte den Betrachter, und ihr Blick räumte dem Redefluss sämtliche Hürden aus dem Weg." (Ro18) Das Erzählen ist ein Teil von Rosas Wesen, was auch darin deutlich wird, dass die Wasserfrau Rosa offenbar auch dabei ganz in ihrem Element bleibt: „Ihre Worte kamen unermüdlich wie das Wasser des Brunnens." (Ro39)

Damit erweist sich Rosa nicht nur als Nachfahrin von Loreley und Undine, sondern auch der Sirenen, jener Mischwesen des antiken Mythos, deren Gesang alle, die ihn hören, ins Verderben lockt. In Homers Sirenen-Episode der *Odyssee* liegt eine Dimension des Wasserfrauen-Motivs begründet, das bestimmend wird in der weiteren literarischen Bearbeitung des Stoffs:

> Seit dem ersten Auftauschen der Sirenen in der Literatur (und das heißt, da es um die Odyssee geht, seit den Anfängen der abendländischen Literatur) tragen diese Gestalten zum Großprojekt ästhetischer Autoreflexion bei. Ihre Sphäre ist ein Bereich am Rande des Vertrauten, an der Schwelle zum Jenseits. Sie personifizieren gleichermaßen Kunst und Verlockung, Kunst und Tod, verweisen auf die Differenz zwischen undomestizierter und domestizierter Kunst.[15]

In der *Odyssee* warnt die Zauberin Kirke Odysseus davor, dass der Gesang der Sirenen ihn seine Heimat, Familie, seine kulturelle Identität vergessen lassen und somit ins Verderben locken wird. Der Sirenengesang erscheint als Angriff:

> Wer auch immer sich naht, unwissend, und hört der Sirenen
> Singenden Laut, dem treten nicht Frau und unmündige Kinder,
> Wenn er nach Hause kehrt, zur Seite und freuen sich seiner.
> Sondern mit hellem Gesang bezaubern ihn die Sirenen,
> Sitzend auf einer Wiese; ringsum ein Haufen von Knochen
> Von vermodernden Männern, und um sie schrumpfen die Häute.[16]

So wie der epische Erzähler Odysseus im Gesang der Sirenen einer identitätsbedrohenden ‚undomestizierten' Kunst, einem ‚anderen', den eigenen Text bedrohenden Text begegnet, so wird auch der Ich-Erzähler in Fritz' Roman in den Erzählungen Rosas mit einer faszinierenden und verlockenden Kunst des Erinnerns konfrontiert, die er mehr und mehr als bedrohlich empfindet und der er sich schließlich durch Flucht (denn anders als bei Odysseus hilft das Verstopfen der Ohren hier ausdrücklich nicht) entziehen muss.

Die Stationen von Rosas Erzählungen finden in verschiedenen Situationen und verschiedenen Räumen der Villa statt, u.a. auch im Garten des Hauses. Dieser parkähnliche Garten ist ein verwunschener Ort mit Putten und einer Diana-Statue. Vom staubigen, muffigen Inneren des Hauses hebt sich der Garten als Ort der Frische und Kühle ab. Der Pavillon, in den Rosa den Erzähler ruft, um ihre Geschichte zu erzählen, erscheint damit als idyllischer Ort der Begegnung zweier Liebenden. Da Fritz seine Titelheldin so deutlich als Undine gestaltet hat, liegt es nahe, dass er auch hier Fouqué zitiert. Dessen Undine führt den Ritter Huldbrand auf eine idyllische Insel und beginnt ihre Erzählung, in der sie ihre nicht-menschliche Herkunft enthüllt:

> Manch einem Fischer ward es schon so gut, ein zartes Wasserweib belauschen, wie sie über die Fluten hervorstieg und sang. Der erzählte dann von ihrer Schöne weiter, und solche wundersamen Frauen wurden von den

> Menschen Undinen genannt. Du aber siehst jetzt wirklich eine Undine, lieber
> Freund.[17]

Undine erzählt nicht nur ihre Geschichte, sondern macht sie auch als
Erzähltes deutlich. In dieser Textstelle der *Undine* werden die
Selbstbespiegelungsstrategien der Reflexionstheorie nach dem Muster der
Frühromantik des Fouquéschen Texts erkennbar:

> Getreu der Devise von Friedrich Schlegel, daß romantische Dichtung Poesie
> und zugleich Poesie der Poesie sei, transzendiert und ironisiert Undine ihre
> eigene Geschichte. Sie macht sich damit selber zum Medium der Poesie.[18]

Mit dem intertextuellen Verweis auf Fouqué übernimmt Fritz in *Rosa
oder Die Liebe zu den Fischen* auch dessen reflexive Geste. Rosas
„seltsamer Mitteilungsdrang"[19] macht also Sinn, weil Fritz mit Rosa der
Wasserfrau-Erzählerin auf ein Kernelement zurückgreift, das spätestens
seit der Romantik die Geschichte des Motivs bestimmt. In der
literarischen Verwendung des Elementargeisterstoffs verknüpft die
romantische Literatur „die Thematisierung des Fremden mit poetischer
Selbstreflexion,"[20] ein Grund, weshalb auch die Gegenwartsliteratur
offensichtlich weiterhin so großes Interesse an Geschichten von
Wasserfrauen hat. Das ist es wohl auch, was Fritz am
Elementargeisterstoff interessiert und weshalb er seine Titelheldin zu
einer Undine macht. Es geht ihm ums Erzählen, oder präziser: um das
literarische Erinnern.

Mit Rosas Geschichte endet dann auch konsequenterweise die
Liebesbeziehung zwischen ihr und dem Ich-Erzähler, ein Ende, das sich
mit dem Tod der Fische bereits ankündigt. Der Erzähler meint nun mehr
zu wissen, als er erfahren wollte, er glaubt sich beobachtet und flieht so
vor Rosas Geschichte und ihrer Liebe, indem er sich, während Rosa
Ersatz für ihre geliebten Fische sucht, davon macht.

Ist Rosas Aquarium, auch wenn es recht groß ist, ein Wasserreich
von eher bescheidenen Ausmaßen, sind es etwas größere Wasser, die in
Julia Schochs Erzählungen eine zentrale Rolle spielen. Die Erzählungen
des Bandes *Der Körper des Salamanders* spielen am Schwarzen Meer,
am Donaudelta oder den Havelseen, aber auch in anderen „Territorien der
Unbehaustheit"[21] wie einer stillgelegten Fischfabrik oder einem
verfallenden Kino.[22] Und damit wird bereits deutlich, dass es auch bei
Schoch um Fremdheit geht.

Konzentrieren möchte ich mich hier auf die Titelerzählung *Der
Körper des Salamanders*. Der Salamander ist nach der
Elementargeisterlehre zwar dem Feuer zugehörig, wird aber auf Grund
seiner kalten, amphibienhaften Natur auch dem Wasser zugeordnet und
so spielt diese Erzählung auch am und im Wasser. Die Erzählung sei „so
naß, daß das Wasser aus den Seiten fließt",[23] bemerkt ein Rezensent des
Bandes. Sie spielt im Februar und die Havelseen präsentieren sich nicht
als besonders idyllischer Ort, sondern als nasskalte, in dichten Nebel ge-

hüllte Welt, so dass die Erzählerin sich an die Unterwelt erinnert fühlt: „Ich dachte, daß die Havel auch der Styx sein konnte, denn wir durchquerten feuchte Nebelfelder in eine andere Welt." (KS23)

Diese Erzählerin ist Steuerfrau einer Rudermannschaft in einem Sportinternat im Osten, vor der Wende. Täglich wird trainiert und bei dem ständigen Aufenthalt auf dem Wasser scheint sich die jugendliche Steuerfrau selbst bald in ein Wasserwesen zu verwandeln:

> Ich besah meine Hände. Hier und da hatten sich bereits winzige Schuppen gebildet, die zu Schwimmhäuten werden konnten, wenn sie sich mit den weißen Stellen an den Fingern verbänden. (KS9)

Klein und zierlich unterscheidet sich die Erzählerin von den anderen Mädchen. Während sie intelligent ist und gute Noten hat, sind die anderen muskulös und träge mit „kräftige[n], breite[n] Hintern" (KS10) und algigem Geruch; stets schlecht gelaunt und müde vom kräftezehrendem Training beneiden sie die Erzählerin um ihren „ewig ausgeruhten Körper". Verglichen mit ihnen ist die Steuerfrau „fast durchsichtig" (KS18), ein ätherisches Wesen: tatsächlich erinnert sie sich daran, als Kind fast einmal im Wind davon geflogen zu sein.

Während die anderen Mädchen zwar murrend, aber ohne Widerstand dem strengen Trainingsregime folgen, widersetzt sich die Erzählerin manchmal. Wegen dieser Disziplinlosigkeit darf sie auch nicht an Wettkämpfen im Ausland teilnehmen. Widerstand leistet die Erzählerin vor allem, in dem sie sich in das Reich der Phantasie zurückzieht. So träumt sie sich in den Urwald und die Landschaft um die Havel wird ihr zur exotischen Kulisse. Da ist es kein Wunder, dass sie über ihren Phantasien schon mal ihre eigentliche Aufgabe vergisst und das Boot in eine Vogelinsel steuert. Das Abtauchen in die Phantasie hilft auch, wenn die Wirklichkeit unerträglich wird, wenn z.B. die breiten Bugwellen der Ausflugdampfer anrollen, die das Mädchen überspülen:

> Dann versuchte ich in meiner Wasserschale ein Fisch zu werden, dem dieses flüssige Material gefallen konnte. Oder ich stellte mir vor, daß ich nur ein Kopf wäre, dessen Körper zu rein maschinellen Zwecken genutzt wurde und keine Sensoren auf der Haut trug. (KS21)

Eigentlich will die Erzählerin gar nicht rudern bzw. steuern. Was sie will, ist erzählen, schreiben. Sie hat sich bereits vor einiger Zeit ein blaues Buch angelegt, aber bisher blieb dieses Buch leer und die leeren Seiten scheinen die Erzählerin zu verspotten: „Als ich es aufschlug, wurden die Linien zu kleinen Wellen, die sich launig über die leeren Seiten bewegten." (KS10) Am Abend nach dem Training fehlt ihr die Inspiration, daran ändert auch die Schwanenfeder nichts, die sie von ihrem unfreiwilligen Besuch auf der Vogelinsel mitgenommen hat und von der sie hoffte, sie sei das passende Gerät für ihre Erzähllust:

> Ich nahm das blaue Buch heraus und legte es vor mich auf den Tisch. Eine Melusine schwebte über dem dunklen Deckel. Ich betrachtete ihre gesenkten

> Lider und dachte nach. Aber kein einziger Buchstabe kam aus dem Füller. (KS16)

Schließlich aber findet sie die erste Zeile ihres Textes: „Laß den Salamander". Und sie entdeckt dann auch tatsächlich einen Teichmolch, also einen Wassersalamander in einem der Bootshäuser, und mit ihm als Verbündeten beschließt sie dem Drill im Sportinternat und der verhassten „Jahreszeit selbst ein Ende zu bereiten." (KS21) Bei der nächsten Trainingsfahrt lässt sie das Boot kentern, und während sie sich schnell selbst befreien kann, sind die anderen Mädchen in ihren Sitzen gefangen:

> Das Boot lag mit dem Rumpf nach oben, und unten im Wasser, unter der Nebelwand, saßen die Mädchen im Boot wie ein Spiegelbild, als wollten sie – eine stumm gewordene Galeere – ihre Berufung in die Unterwelt retten. (KS27 f.)

Vom Boot und den verhassten Ruderinnen befreit, lässt sich die Erzählerin treiben und kann nun endlich abtauchen in die Welt ihrer Dichtung:

> Als fiele der Nebel herab, um unter den Fluß zu steigen, zog er mich in eine feuchte Wolke hinein. Meine Augen konnten geöffnet oder geschlossen sein, als etwas begann:
>
> > Laß den Salamander, in Stein
> > gehaunes Untier,
> > er sinkt zum Grund und anderes fällt mit.
> > Das braune Haar der Frau hängt noch
> > im Schilf, der Sumpf nimmt es nicht auf.
> > Um jeden Halm ist es gewunden und blüht im nächsten Jahr.
> > Der Salamander irrt ...
>
> Schweigend trieb ich durch den Nebel, der sich an diesem Tag erst gegen neun Uhr dreißig aufzulösen begann. (KS28)

So wird am Schluss der Erzählung eigentlich nichts gelöst, das Gedicht, mit dem der Text endet, verstärkt im Gegenteil noch einmal die Atmosphäre des Rätselhaften, die diese Erzählungen wie auch die anderen in der Sammlung bestimmt.

Das Salamander-Gedicht, das die auf dem Wasser treibende Erzählerin verfasst, verweist auf eine Reihe von Bezügen literarischer Art. Ein möglicher Ansatz zur Deutung kann sich vielleicht aus dem Bezug zum Motiv der Elementargeister ergeben. Im Zusammenhang mit der Rätselpoetik wäre dann wohl auch die Verwendung des Motivs des Salamanders zu sehen. Der Salamander trägt eine Reihe von z.T. widersprüchlichen Bedeutungen: Im Volksaberglauben ist er ein dämonisches Tier, ein Unglücksbringer, er gilt als hochgiftig, was ihn mit Zauberei und Giftmorden, aber auch mit der magischen Heilkunde in Verbindung bringt. Gleichzeitig aber fungiert er auch, da er unbeschädigt im Feuer leben können soll, als Symbol des Gerechten, der die Seelenruhe trotz aller Anfechtungen bewahrt oder als Sinnbild für die Seele im Fegefeuer, denn man glaubte, dass der Salamander sich wie der

Phönix im Feuer verjünge.[24] Der bekannteste Salamander der Literatur ist wohl der Archivar Lindhorst in E.T.A. Hoffmanns *Der goldene Topf*, der in seiner zweiten Existenz ein Feuergeist ist. Er führt den jungen Anselmus in das Reich der Poesie und erscheint als eine Personifikation des Literarischen überhaupt.[25] Als Metapher für den utopischen Charakter der Liebe, aber auch für die poetische Sprache, in der eine Annäherung an diese Utopie möglich ist, erscheint der Salamander z.B. ebenfalls in Ingeborg Bachmanns Gedicht ‚Erklär mir, Liebe'.

Die Erzählerin in Schochs Text findet über das Bild des Salamanders ebenfalls den Zugang zum Poetischen, es bildet den Anfang ihrer Dichtung. In dem noch halb im Winterschlaf befindlichen Teichmolch im Bootshaus scheint sie auch etwas wie eine verwandte Seele zu erkennen, zumindest motiviert er ihren Beschluss, sich auf recht drastische Weise aus dem Trainingsalltag zu befreien.

Kehren wir noch einmal zurück zum Salamander-Gedicht. Besonders naheliegend ist hier die Assoziation zu Gottfried Benns ‚Schöne Jugend', aber auch mehr noch zum Ophelia-Motiv, was uns wieder zurückführt zu den poetologischen Autoreflexionen, die sich auch im Ophelia-Motiv, im Bild der weiblichen Wasserleiche, der verstummten Wasserfrau finden lassen. Dies könnte darauf hindeuten, worin die Funktion des Motivkreises der Elementargeister bei Schoch liegt. Wie Fritz erzählt auch Schoch nicht nur von der (DDR-)Vergangenheit, sondern sie markiert dies deutlich als Erzähltes, als literarisch Vermitteltes. So beginnt auch die Erzählung *Der Körper des Salamanders,* die den Erzählband einleitet, mit einer metatextuellen Passage:

> Jetzt ist es vorbei, das Geräusch, das Rauschen, wenn das Wasser sich in meine Gehörgänge schleckt, um mit einem tiefen Gurgeln immer wieder von sich hören zu lassen. Nach der Entscheidung schlägt keine Brandung mehr von innen an meine Haut, keine Welle bricht sich Bahn, kein Tropfen dringt in keinen Spalt, nichts fließt, nichts bewegt sich, endlich kann ich beginnen. (KS7)

Damit unternimmt Schoch eine raffinierte Umwertung des Ophelia-Motivs: während im „Paradigmenwechsel von Undine zu Ophelia",[26] also von der Nixe zur Wasserleiche der einst so mächtige Sirenengesang verstummt, scheint bei Schoch das Ertrinken und Versinken im Wasser gerade die Möglichkeit zur Erzählung zu eröffnen: „endlich kann ich beginnen." Damit verweist Schoch auch auf die ‚unter Wasser' sprechende Undine Ingeborg Bachmanns und den wohl bekanntesten autoreflexiven Wasserfrauen-Text, in dem die Nixe „sozusagen in der Idee einer weiblichen écriture präsent"[27] ist.

Während Schochs Erzählung mit dem Bild des im Wasser treibenden Mädchens endet, beginnt Karen Duve ihren *Regenroman* mit dem Ophelia-Motiv, als sie nämlich die beiden Hauptfiguren Leon und

Martina Ulbricht gleich auf den ersten Seiten auf eine Wasserleiche stoßen lässt:

> Wahrscheinlich war sie jung. Wahrscheinlich war sie gut aussehend gewesen, bevor sie sich in einen Haufen Glibber verwandelt hatte. Sie besaß unerhört lange Haare. Schwarze Haare. Pechschwarze Haare, die ihr einmal bis auf die Hüften gefallen sein mußten. Jetzt wiegten sie sich in der trägen Strömung. (R13)

Die zentrale Wasserfrau-Figur im *Regenroman* ist aber die Nachbarin der Ulbrichts, Isadora Schlei, deren Nachname, der an den Karpfenfisch erinnert, sie bereits als Nixe charakterisiert. So liest sich auch ihr erster Auftritt im Roman als parodistische Anspielung an die mittelalterliche Melusinen-Sage. Dort beobachtet Raimundin seine Ehefrau heimlich durch ein Loch in der Tür beim samstäglichen Bade – und entdeckt dabei nicht nur den Drachenschwanz Melusines, sondern bricht auch das Tabu, an das die Ehe der beiden geknüpft ist. Auch Leon beobachtet Isadora beim Bad im Moor und hält sie zunächst für die Wasserleiche:

> Direkt hinter dem Zaun saß die Wasserleiche – in einem der Moorlöcher. Sie steckte bis zum Bauch im Schlick, und ihre Haut war so weiß, daß sie leuchtete. Auf ihren Oberkörper fiel das schwarze, lange Haar. Als sie es mit Schwung über die Schulter zurückschüttelte, erkannte Leon, daß er sich getäuscht hatte. Diese Frau war viel dicker. (R82)[28]

Als Wasserfrau kennzeichnet Isadora auch ihre Verbundenheit mit dem Moor und seinen Bewohnern, den „glänzenden Salamandern und leuchtenden Fröschen". (R156) Isadora „gluckst" und „plätschert", sie mag keine trockenen Räume, und auch ihre äußere Erscheinung charakterisiert sie als Nixe:

> Alles an ihr wirkte weich und üppig. Sie trug einen Rock aus grünem Samt, der so lang war, daß er auf dem Boden schleppte und der Saum sich mit Wasser vollgesogen hatte. (R97)[29]

Auch der Garten der Schwestern Schlei, der auf wundersame Weise nicht von der Schneckenplage, die Leon und Martinas Haus und Grundstück heimsucht, betroffen zu sein scheint, ist mit Statuen von Misch- und Zwitterwesen und damit mit den Requisiten des Mythischen dekoriert. Isadoras Schlafzimmer ist schließlich als märchenhafter Naturraum gestaltet, so dass es Leon so vorkommt, „als wäre das Bett selbst eine Pflanze." (R149)

Isadora ist nicht nur der Natur zugeordnet, in ihr verschwimmen Mensch und Natur. Sie hat einen „amphibienhaften Ansatz zum Doppelkinn" (R99) und „Krötenschenkel" (R153), isst „wie ein Schwein" (R104) und rekelt sich wie eine dicke Katze. Ihre „elementare Schlampigkeit" (R147) wirkt wie ihre Fettleibigkeit auf Leon ebenso abstoßend wie attraktiv. Als er mit ihr schläft – als Wasserfrau gelingt Isadora die Verführung problemlos – vermischen sich in Leons Phantasie Frau und Natur:

> Als würde er mit dem Moor schlafen. Als wäre der Morast und der Torf und die verfaulten Blätter, die Pustelpilze und die vollgesogene Rinde und all das kleine Gekriech, Kröten, Unken, Molche und Olme und was da sonst noch herumkroch und schiß und sich fortpflanzte, all das Kaulquappenzeug und der Laich und nicht zuletzt der Regen, der endlose alles auflösende Regen, der sich im Moor fing – als wäre das alles zu einer einzigen Frau geworden. (R152 ff.)

In dieser Gleichsetzung von Moor und Frau folgt Leon ganz der kultur-geschichtlichen Konstante der Gleichsetzung von Natur und Weiblichkeit. Diese Gleichsetzung begegnet uns immer wieder im Bild der Wasserfrau, die durch ihren Lebensraum am Ufer (dem Grenzbereich zwischen Zivilisation und Natur), vor allem aber durch ihre Gestalt als Mischwesen, dessen Oberkörper menschlich und dessen Unterkörper als Fisch- oder Schlangenschwanz erscheint, besonders geeignet zur Illustrierung dieses Konzepts zu sein scheint. Bei Duve aber nimmt dieses Konzept die Wendung ins Monströse und damit ins Groteske. In Isadora scheinen die Grenzen zwischen Mensch, Tier und Pflanze zu verschwimmen – diese Aufhebung eigentlich getrennter Bereiche, ist ein Merkmal des Grotesken – wie auch die Tiere, mit denen sich Isadora umgibt (Kröten, Molche, Schnecken etc.) zum Inventar des Grotesken gehören.[30] Auch karnevaleske Züge im Bachtinschen Sinne lassen sich bei Isadora finden, ihr grenzenloser, überbordender Körper, in dem Menschliches und Tierisches ineinander übergehen, entspricht Bachtins Konzept von der grotesken Gestalt des Leibes.[31]

Neben der ins Monströse gewandelten Wasserfrau erscheint im *Regenroman* mit dem Salamander nicht nur ein weiteres Tier aus dem Inventar des Grotesken, sondern eben auch ein weiterer Elementargeist. Leon entdeckt im Garten des Hauses einen „fette[n], samtschwarze[n] Salamander von tropischer Größe" (R42). Als Leon den Salamander anfassen will, verätzt dessen Schleim seine Haut. Während Martina den Salamander „süß" findet und aus der Salamanderspucke Enthaarungscreme gewinnen will,[32] kann Leon das „Schleimvieh" gar nicht schnell genug loswerden. Ein reales Tier zwar, bleibt der Salamander auch im *Regenroman* mysteriös. Isadora antwortet später auf Martinas Frage nach dem Tier: „So was gibt es hier gar nicht. Vielleicht in Asien. [...] Und giftige Salamander schon gar nicht. Das sind mittelalterliche Vorurteile." (R102)

Dass sich Duve auskennt mit der symbolischen Bedeutung von Salamandern und Nixen, das belegt nicht zuletzt das 1997 gemeinsam mit Thies Völker veröffentlichte *Lexikon der berühmten Tiere*, in dem sich nämlich zu beiden Einträge finden. Zusammen mit anderen mythischen Wesen wie der Sphinx und dem Phönix stehen die Elementargeister hier friedlich neben beispielsweise Donald Duck, Lassie, und dem Bärenmarkenbär. Der Versuch, berühmte Tiere aus Geschichte, Film,

Märchen, Literatur und Mythologie in einem Handbuch zu erfassen, erinnert an Jorge Luis Borges *Buch der imaginären Wesen*, das mit dem *Lexikon der berühmten Tiere* nicht nur einige der erfassten Wesen gemein hat, sondern auch dessen Grundhaltung teilt, die Schmitz-Emanns folgendermaßen charakterisiert:

> Der Lexikograph der imaginären Wesen insistiert auf deren Realität. [...] Was im Artikel über den Kafkaschen ‚Odradek‘ mit provokanter Lakonik behauptet wird – „Natürlich würde sich niemand mit solchen Studien beschäftigen, wenn es nicht wirklich ein Wesen gäbe, das Odradek heißt." – charakterisiert die Attitüde des Lexikographen gegenüber den Wasserwesen: Natürlich gibt es sie, denn würden wir uns sonst mit ihnen beschäftigen? Für Borges sind imaginäre Wesen die Figuration ‚wirklicher‘ Erfahrung und ihre Existenz verbürgt durch die literarische Tradition. Nichts könnte wirklicher sein als das Imaginäre, denn nichts ist imaginärer als das Wirkliche.[33]

Das Verschwimmen von Realem und Imaginären führt uns zurück zum *Regenroman*, dessen Erzählhaltung gekennzeichnet ist durch eine Mischung des Phantastischen mit einer Art „dirty realism".[34] Und diese Verbindung von Realem und Imaginärem, das Verschwimmende, nicht Festlegbare scheint zumindest ein wesentliches Moment in der Verwendung des Elementargeister-Motivs bei Duve zu sein, was sich wiederum als poetologische Selbstreflexion lesen lässt. Schließlich ist *Regenroman* ein Roman über einen Autor, der schreiben will (und muss) und es nicht kann. Es geht um die „Demontierung des männlichen Schriftstellers"[35] und in der Parodie des männlichen Künstlerromans fügt sich das ins Groteske gewendete, ironisierte Motiv der Wasser- und Elementargeister seiner Deutung seit der Romantik als Reflexion des Ästhetischen gemäß sinnvoll ein.

Und so ganz können wir uns auch nicht sicher sein, ob Isadoras mythische Züge nicht allein der Phantasie Leons, des Schriftstellers auf der Suche nach seiner Muse, entspringen. Sein Tod im Moor jedenfalls liest sich als Parodie des lustvollen Versinkens, das uns aus den Wasserfrauen-Texten der Romantik vertraut ist:

> „Komm, mein einsamer Leon", rief sie und breitet die Arme aus. Ihre Stimme war ein Rauschen und ein Raunen. [...] Leon richtet sich auf und ging auf sie zu, ging mitten hinein in die sumpfigen Untiefen. [...] ‚Komm, mein armer Leon‘, rief Isadora. „Komm! Du sollst nie mehr allein sein und dich nie mehr fürchten müssen." Sie lächelte und spielte mit einer Hand an ihrem Busen. Ihre langen, schwarzen Haare waren aufs innigste mit den Zweigen der Bäume verflochten. Voller Sehnsucht streckte Leon seine Arme nach ihr aus. Noch einen Schritt tat er und noch einen. Er verlor den Grund unter den Füßen. [...] Seufzend ergab er sich in die feuchte Umarmung. Sofort brach der Morast mit grellem Schmerz in seine Lungen ein. Leon rang nach Luft und fraß bloß Sumpf. (R297)

Das Wiederauftauchen des Elementaren in der deutschen Gegenwartsliteratur ist in den Werken von Fritz, Schoch und Duve unübersehbar. Die Analyse der ausgewählten Texte zeigt, dass der Umgang mit dem

Motivkreis der Elementargeister dabei ausgesprochen vielfältig ist und sein Einsatz, der von der zitathaften Übernahme bis zur parodistischen, grotesken Verzerrung der Tradition reicht, geradezu dem schillernden Charakter des Motivs entspricht: Es ist nicht ein einzelner Motivstrang, wie z.B. der Undinen- oder Melusinenstoff, sondern es ist das Vermengen und Sichüberlagern der verschiedenen literarischen Erscheinungsformen des Elementaren, das sich als besonders fruchtbar erweist. Und doch gibt es bei allen Unterschieden in der Verwendung des Motivkreises Gemeinsamkeiten in seiner Funktion, die das an der Jahrtausendwende neu erwachte Interesse an den Elementargeistern erklären: „Was sich nicht festlegen lässt",[36] so charakterisiert sich Bachmanns Undine und benennt damit eine zentrale Eigenschaft der literarischen Elementargeister. Für die neuen, jungen Autorinnen und Autoren, die – wenn auch mit mehr oder weniger starker Betonung des zeitgeschichtlichen Hintergrunds, – ihre Texte über den Osten Deutschlands in der Zeit um die Wiedervereinigung ansiedeln, scheint der Mythos ein besonders attraktives Gebiet für die literarische Auseinandersetzung mit eben jener Zeit des Wandels zu sein. Und bei dem Unterfangen eine Zeit des Umbruchs zu verarbeiten sind wiederum Wasserfrauen und Salamander auf Grund ihres amphibienhaften Wesens als Projektionsfiguren besonders geeignet: Das Unheimliche, Vage, Unwirkliche dieser Wesen bietet sich den Autoren geradezu an für ein Bild einer Gegenwart, die als sich wandelnd und nicht festlegbar empfunden wird.

Aber die Analyse des Gebrauchs des Motivkreis der Elementargeister hat auch gezeigt, dass ein anderes Element noch wichtiger zu sein scheint. In den drei Texten, so unterschiedlich sie auch in der Verwendung der Wasserfrauen- Elementargeister-Motive sind, übernimmt der Motivkreis eine autoreflexive Funktion. Damit folgen sie der Deutung des Motivs, wie sie seit der Romantik, aber auch besonders in der Literatur des 20. Jahrhunderts relevant wird. In den Zusammenhang der poetischen Selbstbespiegelung gehören auch die vielfältigen intertextuellen Verweise, die die Texte kennzeichnen. Vor allem die Literatur der Romantik ist dabei ein wichtiger Bezugspunkt; bei Fritz und Duve scheint es wieder insbesondere E.T.A. Hoffmann zu sein. Die Verbindung von Phantastik und Wirklichkeit, vom Imaginären und dem Realen eröffnet für diese neuen Autoren besonders reizvolle Möglichkeiten der literarischen Äußerung. Und dies sollte auch nicht überraschen bei einer Literatur, die von der Kritik als „Rückkehr des Epischen"[37] gefeiert wurde und die an der Jahrtausendwende bewusst anknüpft an das Erzählen des 19. Jahrhunderts.

Anmerkungen

1 Der Salamander ist ein Sonderfall unter den Elementargeistern, da er auf Grund seiner Existenz in der Realität eigentlich nicht zu den imaginären Wesen und Fabeltieren gehört. Jedoch macht „ihn der Glaube an seine magischen und übernatürlichen Kräfte zu einem Tierwesen der besonderen Art". (Hans Schöpf, *Fabeltiere*, VMA-Verlag: Wiesbaden, 1988, S. 135.) Somit wird er in die Enzyklopädien der magischen Wesen aufgenommen.

2 Beate Otto, *Unterwasserliteratur. Von Wasserfrauen und Wassermännern*, Königshausen & Neumann: Würzburg, 2001. Monika Schmitz-Emanns, *Seetiefen und Seelentiefen. Literarische Spiegelungen innerer und äußerer Fremde*, Königshausen & Neumann: Würzburg, 2002. Die ‚ganz neue Literatur', die ich hier mit den Texten Karen Duves, Julia Schochs und Michael Fritz' besprechen möchte, wird allerdings in keiner der beiden Studien behandelt.

3 Michael Fritz, *Rosa oder Die Liebe zu den Fischen*, Reclam Verlag: Leipzig, 2001; Julia Schoch, *Der Körper des Salamanders. Erzählungen*, Piper: München, 2002; Karen Duve, *Regenroman*, Ullstein Taschenbuchverlag: München 2001 (3. Auflage), im Folgenden werden folgende Kürzel im Text verwendet: ‚Ro', ‚KS', ‚R'.

4 Otto beschreibt in der Einleitung zu ihrer Untersuchung das andauernde Interesse an Wasserfrauen: „Die Wasserfrau – die heute auch als Alltags-Mythos verstanden werden kann – zählt zu den aufregendsten Figuren der mythischen Phantasie, ihre Doppelnatur wirkt erotisch, geheimnisvoll und herausfordernd. In ihr kristallisieren sich weibliche Identifikationssehnsüchte ebenso wie die ‚Sehnsüchte und Ängste des Mannes gegenüber Weiblichkeit'." Otto, *Unterwasserliteratur*, S. 10.

5 Vgl. zum Motiv des weiblichen Wassertodes: Anna Maria Stuby, *Liebe, Tod und Wasserfrau. Mythen des Weiblichen in der Literatur*, Westdeutscher Verlag: Opladen, 1992, S. 163.

6 Vgl.: Manfred Schmeling, ‚Verlockungen – Der Mythos der Wasserfrau und die Kunst der Imagination,' in: Konrad Hilpert, Peter Winterhoff-Spurk, Hgg., *Der Traum vom Glück: Orte der Imagination*, Röhrig Verlag: St. Ingbert, 2002 (Annales Universitatis Saraviensis 15), S. 59-79 (hier: S. 64 f.).

7 Vgl.: Schmitz-Emanns, *Seetiefen*, S. 56 f.

8 Schmitz-Emanns, *Seetiefen*, S. 25.

9 Zur vielfältigen kulturgeschichtlichen Bedeutung des Wassers vgl.: Hartmut Böhme, Hg., *Kulturgeschichte des Wassers*, Suhrkamp: Frankfurt am Main, 1988.

10 Schmitz-Emans, *Seetiefen*, S. 60.

11 Mit der Wahl Rosa Luxemburgs, deren Leiche nach ihrer Ermordung in den Berliner Landwehrkanal geworfen wurde und die erst Monate später als unbekannte Wasserleiche geborgen wurde, als Namensgeberin für seine Heldin verweist Fritz auch auf den Opheliamythos und den sich daran anschließenden Motivstrang der ‚Inconnue de la Seine', einer geheimsvollen Ertränkten, der in Reinhold Conrad

Muschlers Novelle *Die Unbekannte* (Dresden 1936) ihren Höhepunkt findet. Vgl. dazu: Stuby, *Liebe, Tod und Wasserfrau*, S. 209.

12 Thomas E. Schmidt, ‚Als das Boot gekentert war. Die jungen Autoren Ostdeutschlands erzählen kühl vom Leben in der Zone,' *Die Zeit*, 37, 5. Sept. 2003, S. 52.

13 Peter von Matt, *Liebesverrat. Die Treulosen in der Literatur*, Carl Hanser Verlag: München, Wien, 1989, S. 231.

14 Schmidt, ‚Als das Boot gekentert war', S. 52.

15 Schmitz-Emanns, *Seetiefen*, S. 50.

16 Homer, *Odyssee*, Übersetzung von Roland Hampe, Reclam: Stuttgart, 1979, xii, 39-46, S. 194.

17 Friedrich de la Motte Fouqué, *Undine*, Reclam: Stuttgart, 2001 (erste Auflage 1953), S. 46

18 Manfred Schmeling, ‚Verlockungen', S. 69.

19 Schmidt, ‚Als das Boot gekentert war', S. 52.

20 Schmitz-Emanns, *Seetiefen*, S. 99.

21 Claudia Kramatscheck, ‚Julia Schoch, Malin Schwerdtfeger und Juli Zeh: Drei Debüts, die den Untergang des sozialistischen Ostens verhandeln,' *Wochenzeitung*, Zürich, 4. Okt. 2001.

22 Schoch sagt selbst über die Orte, von denen sie schreibt: „Osten, für mich, ist ein Prinzip und kein Staat. Eine Himmelsrichtung, [...] [a]us der ich Fragen und Probleme ziehe, die ich für die Gegenwart diskutieren will. Letztere ist überfüllt mit Dingen und Materie, die über die Ideen herrschen. Deshalb nehme ich sie auch wahr als einen verstellten Ort, in dem es nahezu unmöglich ist, visionär zu denken. Ich suche statt dessen die kargen, spröden Gegenden, die noch nicht vollständig mit Bildern besetzt sind [...]. Auch meine Vergangenheit ist eine solche Gegend." Julia Schoch, ‚Orte, von denen ich schreibe', http://www.mynetcologne.de/~nc-contzeha/lithaus/200202/-schoch.htm (04.03.2004).

23 M. Kurtz, ‚Unter der Nebelwand.' http://www.i-lit.de/rezension/julia_schoch_salamder.html (19.04.2004).

24 Vgl.: Schöpf, *Fabeltiere*, S. 142 f.

25 Vgl.: Schmitz-Emanns, *Seetiefen*, S. 119 ff.

26 Stuby, *Liebe, Tod und Wasserfrau*, S. 165.

27 Schmeling, *Verlockungen*, S. 27.

28 Einen Drachenschwanz entdeckt Leon zwar nicht, wohl aber ein seltsames kleines Wesen. In ihrem Spiegel-Interview erklärt Karen Duve, dass die mysteriöse Gestalt als Waldschrat geplant war, ein Zitat aus Ina Seidels *Regenballade*, auf die sich auch der Titel *Regenroman* bezieht. Diese Figur fiel jedoch denen vom Verlag geforderten Streichungen zum Opfer. Vgl.: Karen Duve, ,Ich stehe gern im Regen,' in: *Der Spiegel*, 41, (1999).

29 Der stets feuchte Rocksaum zeichnet sie als Nixe aus, denn diese sind nach dem Volksglauben daran zweifelsfrei zu erkennen. Vgl.: Hanns Bächtold-Stäubli, *Handwörterbuch des deutschen Aberglaubens*, Hg. von E. Hoffmann-Krayer und Hanns Bächtold-Stäubli. Berlin/ New York, 1987 (Nachdruck), Bd. iii, S. 130.

30 Vgl. hierzu Wolfgang Kayser, *Das Groteske in Malerei und Dichtung*. Rowohlt: Reinbek bei Hamburg, 1960, S. 135: „Es gibt von dem Grotesken bevorzugte Tiere, wie Schlangen, Eulen, Kröten und Spinnen – das Nachtgetier und das kriechende Getier, das in anderen, dem Menschen unzugänglichen Ordnungen lebt. Das Groteske liebt weiterhin alles Ungeziefer."

31 Vgl.: Ulrike Schnaas, *Das Phantastische als Erzählstrategie in vier zeitgenössischen Romanen*, Almquist & Wiksell International: Stockholm, 2004 (Acta Universitatis Stockholmiensis/ Stockholmer Germanistische Forschungen 63), S. 51 f.

32 Tatsächlich sollen römische Damen „gebrannten Salamander in Öl" als Enthaarungscreme eingesetzt haben. Vgl.: Schöpf, *Fabeltiere*, S. 138 und Bächtold-Stäubli, *Handwörterbuch des deutschen Aberglaubens*, S. 455. Dies belegt nicht nur Duves detaillierte Kenntnis des Motivs, sondern zeigt, dass sie es sehr bewusst und häufig ironisiert einsetzt.

33 Schmitz-Emanns, *Seetiefen*, S. 15.

34 Vgl.: Schnaas, *Das Phantastische*, S. 38 ff.

35 Schnaas, *Das Phantastische*, S. 70.

36 Ingeborg Bachmann, *Undine geht*. In: Dies., *Das dreißigste Jahr*, Pieper: München, 1999 (1. Auflage 1991), S. 176-186 (hier: S. 182).

37 Karl-Wilhelm Schmidt, ,Zur Rückkehr des Epischen in der deutschsprachigen Literatur der neunziger Jahre. Die Welt als Chaos in Karen Duves *Regenroman*,' in: *Zeitschrift für Literaturwissenschaft und Linguistik*, H. 118 (2000), 164-177.

Heike Bartel

Von Jonny Rotten bis Werther: Karen Duves *Dies ist kein Liebeslied* zwischen Popliteratur und Bildungsroman

Karen Duve's *Dies ist kein Liebeslied* is a novel that interweaves intertextual elements from so-called 'low' and 'high' culture. Goethe's Werther meets the English footballer Gareth Southgate and Hartmann von Aue rubs shoulders with Jonny Rotten in this text that is as much a literary composition as it is a cultural study of the FRG of the 80s. This essay aims to establish the position of Duve's novel in relation to the genres of *Bildungsroman* and *Popliteratur*. In three chapters, particular emphasis is placed upon Duve's critical engagement with consumerism – including the voracious consumption of food by the bulimic protagonist Anne Strelau – the use of intertextual elements and the musical and cultural importance of the 'mixtape'.

„Cross the Border – Close the Gap" forderte Leslie A. Fiedler 1968 in seinem gleichnamigen Essay,[1] in dem er für eine neue Literatur postulierte, sie solle anti-künstlerisch und anti-seriös sein. Fiedler schlug damit eine Bresche für die Popliteratur, die im „Zeitalter der neuen Literatur [...] Indianer, Science Fiction und Pornographie"[2] in einer Kombination sowohl der Genres als auch der ‚High' und ‚Low Culture' miteinander vermischen sollte. Diese Forderung nach einer neuen Literatur, in der die Dichotomie zwischen ‚hohen' und ‚niederen' kulturellen Ausdrucksweisen überbrückt werden sollte, kam zuerst in Amerika und mit einiger Verspätung auch in der Bundesrepublik dem Trend nach einer Popliteratur entgegen, die provokant und exzentrisch gegen einen Eliteanspruch und die etablierten Normen einer Literaturtradition anschrieb, wie es im Bereich der visuellen Kunst die Popart mit Vertretern wie Roy Liechtenstein und Andy Warhol taten. Auf diesem umstrittenen Neuland wuchsen in den 60er und 70er Jahren Werke deutschsprachiger AutorInnen wie Rolf Dieter Brinkmann, Paul Gerhard Hübsch, Wolf Wondratschek, Elfriede Jelinek oder der frühe Peter Handke. Das Eindringen von Umgangssprachlichem, Trivialem oder Obszönem in den Bereich der Kunst und Literatur wendete sich in der Kombination von ‚high' und ‚low' gegen ästhetische und politische Normen und löste heftige Debatten aus. Popliteratur war bis dahin vor allem mit dem Begriff der Trivialliteratur im Sinne der Heftchenromane, Zeitschriften und Comics und mit einer von der Frankfurter Schule kritisierten „Kulturindustrie" verbunden und nicht mit der Idee von Avantgarde und dem innovativen Vordringen in neue ästhetische Bereiche.

Im 21. Jahrhundert hat sich die Situation deutlich verändert. Das meint nicht, daß der Begriff ‚Popliteratur' nun klarer umrissen wäre, im Gegenteil trägt seine vielfache und oft unreflektierte Anwendung auf verschiedenste literarische Werke besonders jüngerer AutorInnen – wie

Karen Duve – zur Definitionsverwirrung bei. ‚Popliteratur' umfaßt nun
auch Werke, die mit ihren Zügen klassischer Trivialliteratur gerade das
Gegenteil des Avantgardistischen ihrer Vorgänger der 60er Jahre
vertreten. Die entscheidende Entwicklung der Popromane jüngster Zeit ist
jedoch, daß sich hier das literarische Stoffrepertoire stark erweitert hat
und deutlich und bewußt aus dem Kanon der Medien- , Marken- und
Alltagskultur schöpft, womit es besonders ein junges und jung geblie-
benes Lesepublikum anspricht. Titel wie *Mein erster Sanyo* von Christian
Grasser (2000), Karen Duves aus dem Englischen eines Popsongs
übersetzter Titel *Dies ist kein Liebeslied* oder auch *High Fidelity* (1995)
des britischen Autors Nick Hornby legen deutlich Zeugnis davon ab. Die
Themenbereiche haben sich derart erweitert, daß sie nicht mehr nur ein
wie auch immer geartetes Schöngeistiges, sondern auch Werbung,
Markennamen, Verweise auf Fernsehen, Film und Musik umfassen.
Daraus folgt notwendigerweise auf formaler Ebene, daß diese Texte mit
ihren Verweisen auf Prätexte und präexistierende Zeichensysteme der
Jugend- und Alltagskultur Intertextualität für literarisches Schaffen
nutzen. Neben diesen inhaltlichen und formalen Aspekten, geht auch die
Theorie insbesondere mit der Disziplin der Cultural Studies auf die aus
diesem literarischen Diskurs nicht mehr wegzudenkende Verknüpfung
von Alltags-, Medien- und Wissenschaftskultur ein.[3] Kulturtheoretiker
wie Stuart Hall, John Fiske und vor allem Michel de Certeau setzen sich
mit dem Phänomen der Populärkultur auseinander, deren Konsum nicht
mehr als bloß stumpfsinnige und unreflektierte Beschäftigung mit
Produkten der Kulturindustrie ohne jegliche ästhetische Qualität gewertet
wird. Vielmehr wird – so bei de Certeau – die Seite produktiver
Rezeption am Konsum hervorgehoben, was sich als „andere, lautlose
Produktion" äußere, die zwar keine Produkte hervorbringe, aber den
Blick freigäbe auf die „Umgangsweise mit den [bestehenden] Produkten,
die von einer herrschenden ökonomischen Ordnung aufgezwungen
werden", wobei immer neue „Lesarten und Bedeutungszuschreibungen"
entstünden.[4] Das Populäre, im weitesten Sinn verstanden als alles
außerhalb von Arbeit und Kunst – vom Fußball über die Massenmedien
bis zu Mode und Markenamen – dringt im 20. und 21. Jahrhundert auf
inhaltlicher, formaler und theoretischer Ebene in den Bereich des
Literarischen.

Der folgende Essay wird sich damit auseinandersetzen, wie Duves
Roman *Dies ist kein Liebeslied* (2002) in den Zusammenhang der
Popliteratur mit seinen verschiedenen, hier nur kurz angrissenen Facetten
und Hintergründen paßt. Der Titel dieses Essays deutet bereits an, daß
neben der Popliteratur ein weiteres, wesentlich traditionelleres
literarisches Genre bei der Auseinandersetzung mit diesem Roman in
Betracht gezogen werden wird, der Bildungsroman. Die These ist dabei,

daß Duves *Dies ist kein Liebeslied* zwischen diesen beiden Genres changiert, die markiert werden durch die intertextuellen Eckpfeiler Jonny Rotten und Werther.

Der Anti-Bildungsroman des hungernden Individuums

Auch wenn Duves Roman fast 40 Jahre nach Fiedlers Forderung „Cross the Border – Close the Gap" geschrieben ist, so kann doch von ihm gesagt werden, daß er mit seiner Kombination verschiedener Prätexte eine Brücke zwischen Hoch- und Populärkultur schlägt. Dies äußert sich allein schon darin, daß am Romanende der Protagonist aus Goethes Briefroman *Die Leiden des jungen Werther* und Gareth Southgate, der englische Fußballspieler, der im Halbfinale der Europameisterschaft 1996 das entscheidende Elfmeter gegen Deutschland verschoß, in einen Kontext gebracht werden. Dieser Kontext bildet den Rahmen für die Liebesnacht der mittlerweile Anfang dreißigjährigen und 117 kg schweren Protagonistin und Ich-Erzählerin Anne Strelau mit ihrer inzwischen in London lebenden Jugendliebe Peter Hemstedt. Diese Nacht bildet den Zielpunkt von Annes Reise im Flugzeug von Hamburg nach London, während der wir in Rückblenden durch ihre Kindheit, Jugend und ihr frühes Erwachsenenalter geführt werden. Im Bruch mit einem der prominentesten Vertreter der deutschen Kulturtradition, Goethe, greift Duves Romanende folgende Passage im *Werther* auf:

> Wir traten ans Fenster. Es donnerte abseitwärts, und der herrliche Regen säuselte auf das Land, und der erquickendste Wohlgeruch stieg in aller Fülle einer warmen Luft zu uns auf. Sie stand, auf ihren Ellenbogen gestützt, ihr Blick durchdrang die Gegend, sie sah gen Himmel und auf mich, ich sah ihr Auge tränenvoll, sie legte ihre Hand auf die meinige, und sagte – Klopstock![5]

Bei Duve steht jedoch, nachdem er mit Anne geschlafen hat, Hemstedt auf, „um eine neue CD einzulegen." Dann tritt er, wie Werther, ans Fenster und sieht hinaus. Anne stützt – wie Lotte – die Ellbogen auf. Wie bei Goethe „donnert [es] abseitwärts" – nicht wegen des Gewitters (wie bei Goethe,) sondern weil bei Duve „die Boxen [...] auf dem Fußboden [stehen]", und dann singt „eine traurige Männerstimme" „Don't try so hard to be different", und wie dereinst Lotten ergreift Anne das Wort. Statt der empfindsamen Losung „Klopstock" fällt jedoch eine andere, im Sommer 1996 nach dem Halbfinale Deutschland/England nicht minder zeitgenössische: „‚Southgate', sage ich. Southgates Schicksal hat zwar nicht allzuviel mit dem Songtext zu tun, aber Peter versteht trotzdem sofort, was ich meine."[6] Diese Übereinkunft beim Nennen des Losungswortes steht beim Paar in London – anders als beim Paar in Wahlheim – am Ende und nicht am Anfang einer hier wie dort höchst problematischen und selbstzerstörerischen Liebesbeziehung. Am Ende von *Dies ist kein Liebeslied* nimmt sich Anne zwar nicht wie Werther das Leben, sondern nur ihre Pyjamahose und ihren Koffer, aber die

Geschichte von Anne und Hemstedt hat wie die von Lotte und Werther von Anfang an keine Chance: „ich [...] kaufte mir einen Flugschein nach London, wie sich andere Leute einen Strick kaufen." (L8)

Lässig und respektlos überschreitet Duve hier „Grenze" und „Graben", die die Markierungen zwischen ‚hohen' und ‚niederen' Formen von Kultur und Literatur bilden. Aber im Verweis auf Goethes *Werther* liegt mehr als das bloße Heranzitieren und dann Brechen mit der altehrwürdigen Vorlage. *Werther* – der auch an anderer Stelle im Buch vorkommt, dort jedoch als unfruchtbares Thema einer Klassenarbeit – kann in gewisser Weise als Parallelfigur zu Anne gelesen werden. Denn trotz aller Gebrochenheit dieser Spiegelung und trotz Annes ober-flächlicher Abneigung gegen den Schulstoff, gegen Goethes „empfindsames Gewinsel" und die „ekelhaften Stelle, wie [...] sie dann bloß ‚Klopstock' sagt und er sofort weiß, was sie meint" (L163), versteht Anne, was Werther auszudrücken versucht: „als er anfing von seiner Liebe und seinem Unglück zu sprechen, da war mir als sähe ich mein eigenes Herz. Es spricht so klar und wahr und traurig." (L163) Wie Werther läßt sich auch Annes Geschichte als eine Art Bildungsroman lesen, jedoch einer, in der wir keinesfalls „des Helden Bildung in ihrem Anfang und Fortgang bis zu einer gewissen Stufe der Vollendung" folgen.[7] In beiden Romanen scheitert die Bildung, weil die ProtagonistInnen sich nicht wirklich weiterentwickeln, sondern immer wieder auf die eigenen Fehler und Neurosen zurückverfallen.[8] Bei Duve wie bei Goethe sind es die verschiedenen Sozialisationsinstanzen, an denen Held und Heldin scheitern; hier: Familie, Schule, Sportunterricht, Parties und Psychotherapie; dort: Hof, Gesellschaft, Bälle und Kunstausübung. Der Verweis auf Goethes *Werther*, der vordergründig bloß eine Pointe zu sein scheint, entpuppt sich als wichtige Vorlage, mit deren Hilfe *Dies ist kein Liebeslied* die Tragik seiner Protagonistin entfaltet. Deren gescheiterter Bildungsgang ist vielfach gebrochen in den Sprüngen von Klopstock zu Southgate und wird als die Geschichte der neuen Leiden der Anne Strelau lesbar. Evelyn Finger unterstreicht diesen Charakter von Duves Roman mit Bezug auf Karl Philip Moritz' Roman aus dem 18. Jahrhundert, *Anton Reiser*, der ebenfalls die Schwierigkeit der Bildung des Individuums thematisiert. Finger betont, Duves Roman sei „eigentlich [...] ein Verbildungsroman, dessen Heldin sich keine Entwicklung zutraut und auch keine Chance dazu bekommt, gehetzt vom Unbehagen an sich selbst und von der feindlich gesinnten Gesellschaft – ein weiblicher Anton Reiser."[9]

Das Streben, dem „Kerker des Körpers" zu entkommen, das Werther mit seiner Todessehnsucht zum Ausdruck bringt und schließlich mit seinem Selbstmord realisiert, bildet bei Duve das facettenreiche Zentrum des Romans, dessen Protagonistin mit Bulimie, Tablettensucht,

Selbstverstümmelung und Selbstmordversuchen gegen ihren dicken, gehaßten Körper vorgeht. Der Kreislauf der Bulimikerin von Fressen und Erbrechen, der aus keiner Krise hinaus-, sondern nur tiefer in sie hineinführt, karikiert dabei auf prägnante Weise das Konzept des Bildungsromans. An die Stelle der Reifung tritt die Reifungsneurose im Anti-Entwicklungsgang der Protagonistin Anne mit ihrer zutiefst gestörten Körperwahrnehmung. Ein weiterer Twist im Umgang mit der tradierten Gattung ist dabei, daß es bei Duve um die Entwicklung einer weiblichen Protagonistin geht, die sich in ihren Sozialisations- und Entwicklungsversuchen vor allem und vergeblich einem von den Medien diktierten Körperideal anzunähern versucht. Prägnant ist dabei die Beschreibung von Annes Entschluß zu ihrer ersten Diät, die beschrieben wird als „Initiationsritus", ein

> einschneidender, wenn nicht sogar der wichtigste Moment im Leben eines Mädchens. Jedenfalls ist er bedeutender als das maßlos überschätzte Ereignis der Entjungferung. Eine Art Initiationsritus, nur, daß du nicht als fertige Frau daraus hervorgehst, sondern immer wieder von vorn anfangen mußt. [...] Fortan wirst du versuchen, anders zu sein, und zwar besser – also weniger. (L43-44)

Mit seinen Verweisen auf Eßstörungen erlaubt Duves Roman Rückbezüge zum umfangreichen Diskurs der Forschungsliteratur zum Thema Essen und Eßstörungen, in dem zum Beispiel Kim Chernin die weibliche Obsession mit Essen, die sich in Diäten, Magersucht und Bulimie widerspiegelt, als „puberty rite" beschreibt.[10] Die Aufnahme des Kindes in die Gesellschaft, besonders des Mädchens in den Kreis der Frauen, erfolgt mit der ersten Diät. Dieses selbstauferlegte Weniger-Werden wird im Verlauf des gesamten Frauenlebens immer stärker ritualisiert, das heißt es verliert jegliche Zweckhaftigkeit, verselbständigt sich und nimmt Züge eines zwanghaft übertriebenen Verhaltens an. Das Tragische dieser Entwicklung ist dabei, daß sie nie zu einem befriedigenden Endpunkt, einer wahren Entwicklung zum Selbst führt. Das Scheitern von Anne Strelaus Bildunsgroman ist mit der ersten Diät im Grundschulalter vorprogrammiert. Nach dieser wird fast jede Lebenssituation und Entwicklungsstation mit dem korrespondieren Gewichtsstand konnotiert: „Als ich vierundfünfzig Kilo wog, sprach Hoffi Hoffmann mich an" (L87-88), „[w]enn ich erst unter 60 Kilo wog, würde ich mit keinem dieser Jungen mehr im Bett landen" (L179) und „nachdem ich sechs Kilo abgenommen hatte, fühlte ich mich imstande, Hemstedt aufzusuchen" (L193). Diese lebenslange Hungerkur führt jedoch nie aus der Krise hinaus, sondern wie der Jo-Jo Effekt von Ab- und Zunehmen bei den meisten Diäten, immer tiefer in sie hinein. Dabei bleibt das Subjekt hungrig in jeder Beziehung und im ständigen Zustand der Selbstreduktion. Duve fächert auf verschiedenen Ebenen eine Palette von Eßstörungen und -verhaltensweisen auf. So greift der gelb-rote

Umschlag des Einbandes das Thema in poppiger Bildhaftigkeit auf und bildet eine Frau im geblümten Bikini ab, die geradewegs einem Reader's Digest Heft entsprungen sein könnte, in sechs verschiedenen Stadien ihres Körpergewichts, von 108,0 bis 49,0 Kilo. Mit Annes Freundin „Klein-Doris" kontrastiert Duve Annes Bulimie mit der Magersucht der a-sexuellen und ewig-kindlichen Schulkameradin mit ihren „knochigen, beflaumten Armen", deren größter „Kick" es ist, „wenn sie zusah, wie ich ihr [Nutella-] Brot aß. Was sie nicht wußte, war, daß ich es hinterher auskotzte" (L123). Im Gegensatz dazu wird die „Hemmungslosigkeit" im Eßverhalten der Jungen beschrieben, „mit der sie in ihre Fleischstücke hieben, während Molle und ich unsere Salate hin und her sortierten" (L152).

In diesem Zusammenhang wird das gesellschaftskritische Element von Duves Schreiben deutlich, das nicht mit erhobenem moralischen Zeigefinger und deutlicher Opfer-Täter-Dichotomie auftritt, aber doch im Kontext des (Selbst-)Bildungsromans die Chancenlosigkeit der Protagonistin zeigt angesichts der Perfektion artifizieller, durch die Medien vermittelter weiblicher Schönheitsideale. Duve hat auch ohne dezidiert theoretische Verweise Teil am feministischen Diskurs, indem sie mit Annes Geschichte auf das verweist, was Sarah Sceats als Gesellschaft bezeichnet, die von Frauen kein „work to produce" verlangt, sondern ein „work to reduce".[11] Während in theoretischen Diskursen, zum Beispiel bei Luce Irigaray, gestörtes Eßverhalten oft in Zusammenhang mit einem gestörten Mutterverhältnis gebracht wird – was auch auf Mutter und Tochter Strelau zutreffen könnte – betont Duve auch die Rolle des Vaters in Annes gestörtem Entwicklungsprozeß. Die erste Diät, angeregt durch die Mutter, ist eine ebenso einschneidende Station im Anti-Bildungsroman wie das gestörte Verhältnis zum Vater, das mit dem beschämenden Vorwurf des Ödipuskomplexes vollends zerbricht: „‚Kannst du mich nicht in Ruhe lassen? Sag mal, hast du einen Ödipuskomplex, oder was ist los?' [...] Ich wußte, was ein Ödipuskomplex war. Etwas mit Sex. [...] Ich war meinen Vater angegangen. Oh Gott, war ich widerlich." (L72) Auch hier führt die Flucht zum Essen:

> Vermutlich schmierte ich mir ein Marmeladentoast, während meine Seele brach und brach und brach. Vielleicht löffelte ich einen Joghurt – einen Löffel für die Erniedrigung, einen Löffel für die Enttäuschung, einen Löffel für den Selbstekel und einen großen Löffel für den Haß. (L73)

In diesen Bereich des selbstzerstörerischen Fluchtverhaltens gehören auch die halb vorgetäuschten, halb autosuggestiv erzeugten Krankheiten Annes.

Es gibt jedoch noch weitere literarische Lesespuren in diesem verweiskräftigen Roman. So wie Werther legt auch die Widmung des Buches, „Für den armen Heinrich", eine Fährte aus zu einem literarischen

Vorbild. Der arme Heinrich ist ein Werk Hartmann von Aues aus dem 13ten Jahrhundert. Er ist insofern ein Bildungsroman als er vom Lebens- und Leidensweg Heinrichs handelt, der von Lepra befallen als Aussätziger von der Gesellschaft gemieden wird und dessen Weg von den Rändern dieser Gesellschaft zurück in ihr Zentrum führt – nach seiner Heilung. Das, was den armen Heinrich ‚arm' macht, ist sein physisches Leiden, die Lepra, die ihn deutlich als Aussätzigen in der Gesellschaft kennzeichnet, durch die von ihr verursachte körperliche Verunstaltung, aber auch weil Lepra im Mittelalter als Strafe Gottes für Sünden gesehen wurde. Die Verbindung von körperlicher Mißgestalt und gesellschaftlicher Ächtung legt den Bezug zur Protagonistin Anne in Duves Roman nahe, denn Anne erfährt durch ihre Dickleibigkeit ein vergleichbares Schicksal. Vielleicht ist Dicksein in unserer Gesellschaft die neue Lepra, angesiedelt zwischen dem Stigma von (Drüsen-)Krankheit und einem verwerflichen Mangel an Selbstbeherrschung. Sowohl bei Anne als auch beim armen Heinrich steht das physisch sichtbare Leiden in engem Zusammenhang mit psychischem oder spirituellem Leiden, bei Heinrich ist es mangelndes Gottvertrauen, bei Anne ein durch Familie, SchulkameradInnen, Männer und Therapien zutiefst unterminiertes Selbstvertrauen. Während am Ende der Legende der arme Heinrich zum „guoten Heinrich" wird und geheilt die schöne Jungfrau heiratet, mit der er glücklich bis an sein Lebensende lebt, erlebt Duves Protagonistin jedoch ihr Happy-End nicht in *Dies ist kein Liebeslied*, sondern erst im nachfolgenden Werk, *Die entführte Prinzessin*.[12] Was die Widmung für den armen Heinrich am Anfang jedoch deutlich macht, ist das Verständnis dieses Buches für den Underdog – besonders den, der in der öffentlichen Sphäre durch seine Inadäquatheit Mißachtung erfährt, der verletzbar und ausgeliefert ist. Der Roman ist gleichsam eingerahmt von solchen Underdogs: dem armen Heinrich, Werther und Gareth Southgate.

Hier wird die im Titel dieses Essays angedeutete Zwischenposition von *Dies ist kein Liebeslied* zwischen dem traditionellen Genre des (gescheiterten) Bildungsromans und dem popliterarischen Bruch mit eben solchen Genres deutlich durch Einsprengsel aus Jugend- und Alltagskultur, auf die wir im folgenden Abschnitt noch weiter eingehen werden.

Poppige Intertextualität

Duves Roman ist „[…] kein Liebeslied", so will es uns der Titel nahelegen. Passender wäre allerdings gesagt „This is not a love song", denn wie so vieles andere im Buch ist auch der Titel des Romans ein Verweis auf einen anderen Text: den eines Liedes der Band Public Image Unlimited mit Jonny Rotten als Sänger, dem ehemaligen Mitglied der Sex Pistols, der Vorzeigeband des Punk, die sich in den späten 70er Jahren nach Sid Vicious' Selbstmord auflöste. Auf andere Texte verwiesen – und *Text* ist hier im weitesten Sinn und nicht nur als literarischer Text zu verstehen – wird im Roman viel, und intertextuelle Einsprengsel spielen eine wichtige Rolle. Sie unterlegen die Handlung mit einer deutlichen Metaebene und ziehen sich als Spuren von Literatur, Popmusik, Markenmanen, Fernsehen und Film durch den Text. Dabei führt der Umweg oder Abweg über diese anderen Texte nicht von Duves Roman fort, sondern gerade in ihn hinein. Die verschiedenen Intertexte tragen wesentlich zur Konstituierung des Textes bei. Wie das Romanende, das Werther und Southgate ins Feld führt, so steht der gesamte Roman gelassen auf der Grundlage eines Mosaiks aus Verweisen sowohl auf populäre als auch auf ‚hohe' deutsche Kultur. Dieses Verfahren, das in seiner radikalen Ausprägung für AutorInnen in den 60er und 70er Jahren noch hart erkämpftes Neuland der deutschsprachigen Popliteratur der ersten Stunde war, steht AutorInnen wie Duve nun selbstverständlicher zur Verfügung. *Dies ist kein Liebeslied* nimmt hier eine Zwischenstellung ein: der Roman gibt sich weder als Werk einer künstlerischen Avantgarde aus, das in der Nachfolge Brinkmanns etwa ganz neue ästhetische Zugänge zu erschließen meint, noch ist er Vertreter der nur konsumorientierten Trivialliteratur einer Spaßgesellschaft. Dabei erlaubt es die bereits zu Anfang skizzierte unscharfe Begriffsbestimmung von ‚Popliteratur' im Zusammenhang mit AutorInnen des 21. Jahrhunderts, Duves Roman trotz (oder gerade aufgrund) der Gegensätze umfassenden Definition dieses Genre als ‚Poproman' zu klassifizieren. Dabei ist es bezeichnend für seine Zwischenstellung, daß manche RezensentInnen den Terminus ‚Popliteratur' für *Dies ist kein Liebeslied* mit Begriffen wie „Postpoproman" oder „Popmoderne" umgehen.[13]

In einem Mosaik der Verweise wirft der Text sogenannte ‚Hochkultur' – wie das literarische Werk Goethes – unter die sogenannte ‚Low Culture' mit Verweisen auf Alltagskultur und Massenmedien. Die ‚Hochkultur' wird in dieser Kombination parodiert, gegen den Strich gebürstet, gleichzeitig aber auch – wie im Falle Werthers – wiederbelebt, indem sie einen aktuellen Bezug erhält, mit Southgate dem authentischen Fußballer im Spiel der Verweise. Duve spielt dieses Spiel noch weiter und wendet es vom Alltäglichen wieder zum Literarischen. So ist zum Beispiel der/die durch die Verweise auf Goethe und Hartmann von Aue sensibilisierte LeserIn versucht, Duves detaillierte Beschreibung des unglücklichen Elfmeterschützens als perspektivenverkehrten Verweis auf Peter Handkes *Die Angst des Tormanns beim Elfmeter* zu lesen.

Bereits Duves Vorwort schärft diese Wahrnehmung, die auf Verweise achtet, indem es mit der Textsorte der Gegenerklärung spielt:

> Was folgt, ist frei erfunden. Orte und Handlungen haben nur wenig mit
> tatsächlichen Orten und Vorkommnissen zu tun. Bücher und Filme werden
> schlampig zitiert. Und ihr seid alle nicht gemeint. (L5)

Dieser *disclaimer*, der alle Bezüge und Verantwortung scheinbar von sich
weist, eröffnet dabei gerade die Möglichkeit, entferntere Bezüge
herzustellen. In diesem Vorwort liegt – gleichsam ex negativo – die
Möglichkeit, sogar Aufforderung, zu einer Parallelisierung von Fiktion
und Autorin-Biographie. Die Gegenerklärung, die sich allen Bezügen auf
Tatsächliches scheinbar widersagt, ist eine ironisch gebrochene, die
gerade auf ihr Gegenteil verweist. Zusätzlich eröffnet der Text jedoch
hier auch die Möglichkeit, als LeserIn in den Prozeß der Textproduktion
einzusteigen und subjektive Bezüge zu Personen und Texten herzustellen,
die „schlampig zitiert" werden und eventuell „gar nicht gemeint sind".

Was das Vorwort zusätzlich verdeutlicht, ist, daß der Text mit dem
Genre der Popliteratur das Merkmal teilt, „eine Literatur über
präfabrizierte Zeichensysteme" zu sein mit einem „Arsenal von
„sekundären Texten". Er ist ein Text, der „keine Anklage gegen die
ausufernde Zeichenproduktion der populären Kultur erhebt, sondern diese
als Ausgangsbasis des literarischen Schreibens nutzt."[14] Hier wird auch
der enge Zusammenhang von Popliteratur und einer
poststrukturalistischen Lektüre deutlich, die davon ausgeht, daß jeder
Text in all seinen Elementen intertextuell sei, indem er auf andere Texte
verweise oder aus deren Echos bestehe. Besonders das „Mood-Mosaic"
der aus mehreren Titeln zusammengeschnittenen Musikkassette, auf die
wir im letzten Abschnitt dieses Essays noch zurückkommen werden,
spiegelt das „mosaique de citations" wider, mit dem Julia Kristeva solche
Intertextualität bezeichnet. Vor allem tun dies aber die ersten beiden
Seiten des Romans, die in atemberaubender Schnellabfolge und mit einer
Technik, die an das musikalische Sampling oder an Collagetechnik
erinnert, ein kulturelles und gesellschaftliches Tableau der
Bundesrepublik der 80er Jahre liefern. Wir werden konfrontiert mit der
Geschichte der Welt und des Individuums auf zwei Buchseiten, wobei
beides, das große Weltgeschehen und scheinbar banale Begebenheiten
des kleinen Leben des Individuums, sich wie die Steine in einem Mosaik
zugleich berühren und doch ungerührt nebeneinanderstehen:

> Alle anderen hatten Freunde und Sex, sie hatten Berufe, gingen auf Parties und
> Reisen, und freuten sich fünf Tage lang aufs Wochenende. Also ging ich
> ebenfalls mit Männern ins Bett und mit Frauen in Bars, scheiterte in diversen
> Jobs, langweilte mich auf Festen und woanders und schnitzte mir sonntags mit
> einem Kartoffelschälmesser Muster in die Oberarme. Unterdessen wurde der
> F.C. Bayern München achtmal deutscher Meister. Alle Leute, die ich kannte,
> kauften sich Uhren mit Digitalanzeige und vertauschten ihre Schlaghosen
> gegen knöchelenge Jeans oder Karottenhosen. Der Iran erklärte die USA zum
> großen Satan, und MTV startete sein Programm mit ‚Video kills the Radio
> Star' von den Buggels. Englische Soldaten marschierten auf den Falk-

landinseln ein und amerikanische auf Granada. Alle Leute, die ich kannte, tauschten ihre Digitaluhren wieder gegen normale Uhren [...] und kauften sich Walkmen. Der Atomreaktor Nr. 4 des Kernkraftwerks Tschernobyl verteilte seine Spaltprodukte über ganz Europa [...]. In Uganda und Liberia und Georgien brachen Bürgerkriege aus, und Aserbaidschan kämpfte gegen Armenien. Und die Schlager handelten weiterhin von Liebe. [...] Die ganze Zeit hielt ich gewissermaßen den Atem an und wartete auf meinen Einsatz [...]. (L7-8)

Der Roman zeichnet die Wirklichkeit und Kultur der 80er Jahre als Collage, in der Historisches, Politisches, Alltägliches, Weltbewegendes und Triviales in schönster Popmanier zusammengeschnitten wird. Modetrends und Fußballerfolge stehen neben historisch-gesellschaftliche Eckdaten wie Tschernobyl, Golf-, Balkan- und Tschetschenienkrieg und werden durchsetzt von äußerst Privatem. Diese Collage wirkt in mehrfacher Hinsicht. Einerseits wirft die schnelle Abfolge der verschiedenen Bilder ein kritisches Licht auf die Schnellebigkeit und das mangelnde Geschichtsbewußtsein einer Gesellschaft, die scheinbar unberührt historischen, politischen und ökologischen Desastern gegen-übersteht. Nach Tschernobyl wird „empfohlen, zwanzig Jahre lang keine Waldpilze mehr zu essen, und zwei Jahre lang aß man tatsächlich weniger Pilze" (L8). Umweltkatastrophen und Kriege werden im gleichen schnellen Takt wie Modetrends genannt und vergessen. Andererseits illustriert das „unterdessen" dieser Passage das unberührte Nebeneinander von Zeitgeschehen und Leidensgeschichte der Protagonistin, die nie zum Zuge kommt und bei der sogar Akte der sonntäglichen Selbstverstümmelung keinen ‚Einschnitt' hervorrufen, sondern mit scheinbarer Beiläufigkeit Erwähnung finden: „ich [...] schnitzte mir sonntags mit einem Kartoffelschälmesser Muster in die Oberarme."

Duve nimmt mit dieser Chronik der nicht nur laufenden, sondern rasenden Ereignisse die Position ein, die Moritz Baßler den AutorInnen von Popromanen im Titel seiner 2002 erschienen Studie, *Der deutsche Pop-Roman. Die neuen Archivisten*,[15] zuschreibt. Duve ist eine solche neue Archivistin, die mit ihrem Schnelldurchlauf durch die Zeitgeschichte authentisches Zeugnis der Bundesrepublik der 80er Jahre ablegt und in literarischer Form speichert. Auch im weiteren Verlauf des Romans setzt sich dieses archivierende Verfahren fort mit Verweisen aus weit gestreuten alltagskulturellen Bereichen – Fernsehen, Kulinarisches, Architektur, Konsumverhalten, Ferienziele – die das Westdeutschland der 80er evozieren: der Quelle–Fernseher, die Haribomischung von Aldi zu DM 1,39, die Fernsehsendungen „Flipper" und „Drei mal Neun", das kalte Buffet mit dem Fliegenpilz aus Ei und Tomate, Katzenzungen, der Urlaub auf den Kanarischen Inseln und das elterliche Eigenheim im Vorort mit Jägerzaun, Glasbausteinen neben der Haustür und einem Panoramafenster „an dem sich kleine Vögel das Genick brachen" (L15).[16]

Vordergründig scheinen dabei die Verweise auf Markennamen und Fernsehen ein reines Wiederholen der Produkte einer Kulturindustrie zu sein. Es zeigt sich jedoch ein anderes Bild, wenn wir Konsum hier in seiner durch die Cultural Studies erweiterten Bedeutung verstehen, auf welche wir zu Anfang dieses Essays bereits hingewiesen haben. Bei Duve entsteht nämlich mit Konsum, verstanden als „andere, lautlose Produktion" (de Certeau), ein System von Bedeutungszuschreibungen. In ihrer literarischen Rezeption von zeitgebundener populärer Kultur schreibt sie die Zeichen dieser Kultur um und neu, so daß sich im Spiegel des Profils der Protagonistin Anne das Profil einer ganzen Generation zeigt.

Duve ‚archiviert' Konsum nicht stumpfsinnig, sondern schreibt ihm in der Geschichte Anne Strelaus neue Bedeutungen zu, die in ihrer ironischen Gebrochenheit auch teilweise subversiv sind, indem sie der Schnellebigkeit und Gedankenlosigkeit der Gesellschaft einen kritischen Spiegel vorhalten. Damit steht sie in Gegensatz zur Literatur der, um es mit dem Titel von Florian Illies' Studie zu sagen, „Generation Golf",[17] die ihre deutlichste Ausprägung wohl in Christian Krachts *Faserland* findet. Während die plumpe Anne Strelau gerade den Inbegriff des Anti-Imageträgers repräsentiert, steht bei Kracht die Egomanie, Selbstzelebrierung und das daran geknüpfte Konsumverhalten einer mit den verschiedenen Modellen des VW-Golf großgewordenen Generation im Vordergrund. Das macht besonders die am Anfang von *Faserland* beschriebene Szene deutlich, in der Markennamen wie *product placement* wirken und authentische Ortsnamen eine hippe In-Szene evozieren:

> Also, es fängt damit an, daß ich bei Fisch-Gosch in List auf Sylt stehe und ein Jever aus der Flasche trinke. […] Weil es ein bißchen kalt ist und Westwind weht, trage ich eine Barbourjacke mit Innenfutter. Ich esse inzwischen die zweite Portion Scampis mit Knoblauchsoße […]. Vorhin habe ich Karin wiedergetroffen. Wir kennen uns schon aus Salem, […] und ich hab sie ein paarmal im Traxx in Hamburg gesehen und im P1 in München.[18]

Illies kommentiert die zelebrierte Politiklosigkeit und Egomanie der von Kracht porträtierten Generation: „Nicht nur ich, so durfte man endlich sagen, finde die Entscheidung zwischen einer grünen und einer blauen Barbour-Jacke schwieriger als die zwischen CDU und SPD."[19] Den Gegensatz hierzu bildet die zwar nicht politisch engagierte, aber (unfreiwillig) jedem Trend entgegengesetzten Anne:

> Ich hatte die falsche Figur und die falschen Jeans, ich lachte falsch und sagte die falschen Sachen; selbst das Fahrrad, das mir gehörte, war gar kein richtiges Fahrrad, sondern ein Klapprad. Es wäre müßig gewesen, alle meine Fehler aufzuzählen – ich selbst war der Fehler. (L53)

Sie ist keinesfalls Imageträgerin, und die Marken, die sie gierigst konsumiert, zeigen nicht ihre Rolle als modebewußte Trendsetterin, sondern sind authentische Requisiten ihres unglücklichen Lebens:

Nutella, Milky-Way, Haribo Konfekt und der Appetitzügler Recatol im Zusammenhang ihrer Eßstörung; Bravo, Apfelshampoo und das schäumende Verhütungszäpfchen Patentex Oval im Zusammenhang ihrer unschönen sexuellen Erfahrungen. Die Bedeutungszuschreibungen, die Konsum hier im Sinne de Certeaus erfährt, sind die von Trostlosigkeit und Selbstentwertung. Das zeigt sich insbesondere in Annes Eßstörung, die sich im weiteren kulturellen Kontext als Form von Konsum lesen läßt, der das weibliche Individuum hineinführt in den Teufelskreis von Heiß-hunger und Übersättigung:

> bingeing and self-starvation […] occur in a cultural context of rampant consumerism in which consumption (literal or metaphorical) is promoted as wholly desirable, while overweight women are stigmatised and often portrayed as as joke figures, as coarse, stupid or sexually promiscuous.[20]

Der kritische Blick auf Konsum bei der Entwicklung der jugendlichen Protagonistin wird auch im Spiegel von Annes Leseverhalten deutlich. Hier scheint Duves ‚Poproman' paradoxerweise gerade Horkheimer und Adornos Kritik an der „Kulturindustrie" nachzuvollziehen, die die RezipientInnen manipuliert, abstumpft und verdummt. Diese Kritik trifft nämlich gerade auf die Mädchenliteratur zu, die Anne im wahrsten Sinnes des Wortes verschlingt, denn

> Lesen allein genügte einfach nicht. Ich hielt es mit den Süßigkeiten wie mit den Büchern – der Inhalt war zweitrangig. Ich brauchte vor allem eine Quantität, die mich sicher über den Nachmittag brachte. Was ich eigentlich gebraucht hätte, wäre Alkohol gewesen, aber Schnaps zu trinken fiel mir einfach nicht ein. (L58)

Der vergebliche Versuch, eine innere Leere mit Schokolade und Weingummi zu stopfen, geht Hand in Hand mit dem vergeblichen Streben nach der perfekten Welt einer Britta, Billie oder Gundula, über die in der klassischen Trivialkultur der Mädchenromane „ein gütiger Gott [wachte, der] dafür sorgte, daß sie beim Reitturnier trotz eines schlechten Starts doch noch den ersten Preis machen" (L58). Ebenso wie auf die Freßanfälle das selbstherbeigeführte Erbrechen der Bulimikerin folgt, liefert auch die Lektüre keine Erfüllung. Anne nimmt deutlich die mindere Qualität der in Widerspiegelung ihrer Freßanfälle gleich stapelweise aus der Bücherhalle entliehenen Mädchenromane wahr, ohne sich jedoch von der Sucht nach ihnen befreien zu können. Gieriges Verschlingen und nachfolgender Brechreiz geben sich auf beiden Ebenen die Hand: „Es war wieder so ein Buch, bei dem ich am liebsten erbrochen hätte. Zum Glück war ich sowieso schon krank." (L77) Die Protagonistin perfektioniert ihre Weltflucht ins heimische Kinderbett auf dreifache Weise mit Krankheit, Trivialliteratur und Freßsucht. Hier artikuliert sich Duves kritische Perspektive, mit der sie den Zusammenhang von Kulturindustrie und dem Verlust eines Ich deutlich macht, das als Kind im „stetigen Strom von Weingummi und Schokolade" (L58) und stereotypischen Mädchenbüchern zu ertrinken droht und als Erwachsene an Drogen, Psychotherapien und Beziehungen scheitert.

„The Mood-Mosaic" des Mixtapes

Bereits der Titel *Dies ist kein Liebeslied* verdeutlicht die wichtige Rolle, die Popmusik in diesem Roman spielt als wesentliches Versatzstück in der Collage des Zeitgeschehens. Dazu gehören neben deutschen Schlagern wie „Ich wünsch mir eine kleine Miezekatze" von Wum vor allem britische und amerikanische Titel der 80er Jahre von den Sisters of Mercy über David Bowie bis hin zu Flash and the Pan. Das Nennen eines bestimmten Titels markiert dabei zugleich ein historisches Eckdatum, das einen (musik-)kulturellen Referenzpunkt bildet.[21]

Einen wichtigen Verweis auf die Bedeutung von Platten im Prozeß der Archivierung von Zeitgeschehen im Poproman liefert Duve mit dem Nennen von Diedrich Diederichsen: „Da! Das ist Diedrich Diederichsen", raunte er mir [...] vor dem Broadway-Kino zu. [...]. Ein junger Mann in einem Kohlenklau-Mantel [...] ging in schlechter Haltung zur Kasse und verbreitete Glanz." (L176) Diederichsen, geboren 1957 in Hamburg, ist Autor, Kulturwissenschaftler, Journalist und Poptheoretiker, der Kunstproduktion und Alltagskultur ästhetisch und machtkritisch analysiert und bis heute wesentlich zum kritischen zeitgenössischen Popdiskurs beigetragen hat. Er analysiert das, worüber Duve schreibt: Jugendkultur, Fernsehserien, Filme und vor allem Popmusik. Seine Plattenkritiken sind in einschlägigen Musikzeitschriften wie *Spex* und *Sounds* erschienen, an deren Herausgabe er auch beteiligt war. Es ist also sicher kein Zufall, wenn Duve auf Diederichsen verweist, der sowohl inhaltlich als auch theoretisch ins Konzept des Romans paßt. Besonders signifikant scheint dabei Diederichsens im Jahre 2000 erschienene Studie *2000 Schallplatten. 1979-1999*[22] zu sein mit Essays zur Musik der 80er und 90er Jahre, mit der er als Beobachter und Kommentator der Popkultur das nachvollzieht, was Duve in literarischer Form als ‚neue Archivistin' (Baßler) vornimmt. Dieses Phänomen der Popliteratur als Archiv zeigt sich auf ganz anderer Weise übrigens auch in Duves Lexika „der berühmten Tiere" und „berühmten Pflanzen".[23] Im ersteren listet sie mit Thies Völker tierische Kulturträger auf, von Meteor, dem „Spring-pferd mit Paul-Gascoigne-Qualitäten", dem Fernsehdelphin Flipper und Disneys Bambi – die alle drei auch kleine Statistenrollen in *Dies ist kein Liebeslied* haben – bis hin zu den „Protestlern, Souvenirjägern und Geschäftemachern" als Mauerspechte und dem „Markensymbol" Bärenmarkenbär.[24] Ähnlich verfährt sie im zweiten Lexikon mit „berühmten Pflanzen" wie Adventskranz, Dorn im Auge und „Zonen-Gabys erste[r] Banane".[25]

Im Zusammenhang der Popmusik entfaltet der Roman die Heterogenität der unter dem weiten Schlagwort ‚populäre Kultur' zusammengefaßten ästhetischen Produkte, die Diederichsen wie folgt zusammenfaßt:

> Pop ist immer Transformation, im Sinne einer dynamischen Bewegung, bei der kulturelles Material und seine sozialen Umgebungen sich gegenseitig neu gestalten und bis dahin fixe Grenzen überschreiten.[26]

Mit Verweisen auf David Bowie, Nick Cave und Leonard Cohen, die alle den genreüberschreitenden Schritt von der Musik zur Literatur unternommen haben, fächert Duve die große Spannbreite der Kulturformen noch weiter auf. *Dies ist kein Liebeslied* zeigt deutlich die kulturelle Bandbreite der Popmusik, auf deren einer Seite die altmodische Musiktruhe aus den frühen Ehejahren der Eltern steht, welche Schlager wie Bill Ramsays „Pigalle" oder „Banjo Boy" des Knabenduos von Jan und Kjeld abspielt (L25). Am Parameter dieser altmodischen Musiktruhe zeichnet sich Annes Heranwachsen ab. Prägnantes Beispiel für einen Wechsel der Generation von den Wirtschaftswunderkindern zu den 68ern Jahre, ist hier die vom Freund der großen Schwester geborgte Platte von Franz Josef Degenhardt, „Lieber Rudi Dutschke würde Vati sagen", die die junge Anne auf der Musiktruhe der Eltern abspielt. Als Kind der 80er gehört Anne jedoch weder zur Kulturwelt ihrer Eltern noch zu der der Studentenbewegung, eine Unzugehörigkeit, die von Kulturtheoretikern als maßgeblich für die „Generation Golf" gesehen wird. Annes musikalische Sozialisation ist bestimmt von der Musik der 80er und einem anderen musikalischen Parameter: dem Mixtape.

Das Mixtape, diese selbstaufgenommene Kassette mit einer Auswahl von Liedern, stellt allein schon aus technischer Sicht ein Stück vergangener Zeitgeschichte dar, die im Roman archiviert wird, denn längst haben CD und I-Pod Kassette und Walkman als Marktführer verdrängt. Im Mixtape treffen Popmusik, Eigenkreativität und Medienumgang aufeinander. Mixtapes markieren prägnant die kulturtheoretisch relevante Schnittstelle von Konsum und Produktion, denn sie sind sowohl Reproduktion als auch kreative Produktion, indem sie Material von einem auf einen anderen Tonträger überspielen, dabei jedoch höchst persönliche und einzigartige neue Misch-Kassetten erschaffen. Das Mosaik von Titeln auf einem Mixtape ist trotz seiner technischen Reproduzierbarkeit und beliebigen Abspielbarkeit weniger Zeichen bloß reproduzierter Massenkultur, sondern vielmehr höchst individueller und innovativer (Jugend-) Kulturträger. Dabei ist die selbstgemachte Verpackung der Kassettenhülle ebenso wichtig wie das Datum, das den, der sie aufnimmt, als Trendsetter oder -folger ausweist. Auch die Kurzlebigkeir dieser Kultur gehört wesentlich zu ihrem Stil und prägt die Schnelligkeit, mit der sie sich immer wieder neu konstituiert und inszeniert. „Wenn du dir von einem Mann eine Kassette aufnehmen läßt, erfährst du mehr über ihn, als wenn du mit ihm schläfst" (L45), legt Duve dann auch ihrer Protagonistin in den Mund als Beschreibung dieser besonderen Art von Kassette.

Es sind sechs solcher Kassetten, aufgenommen von den sechs Männern, mit denen Anne zusammen war, welche gleichsam den Soundtrack zum Roman bilden. Diese Kassetten stellen nicht nur ein gespeichertes Stück (Popmusik-) Geschichte dar, das Anne auf ihrem Flug nach London mit sich führt. Vielmehr entfaltet sich mit ihnen zwischen Nick Cave, Sisters of Mercy, Nation of Ulysses, David Bowie und anderen ein „Mood-Mosaic" (L48) – so der bezeichnende Name der ersten Band auf der wichtigsten dieser Kassetten, der von Peter Hemstedt, die Anne auf ihrer Reise hört. Als personalisierte Form des Umgangs mit Medienprodukten weisen die Mixtapes die ganze Bandbreite der jugendlichen Empfindungen auf von Liebeserklärungen und melodiösen Harmonien bis zu „Gezerre, Genöle, Hall und Dissonanzen" (L165): „Es war, als fächerte Hemstedt mir alle Möglichkeiten seiner Seele auf […]." (L165) Während die Mädchen im Roman nie abgeschickte oder verlachte Briefe schreiben, finden die Jungen und Männer im Umgang mit Musik kreative Verständigungs- und Ausdrucksmöglichkeiten. Was für Werther Briefe sind, sind bei Duve Mixtapes.[27] Obwohl Anne selbst keine solchen Kassetten aufnimmt, hat sie doch teil an diesem Diskurs. Hier liegen die einzigen kurzen Momente von Erfüllung der Protagonistin:

> Die Musik drang in mich ein, war in mir, durchströmte mich und füllte mein ganzes Sein. Und ich, all dieses Unerfreuliche, Widerliche, das ich bisher gewesen war, war endlich aus mir heraus. In mir war nur noch das Schöne. Das Wunderbare. Und dann war das Wunderbare auch schon wieder vorbei. (L166)

Mit Blick auf den gesamten Roman verwundert es nicht, daß dieser Zustand, der an sexuelle Erfüllung, Drogenrausch oder frühromantische symphilosophische Zustände erinnert, nicht lange anhält.

Das aus Versatzstücken der Popkultur der 80er zusammengesetzte „Mood-Mosaic" begleitet den gescheiterten Bildungsgang der Protagonistin. Die intertextuellen Einsprengsel zeichnen den Roman nicht nur auf inhaltlicher Ebene aus, sondern sie entwerfen auch das Bild des Individuums, das wie der Text vielfach gebrochen ist und dessen Stimme an die musiktechnische Methode des Samplings erinnert. In diesem Mosaik der Eindrücke kombiniert Duve Zeittypisches und Zeitloses, Spielerisches und Subversives, Komik und Tragik, Egomanie und Selbstironie sowie Konsum und Produktion. Insbesondere das Medium der Mischkassette steht dabei kennzeichnend für die Zwischenstellung von Duves Roman zwischen trivialer Kultur und innovativer Collagenhaftigkeit. Zwar kann Duves Roman im Jahr 2002 seiner Erstveröffentlichung, trotz seiner Verweise auf Eßstörungen, Sexualität oder Pornographie, keine Grenzen zum Tabu mehr überschreiten, wie es noch die erste Generation der PopliteratInnen taten. Die Autorin artikuliert jedoch auf andere Weise ihre kultur- und konsumkritische Perspektive. Dies geschieht im Roman auf vielen verschiedenen Ebenen, die von einer Brechreiz verursachenden Trivialliteratur, welche die Bulimie der Protagonistin in einen kulturtheoretischen Zusammenhang stellt, bis hin zum innovativen Medienumgang im kulturellen Speichermedium des Mixtapes reichen. Mit ihrem Mosaik aus ‚High' und ‚Low Culture' führt die Autorin ihre LeserInnen in eine Kultur ein, die sich wie der Roman selbst weder auf die eine noch auf die andere Seite schlägt, sondern beide produktiv konfrontiert.

Anmerkungen

1 Leslie A. Fiedler, *Cross the Border – Close the Gap*, Stein & Day: New York, 1971.

2 Siehe die deutsche Übersetzung, die als ‚Überquert die Grenze – Schließt den Graben' in zwei Teilen in der Zeitschrift *Christ und Welt* erschien. Leslie A. Fiedler, ‚Das Zeitalter der neuen Literatur. Die Wiedergeburt der Kritik,' *Christ und Welt* 13 (1968), 9-10. Ders., ‚Das Zeitalter der neuen Literatur. Indianer, Science Fiction und Pornographie,' *Christ und Welt* 20 (1968), 14-16.

3 Siehe: Rolf Lindner, ‚Kulturtransfer. Zum Verhältnis von Alltags-, Medien- und Wissenschaftskultur,' in: Wolfgang Kaschuba, Hg., *Kulturen Identitäten Diskurse. Perspektiven Europäischer Ethnologie*. Akademie Verlag: Berlin, 1995, S. 31-44.

4 Michel de Certeau, *Kunst des Handelns*, Merve: Berlin, 1988, S. 13.

5 Johann Wolfgang Goethe, *Die Leiden des jungen Werther*, Goethes Werke. Hamburger Ausgabe hg. und kommentiert von Erich Trunz, xiv Bde, Christian Wegner: Hamburg, 1964, Bd. vi, S. 27.

6 Karen Duve, *Dies ist kein Liebeslied*, Eichborn: Berlin, 2002, S. 280. Im folgenden werden Verweise auf diesen Roman im Text mit ‚L' abgekürzt.

7 Diese „Vollendung" sieht zu Beginn des 19. Jahrhunderts der Dorpater Professor Karl von Morgenstern als ein Ziel des Bildungsromans. Zitiert nach: Jürgen Jacobs, *Wilhelm Meister und seine Brüder*, Wilhelm Fink: München, 1972, S. 10.

8 Zur Gattung des Bildungsromans, die wesentlich komplexer ist als hier beschrieben werden konnte, siehe u.a. auch: Gerhard Kaiser und Friedrich A. Kittler, Hgg., *Dichtung als Sozialisationsspiel. Studien zu Goethe und Gottfried Keller*, Vandenhoeck & Ruprecht: Göttingen, 1978. Klaus-Dieter Sorg, *Gebrochene Teleologie. Studien zum Bildungsroman von Goethe bis Thomas Mann*, C. Winter: Heidelberg, 1983. Hans-Jürgen Schings, ‚Agathon – Anton Reiser – Wilhelm Meister. Zur Pathogenese des modernen Subjekts im Bildungsroman,' in: Wolfgang Wittowski, Hg., *Goethe im Kontext. Ein Symposion*, Tübingen, 1984, S. 43-68.

9 Evelyn Finger, ‚Exzesse der Trostlosigkeit,' *Die Zeit* 47, 4. Nov. 2002.

10 Kim Chernin, *The Hungry Self. Women, Eating and Identity*, Virago: London, 1986. S. 167. Siehe auch: Maud Ellmann, *The Hunger Artists: Starving, Writing and Imprisonment*, Virago: London, 1993.

11 Sarah Sceats, *Food Consumption and the Body in Contemporary Women's Fiction*, Cambridge University Press: Cambridge, 2000, S. 67.

12 Karen Duve, *Die entführte Prinzessin. Von Drachen, Liebe und anderen Ungeheuern*, Eichborn: Berlin, 2005.

13 So zum Beispiel Gustav Seibt, ‚Da! Das ist Diedrich Diederichsen,' *Süddeutsche Zeitung*, 10. Dez. 2002.

14 Jörgen Schäfer, *Pop-Literatur. Rolf Dieter Brinkmann und das Verhältnis zur Populärkultur in der Literatur der sechziger Jahre*, Metzler: Stuttgart, 1998, S. 26.

15 Moritz Baßler, *Der deutsche Pop-Roman. Die neuen Archivisten*, Beck: München, 2002.

16 Vergl. Anthea Bells Beitrag in diesem Band zur Schwierigkeit der Übersetzung dieser kulturellen Verweise, die sie selbst mit einer Sicherheit und Feinfühligkeit vornimmt, von der Lavinia Greenlaw schreibt: „The subtlety with which the abrasive bravura of [Anne Strelau's: HB] voice dissolves [...] depends (in English) upon the skills of her eminent translator, Anthea Bell, whose credits range from Freud to Asterix. Duve is lucky to have her." Lavinia Greenlaw, ‚Teenage Kicks,' *The Guardian*, 10.12.05. *Dies ist kein Liebeslied* ist in seiner englischen Übersetzung durch Anthea Bell erschienen als: Karen Duve, *This is Not a Love Song*, Bloomsbury: London, 2005.

17 Florian Illies, *Generation Golf. Eine Inspektion*, Fischer Taschenbuch Verlag: Frankfurt am Main, 2001 (4. Auflage), und Ders., *Generation Golf zwei*, München: Goldmann, 2005. Der Titel spielt u.a. auf die TV-Werbung für den VW-Golf im 21ten Jahrhundert ab, die einen Durchlauf durch die letzten 30 Jahre liefert mit dem jeweils neuesten Golf-Modell als konstantem Referenzpunkt.

18 Christian Kracht, *Faserland*, Goldmann: München, 1997, S. 9.

19 Florian Illies, *Generation Golf. Eine Inspektion*, S. 154-155.

20 Sarah Sceats, *Food Consumption and the Body*, S. 3. Vergleich auch : Mike Featherstone, ‚The Body in Consumer Culture,' in: Mike Featherstone and Bryan S. Turner, Hgg., *The Body: Social Process and Cultural Theory*, Sage: London, 1991.

21 Ich danke Chris Done für seine Beratung und Hilfe in Fragen der Musik der 80er und 90er Jahre.

22 Diedrich Diederichsen, *2000 Schallplatten. 1979-1999*, Hannibal Verlag: Höfen, 2000.

23 Vergl. Elisa Müller-Adams Beitrag in diesem Band zur Attitüde des Lexikographen.

24 Karen Duve und Thies Völker, *Lexikon der berühmten Tiere. Von Alf und Donald Duck bis Pu der Bär und Ledas Schwan*, Piper: München, 1999 (hier: S. 472, 247, 52, 465, 56).

25 Karen Duve und Thies Völker, *Lexikon berühmter Pflanzen. Vom Adamsapfel zu den Peanuts*, List: München, 2002, S. 10, 84, 317.

26 Diedrich Diederichsen, ‚Pop – deskriptiv, normativ und emphatisch,' in: *Literaturmagazin. Pop Technik Poesie. Die nächste Generation*, Rowohlt: Reinbek bei Hamburg, 1996, S. 36-44 (hier: S. 38-39).

27 Duves Roman ist bei weitem nicht der einzige, der mit dem Motiv des Mixtapes arbeitet. Zu nennen wären hier u.a. *High Fidelity* des Briten Nick Hornby (1995) und Christian Grassers *Mein erster Sanyo. Bekenntnisse eines Pop-Besessenen* (2000). Letzterer bildet in der Taschenbuchausgabe (Heyne, 2003) sogar ein Mixtape auf dem Umschlag ab und evoziert wiederum einen anderen Titel, der auch den Umgang mit Unterhaltungselektronik thematisiert, allerdings nicht mit musikalischem Schwerpunkt: *Benny Barbasch, Mein erster Sony*, Ullstein: Berlin, 1999. Einreihen in diesen Zusammenhang, jedoch mit dem musikalischen Speichermedium der Jukebox, lassen sich auch Peter Handkes *Versuch über die Jukebox* (1990) oder *Der Jukebox-Mann* des Schweden Åke Edwardson (2006).

Lucy Macnab

Becoming Bodies: Corporeal Potential in Short Stories by Julia Franck, Karen Duve, and Malin Schwerdtfeger

Since the mid-90s, the German media have been looking at a new group of younger women writers, among whose texts there are compelling comparisons to be drawn, their protagonists often young women negotiating a space for themselves in a post-feminist, pop-consumerist society. The body is frequently the locus of this struggle, as the scene of both constructed gender and the potential to undermine it. This paper will examine the body and its significance in texts by Julia Franck, Karen Duve, and Malin Schwerdtfeger. It will investigate the female body as a site of resistance to the dominant cultural discourse, and ask to what extent the bodies in these texts are subversive.

In the late 1990s, the German media began examining and promoting a new group of younger women writers that attracted the belittling label 'das literarische Fräuleinwunder'.[1] Their books have been marketed largely on the basis of the authors' youth and good looks and the way in which they supposedly signify the reinvention of German literature as light, readable and popular. The creation of such a category is both misleading and condescending, for what is most striking is 'the artificiality of the grouping'.[2] There are nonetheless compelling comparisons to be drawn between the texts, whose protagonists are often young women negotiating a space for themselves in a post-feminist, pop-consumerist society, in the sense that post-feminism promises a consumerist vision of 'having it all' that it fails to deliver, in a culture where identity is commodified as product.[3] The body is frequently the locus of this struggle, for it has long been the focus of cultural inscription as well as the site of individual agency.

In many of these texts we find the possibility of subverting rigid gender roles. Judith Butler defines gender as an ongoing journey:

> If there is something right in Beauvoir's claim that one is not born, but rather *becomes* a woman, it follows that *woman* itself is a term in process, a becoming, a constructing that cannot rightfully be said to originate or to end.[4]

Butler's becoming bodies are no longer stable, *pre*-discursive material, but rather fragmented and dynamic entities, constituted *through* discourse. Discourse can be defined as a cultural ordering, language statements produced by society's institutions, through which ideologies circulate in a network of power relations. The gendered body is an effect of cultural discourse,[5] not a 'natural' pre-given form but a work in progress, a site under construction. For the appearance of a stable, physical body that is acted on by culture is illusory. Gender styles the body, through repeated and regulated acts that congeal over time, thus producing the appearance of natural matter. The body is gendered by cultural rituals, mundane everyday acts that contour it, making it 'feminine'. This performativity, the way we 'do' our gender, when repeated, solidifies to form what seems to be a pre-given, essential femininity, hiding its own constructedness. It therefore follows, that if the gendered body is constructed, there must be the possibility of re-constructing it, of re-doing the way we act out our gender identity. Rearticulating gender norms can provide the occasion for their critical reworking, yet it is always dangerous to do so. Butler dares to ask what it would mean "to 'cite' the law to produce it differently", expose its contingency and open up possibilities for subversion.[6] One way in which the law can be produced differently is via the re-citing and reinterpretation of the body. This is the corporeal potential of these texts, the possibility of using the body to disrupt the process of the law, to find new ways of doing gender. A number of questions arise, however. Firstly, is the behaviour the texts convey successfully subversive, or does it potentially reinforce and confirm established gender roles and boundaries? Secondly, any act of rebellion must necessarily take place within discursive systems, so is it possible to sustain resistance to prescribed gender norms? Accepting that there is no utopian 'outside' to the social order, any such resistance may have to be located in the margins of what is corporeally acceptable. A liminal position, a state 'in between' at the boundaries, may provide more opportunity for deviance. Thirdly, if gender is 'a stylized repetition of acts', does there have to be a subject that precedes the activity of gender?[7] Finally, what happens to female agency and lived bodily experience if we accept that there *is* no 'doer', only the performance of gender itself (meaning that identity is constituted by the very actions that are said to be its consequences). Whether these texts provide any answers or not, one thing is clear. The body, a prominent and even intrusive presence at times, is a highly contested site of meaning, offering the potential to expose and destabilize gender as a cultural construct.

The gendered body is revealed as an effect of discourse in Julia Franck's novel *Der Neue Koch* (1997). The narrator, a young woman, has inherited a run down sea-side hotel from her mother. This is the building where she grew up, and the inheritance includes its staff and the bizarre group of regulars who stay there. Constantly compared to her mother, she is alternately ordered around or ignored by the guests and the new cook, whom she has employed, but who acquires increasing authority over the running of the hotel. When one of the guests dies in his room, the corpse is not moved for days, and the story becomes progressively more claustrophobic, culminating in a failed attempt by the narrator to escape.

The hotel, nameless like its owner, is a strange place to call home, and its anonymity highlights the uncertain identity of the narrator. A little girl who is staying at the hotel articulates the simple truth that 'das sei hier doch ein Hotel und kein Zuhause'.[8] Yet the narrator has grown up in what is essentially a parody of the domestic space of home. Each room in the hotel mimics the rooms in a normal house, but this is not a private space, it is public, commodified and merely provides the illusion of home. The space of the hotel is strictly delineated, being made up of clearly labelled areas (the dining room, the lobby, the bedroom) where certain activities are meant to take place. The narrator's familial home is further alienated when we discover that her mother managed the hotel by offering sexual favours to the men who worked for her.

The narrator's feminine inheritance, therefore, comes from a mother who effectively sells sex and deals in domesticity as a commodity for the hotel business. This parody of the mother's role finds its physical equivalent in the grotesquely fat Madame Piper, a guest at the hotel who gradually becomes more of a mother figure for the narrator. *Der neue Koch* begins with a description of Madame, a title also suggesting prostitution:

> Ihre Augen sehen auf mich herab, Schweiß rinnt in kleinen Bächen ihre Waden entlang, und auch zwischen den Schenkeln schimmert es klebrig, ihre Augen folgen mir träge, so gut sie können, das Gelb ums Braun ist zäh und dick und trüb, der Schleim, sie kommen mir nach, die ich auf dem Boden krieche und Glassplitter mit der Hand aufsammle. Ich muß aufpassen, mich nicht zu schneiden [...] weil immer noch Sommer ist und ich kurze Hosen trage. (NK5)

The excess of flesh is the image of the female body taken to an extreme; transgressing boundaries, it confronts us with the body's physicality. While we see the narrator here as a child, crawling around on the floor in shorts, Madame takes over the maternal role, her shape more excessive even than the pregnant body. The revulsion of seeing between her legs comes from facing the abject, the body that must be excluded because it suggests the horror of physical engulfment. Her body is permeable, she is constantly sweating or excreting across the boundaries that separate the inner from the outer, the self from the other, and thereby disrupting a system that propagates the illusion of closed bodies. Abject in its liminality, its disregard for borders, her body makes trouble for the dominant discourse. She later becomes a grotesque caricature of femininity, as she makes the narrator shave her armpits for her, pluck her eyebrows off and apply false eyelashes, constantly advising the narrator to wear a dress and make up herself.

If Madame represents the mother in the constructed family home, then the rest of the guests take on equally stylized roles. Herr Hirschmann, whose name speaks of masculinity, takes on an authoritative role, attempting to take control of the hotel. The guests are for the most part bizarre parodies, with designations that invite a satirical reading, such as 'der Dichter Anton Jonas', always referred to as 'der Dichter Anton Jonas' and who self-consciously assumes the role of poet with all its clichés. Wearing only black, highly critical of poetry that is cheerful or rhymes, he also suffers from insomnia, which, in his opinion, elevates his poetic status. His attempt to articulate this exposes him as a ridiculous imitation of a poet. 'Wie beneide ich euch Menschen, die ihr nachts feste schlummert, wie satte – satte, ja Menschen.' (NK39) The hotel's inhabitants gradually become exaggerated versions of themselves that demonstrate how identity is constructed as a copy of a copy, the effect of a rule bound world. We see the full restrictive nature of this when the cook creates a special dish of quails served in wire cages. The guests are delighted, 'sie klatschen, sie kucken' (NK94), and poke their fingers through the holes in the wire to touch the food, evoking the startling image that they themselves are trapped in cages, and furthermore, that they seem to be enjoying it. A bizarre carnival of caricatures, braying with excitement, they expose the prison of social ritual and the pleasure of such conformity. It is at the borders of this rigid system that we find the marginalised narrator, unnamed because she does not fit. She watches the guests from an outsider's perspective, barely eating anything and unable to join in their enjoyment of the cages. She is an outsider when it comes to her own body as well. When she finally complies with Madame's request to be more feminine, and dons black stockings and suspenders, she then puts on a pair of jeans and walking boots over the top, unable to 'do' her gender properly and thus highlighting its contingency.

The narrator is further crushed by the cook's authority in the hotel, whose name titles the book, refusing her the position of the central character. She begins an unsatisfactory sexual relationship with him, her body treated as a reflection of his desire only; in fact, it is an image that falls short of his expectations. As he kisses her body, the cook tells her, 'daß er sich meine Brüste anders vorgestellt habe, er wolle ehrlich sein, auch die Form der Innenschenkel hätte er sich anders gedacht, aber das sei nicht weiter schlimm' (NK71). He defines her body, it is not valid unless it fits with the male imagination. Because it doesn't, she has little physical presence, being constantly ignored, pushed to one side or simply going unnoticed by the other characters. She spends her time literally in the margins of the hotel, sitting far away from the others at mealtimes and constantly retreating to the reception desk. According to the rituals of gender, she is not a body that matters, and must be relegated to the margins. Neither can she leave, because there is nothing outside. There appears to be no real alternative to life as delineated by the hotel, and when she plans to escape, it is for Cuba, and a fantasy town called Esperanza that she has heard about from the cook. The myth of Cuba, and the imaginary place that represents hope of a life outside only exist to sustain the discourse and structure of the hotel itself. Her attempt to reach this utopia fails, and she must return to the location where bodies are constructed and regulated, to her circus-like hotel home.

While *Der neue Koch* highlights the constructed nature of the body to show the impossibility of finding a space outside such construction, Karen Duve's collection of short stories, *Keine Ahnung* (1999), questions whether there are possibilities for subversive acts within the frame of cultural coding. She explores the potential for repeating gender ritual in a different way, asking what happens when our bodies do not conform. The nameless women in Duve's texts do not fit comfortably within prescribed gender roles; the importance of a named body is denied them because of a language that does not recognise the female sexed body as anything other than what it can contain in tired gender conventions. This closed system of signification rejects the body as grotesque, abject or transgressive of dangerous boundaries when it does not, or cannot enact gender 'properly'. Her writing also underlines the violence inherent in the moulding of bodies by discourse. Monique Wittig describes the effect of language on the body: 'Language casts sheaves of reality upon the social body, stamping it and violently shaping it'.[9] It is the female body as maternal that is most violently shaped, because it must be styled as other, if the binary system of gender is to operate successfully. The woman's frame, able to change shape in pregnancy, is penetrable, its borders unreliable and therefore dangerous, a threat to the fantasy of autonomous identity. The maternal body confounds a system that defines Self in opposition to the Other, because it contains the Other within, and because it demonstrates her liminality, the position between categories, thus proving the categories themselves untenable.[10]

Duve's stories are out to distort these binary categories, to expose them as contingent constructs supported by nothing more than the weight of ritual repetition. The texts offer the possibility that gender can be redone in a different way, reconstructed to subvert our expectations. It remains unclear, however, whether these possibilities can be realised by her nameless narrators. Too often, the results of trying to conform are both painful and grotesque. In the title story, 'Keine Ahnung', the narrator has just left school and experiments with sex, drugs and rock and roll to try and locate herself, to form an embodied social identity. Her first sexual experience occurs because she is heavily under the influence of drugs. Markus (a character from the local disco), who has heard from other men that she is 'leicht zu haben',[11] penetrates her twice, first with a syringe to inject drugs and then during sex, which is akin to rape because she is unable to protest. The story she usually tells to put off sex becomes impossible because of the drugs, as she literally loses her power to speak. Her own history and voice are dislocated from her body and she cannot even remember what happens the following day. She literally has 'keine Ahnung', no idea of the event and she lacks any sense of self from which to remember it. She therefore attempts to repeat the process of injecting herself with drugs, with Markus's syringe, in an effort to reconstruct what has happened, to form an idea. Missing the vein, she sticks the needle impatiently in her arm and it results in deformity. 'Ich fühlte nichts. Auf meinem linken Arm bildete sich eine Beule. Ich konnte zusehen, wie sie anschwoll, bis sie schließlich so groß wie ein Hühnerei war.' (KA17) A grotesque parody of pregnancy, a hen's egg cocktail of drugs, replaces the traditional consequence of sex. Similarly, her attempts at embodying other feminine stereotypes result in a skewed and often monstrous imitation of the norm. Her costume for an experiment in prostitution is an ugly 1960s style dress with dirty trainers and unkempt hair; she also disobeys the cultural rule that prostitutes don't kiss on the mouth in an attempt at provoking some meaning: 'weil im Mund die Seele sitzt' (KA23). However, the sex she has, while it is both ridiculous and painful, is not significant, and she is left with no answer as to what she will become. The futility of searching for a finite identity underscores the idea of woman as process, of a body that *becomes*, rather than *is*. The narrator later embarks upon a panic stricken theft of household items, enacting a distorted parody of the housewife role. In her desperation to claim a feminine identity, she steals a pot plant from McDonald's and tries to grab a table lamp from a Chinese restaurant, making do with the lampshade. While these experiments with femininity distort and expose constructed gender identities, they also foreground the violence and pain that comes with performing femininity. The narrator's body is raped, infected, criminalised and stamped with feminine identity, and there is nothing natural about it at all.

Elsewhere in Duve's stories, the potential for enacting gender defiantly is explored. In 'Die Strumpfhose', the protagonist remembers a childhood incident where she pees on the carpet in a strange house. Aged five, she is forced to wear restrictive and uncomfortable white tights, a source of great embarrassment to her, particularly when her mother stops in the street to pull them up. Restrictive in a physical sense, they also prevent her from moving freely because they are expensive and must not be damaged. When she pushes through a bramble bush and slides down a slope, she rips her tights and is subsequently punished for her tomboyish behaviour. Her body is being trained to behave in a certain way, and when it rebels and she wets her pants, bursting its boundaries, she feels the shame of not behaving correctly without prompting. Still relatively young, she is in a liminal state, where she wishes 'ich wäre am liebsten tot oder gar nicht geboren gewesen' (KA77). She considers going either way, back into the womb or forward into death, and her body is also in between a childish disregard for rules and systems and a docile state of conformity. Her saviour is an older boy who radiates power and masculinity. 'In meiner Erinnerung ist er einen Meter neunzig groß, und sein Mund ist von Ernst und Entschlossenheit geprägt.' (KA77) Almost godlike, the nine year old boy takes her home on his bicycle, returning her to where she will be immersed once again in training. Yet a small moment of shared mutiny remains between the two children, when she realises as an adult that he delayed the moment of return by taking her on a long detour.

The concept of rebellion against the conventions of femininity is developed further in 'Besuch vom Hund'. Getting dressed to go out on a date, the narrator opens her door to find a collie dog, who starts talking to her and manages to disrupt her plans for the evening. The collie, in an abject state, fat, shivering, with bloodshot eyes and smelling of wet dog, tells her a hysterical story:

> 'Ich bin ein magerer Wolf und heule nachts an den Mauern eurer Stadt. Dann binden die Jäger ihre Hunde fester. [...] Dann heule ich lauter und die Hunde zittern und sträuben ihr Fell.' (KA47)

The collie, traditionally a highly obedient, trained dog, has turned the image upside down to present a wild version of itself, upsetting all the trained hounds. It is situated at the city walls, in the volatile setting of the border, where it is possible to challenge the dominant discourse. By re-appropriating its role as trained dog and becoming wild, the collie dog begins to affect change among other dogs, to threaten the order of things. Later called 'Lassie', by the narrator's date, defined as part of the reality of conventional American television, it plays a highly rebellious role in the story, inciting the narrator herself to refuse the role of dutiful girlfriend. Since dogs cannot speak, we can assume we are actually hearing the narrator's inner monologue with herself, her subversive side represented in the dog. Her mutiny is all the more powerful because it uses the trope of the trained collie dog, and because it is humorous and irreverent towards a discourse that allows dogs, or women, no voice.

The collie also dramatises the narrator's oppression, giving meaning to the cuts she has from arranging flowers, a typically feminine pursuit. It offers to lick the blood from her fingers, imagining that her nails have been ripped out in the torture of feminine ritual. In offering to lick her fingers, the dog eroticises the situation, making a space for female desire that has been otherwise suppressed. The story ends on a hopeful note, as she dresses in an odd assortment of practical rather than stylish clothes, and skips down the street, the collie at her side. There is a single star in the sky, signalling hope and an empty space not yet colonised by men, although the remaining irony is whether she would be seen as anything other than a hysterical woman dressed in strange clothes, talking to a dog. It seems that doubts can always be raised as to whether parody is truly subversive or whether it merely confirms the stereotypes it seeks to undermine.

In the end, then, Duve's nameless women remain elusive, escaping definition as either defiant or docile bodies. While they tell their own stories, with all the agency of the narrator, they are disempowered by a consensual social order which denies them agency over their own bodies. The violence of this process is clear, both in the physical damage done by rape and drug abuse, and the inscription of the grotesque on any female body that does not conform to the dominant ideal. Yet her protagonists manage to rebel against this in their corporeality, which intrudes into the closed ideals of conformity. They become unidentifiable beings, impossible to name because they elude definition, and painfully disengaged from their own bodies, their own identity and ideas. They quite literally have 'keine Ahnung'.

In contrast, the heroines of Malin Schwerdtfeger's short story collection, *Leichte Mädchen* (2001), would appear to have more agency when it comes to becoming bodies. The protagonists of all the stories are defined as girls and daughters, all undergoing a rite of passage to adulthood. Yet from the start, the rituals of femininity, acted out through the body, are a problematic inheritance. The title phrase 'leichte Mädchen' is heavy with social disapproval and conventional views about female sexuality, although the adjective 'leicht' promises a lightness, a freedom of choice which young women in the twenty first century might expect. We are immediately aware of how discourse both creates and excludes female desire, and therefore prevents the autonomous formation of female identity. However, twisting the phrase to mean what we want it to also shows the potential for subverting the categories of femininity that exist. Schwerdtfeger's 'leichte Mädchen' embody both the conformity and the freedom that the title suggests, in the diverse bodies they are becoming.

The possibilities afforded by occupying the liminal space between child and adulthood are explored in relation to the maternal and sexual body, in 'Für gutes Betragen'. The narrator, Kassandra, takes on the maternal role in her family after her mother has a baby and is taken to hospital because she is still bleeding. The stylisation of the body to become the gendered body begins from birth, as we see when Kassandra goes shopping for a babygro for her new brother and finds that the colours of clothes for baby girls are far more attractive. 'Das kam mir wie eine Strafe für meinen neuen Bruder vor: Sein Leben fing erst an, und er sollte Farben wie fürs Kloster tragen oder für die Todeszelle. Und nur, weil er ein Junge war.'[12] The confinement of a gendered body that is determined by society is underscored by the imagery of the monastery and the death cell. Kassandra refuses to conform to the colour convention, though, and shoplifts a yellow babygro from the girls' department. This is a rebellious act against the styling of the baby's body, signalled also by the fact that she steals it. Later on, the signifying power of the clothes is proved, as Paulina, the household help, mistakes the baby boy for a girl.

Schwerdtfeger suggests that the adult body is equally stylized, and the ritual of menstruation is of central significance to Kassandra. She is reprimanded by her mother for not having started to menstruate, and recognises that to bleed is to become a woman in the sense of being able to have children. 'Man konnte es drehen und wenden, wie man wollte; alles drehte sich nur um Blut und Fruchtbarkeit.' (LM18) There is a sense of frustration in her tone here, a realisation that the central role in a woman's life is supposed to be reproduction, and that however it is expressed, there is no escape from this assumption. The idea extends to the image of the narrator herself turning around and around trying to free herself from this constrictive definition. She finally starts her period when she is stopped for shoplifting, escapes and begins to entertain the fantasy that she has, like her mother, suddenly and unexpectedly given birth.

> Der Bus fuhr los, und ich hockte mich mit Ludwig in eine Ecke [...]. Wie Mama auf dem Küchenboden mit Begonia. Aber anders als Mama hatte ich nur Blut verloren und nichts geboren. Oder doch? Hatte ich ein Kind geboren und es bei den Detektiven fallen lassen? (LM23)

Kassandra then begins to play out the fantasy of having given birth herself, to the extent that she tries to breastfeed her mother's baby, which is disappointing for both of them, but she is strangely compelled to continue. The role of motherhood, assumed to be the most natural instinct for a woman, turns out to be unfulfilling and awkward, a series of rituals that she exposes, through her misbehaviour, as cultural impositions.

This sense of being compelled by what is expected of her as a maternal body, now she has begun to menstruate, is highlighted by the title, 'Für gutes Betragen'. As a child, she was awarded a prize at school for good behaviour, and the awareness of right and wrong affected her physically throughout her childhood. Indeed it continues all through the story, with violent effects on her body. Framed in the Christian convention of sins and confession, with all the patriarchal weight of religion, her childish wrongdoings are categorised as sins that are punished by physical stigmata.

> Jedesmal, wenn ich mit meiner Mutter stritt, wuchsen mir kleine rote Blutschwämmchen in den Hand flächen. Und jedesmal, wenn ich fluchte,

erschienen an meinem Haaransatz juckende rote Abdrücke wie von Dornen.
(LM27)

The only relief from these painful manifestations of what is considered by
the child as terrible sin is to go to confession. In this way, she is
physically tortured by the belief system imposed upon her, and this only
changes when she becomes involved with Paulina in a potentially
rebellious relationship. Paulina, who arrives from social services to help
Kassandra run the house, is in fact useless at household tasks, signalling
some kind of refusal to conform to the way women are traditionally
perceived as homemakers. Kassandra develops feelings for her, and they
begin to behave like a couple. It is Paulina who finally overturns the
conditioning of her childhood. When Kassandra is suffering from
stigmata for the second time in the story and wants to go to confession,
she cures her of the pain on her forehead. '"Da ist nichts", sagte Paulina.
Sie gab mir einen Kuß auf die Stirn. "Für gutes Betragen", sagte sie.'
(LM39) In repeating the phrase that has regulated Kassandra's life until
that point, Paulina breaks the spell. She has rejected her biblical name, as
Paul was responsible for many of the laws that Christianity operates
under. Her voice is invested with more power, as she takes the traditional
means of social definition, the ritual of repetition, and all the weight of
this, and transforms it, skewing its meaning through her own lesbian
voice. Kassandra's own name recalls Christa Wolf's unconventional
heroine and outsider in *Kassandra* (1983).[13] Their relationship is outside
the dominant heterosexual model of parenthood and obedient
daughterhood and disrupts the process of becoming a maternal body.

      With regard to all three of the authors considered here, however,
the question remains, whether these subversive acts successfully
challenge the conventional construction of bodies by discourse. Certainly
they expose the body as a dynamic construct, as 'a process of
materialization that stabilizes over time to produce the effect of boundary,
fixity, and surface we call matter.'[14] Julia Franck's caricature of a hotel
provides the scene for ridiculing the illusion of gender, yet it also
underscores its inevitability. The violence of bodily inscription is also
brought to light. As Karen Duve shows, we punish those who fail to do
their gender correctly, and the results of trying to fit into conventional
femininity are often painful and destructive. Yet there is a subversive
quality to these texts, and the bodies in Malin Schwerdtfeger's stories
skew and disrupt the gender roles they inherit. They do not provide
answers, or alternative gendered bodies, rather they open up questions,
which destabilise corporeal closure, and disrupt the process of becoming
woman. Discourse both prohibits and produces desire and subversion,
and it is the fact that an attempt is made to undermine the cultural fictions
of the body that is important. This attempt, not a conscious act of

rebellion, but nevertheless an effective protest, makes space for female agency, and this potential is attractive. The bodies in these texts are all becoming.

Notes

1 Volker Hage, 'Literarisches Fräuleinwunder,' *Der Spiegel*, 22 March 1999, p. 7.

2 Peter Graves, 'Karen Duve, Kathrin Schmidt, Judith Hermann: "Ein literarisches Fräuleinwunder,"' *German Life and Letters*, 55 (2002), 196-207 (here: 198).

3 See Stuart Taberner, *German Literature of the 1990s and Beyond*, New York: Camden House, 2005, p. 19.

4 Judith Butler, *Gender Trouble: Feminism and the Subversion of Identity*, Routledge: New York, 1990, p. 33.

5 Butler also rejects the distinction between sex and gender, arguing that there is no body that is not always already gendered, that we can only apprehend materiality through discourse. See Judith Butler, *Bodies that Matter: On the Discursive Limits of 'Sex'*, Routledge: New York, 1993.

6 Judith Butler, *Bodies that Matter*, p. 15.

7 Judith Butler, *Gender Trouble*, p. 179.

8 Julia Franck, *Der Neue Koch*, Amman: Zürich, 1997, p. 45. Henceforth abbreviated to 'NK'.

9 Monique Wittig, *The Straight Mind and Other Essays*, Beacon Press: Boston, 1992, pp. 43-4.

10 See Mary Russo, 'Female Grotesques: Carnival and Theory,' in: Katie Conboy, Nadia Medina and Sarah Stanbury, eds., *Writing on the Body: Female Embodiment and Feminist Theory*, pp. 318-36 (here: 325).

11 Karen Duve, *Keine Ahnung*, Suhrkamp: Frankfurt am Main, 1999, p. 14. Henceforth abbreviated to 'KA'.

12 Malin Schwerdtfeger, *Leichte Mädchen*, Kiepenheuer & Witsch: Köln, 2001, p.20. Henceforth abbreviated to 'LM'.

13 Christa Wolf's novel *Kassandra* is an adaptation of a classical myth whose protagonist is an outsider, condemned to being mistrusted and rejected because of her ability to see the future.

14 Judith Butler, *Bodies that Matter*, p. 9.

Katie Jones

'Ganz gewöhnlicher Ekel'? Disgust and Body Motifs in Jenny Erpenbeck's *Geschichte vom alten Kind*

Erpenbeck's 1999 novella *Geschichte vom alten Kind* is characterised by pervasive physical metaphors, in particular depictions of bodily disgust, which can be read allegorically as referring both to the GDR and to post-*Wende* issues. The author's symbolic use of the body is mirrored on a thematic level in that the protagonist communicates primarily through a form of 'body language'. These bodily motifs, especially disgust with its ambiguous double role in both protecting yet threatening boundaries, are extremely successful in expressing the fluidity of social structures. However, the novella may reproduce potentially misogynistic stereotypes of the adult female body as inherently unruly, irrational or disgusting.

Jenny Erpenbeck's 1999 novella *Geschichte vom alten Kind* can be seen as part of a trend among East German writers in the 1990s, such as Monika Maron and Thomas Brussig, of using physical motifs in the allegorical expression of post-*Wende* concerns.[1] However, in contrast to Brussig's overt political satire in *Helden wie wir*, Erpenbeck's satirical project remains rather more understated. Based on a real incident, in which her grandmother, writer Hedda Zinner, befriended a teenage hospital patient, only to learn later that the 'girl' was in fact a 31-year-old woman, *Geschichte vom alten Kind* tells the story of a mysterious child who is not what she seems.[2] Discovered standing in the street holding an empty bucket, and unable to give the police any information other than her age – fourteen years – the protagonist is placed in a children's home, a fenced-in institution on the outskirts of an unspecified city. The girl, whom the third-person narrator never refers to by name, but only ever as 'das Mädchen' or by the neuter pronoun 'es', is large, fat and formless. Unlike the other children who long for the freedom of the outside world, the girl is drawn to the security offered by the home's authoritarian structure, its rigid rules, and guarded gate. In fact, as becomes increasingly apparent and as the title hints, the girl is not a child at all, but an adult woman, whose shapeless body functions as a disguise. She uses her appearance and lack of physical abilities to manipulate her teachers and carers, although ambiguities in the narration leave open the question of whether this is deliberate, or to what extent it is unconscious. The other children, initially less easily fooled by the girl's attempts to integrate herself by copying their behaviour, sense that they have an impostor in their midst. Gradually, however, the girl wins their confidence and attains the position she covets in the classroom hierarchy: the lowest position, the only one which does not have to be defended. Apparently loyal and stupid, the girl is tolerated by her classmates who use her to carry messages or stand guard while they experiment with adolescent sexuality.

While they are beginning to grow up, the girl becomes increasingly childlike. However, her attempt to remain a child ultimately fails, as the more involved she becomes in the lives of the other children, the more the simple, comforting rules of the institution are replaced with complex and often contradictory sets of expectations. Trying to please everyone at once proves too complicated and she finds herself incapable of doing anything at all, becoming slower and slower until she cannot move. After being transferred to a hospital outside of the home, she is put on a strict diet and loses weight. Over a period of two weeks, her body sheds its disguise, and she is recognised as a thirty-year-old woman.

In post-*Wende* context, this brief outline already evokes GDR themes, for example the enclosed physical space of the children's home, or the protagonist's attachment to an authoritarian system. Yet as Nancy Nobile points out, although the GDR references are often so obvious as to verge on caricature, the allegory is more complex than it may initially seem and reviewers have interpreted the novella in different ways, seeing it both as primarily a reflection on the GDR past and as an expression of fears for the future.[3] My intention here is not to attempt an exhaustive 'decoding' of the novella's political symbolism, although certain examples will be discussed. I wish, rather, to explore the type of – predominantly physical – images used, the way they function as metaphors for the GDR, and their particular suitability for representing social structures of any kind.

The allusions to the GDR take two main forms. The girl herself can be taken as a metaphorical representation of a society which, like her body, is both resistant to change, and yet constantly pushing at its boundaries and not always consciously controllable. Furthermore, the enclosed children's home offers a spatial representation of the GDR, and its rules concerning social conduct all aim at maintaining a collective, rather than individualised, corporeality. For example, there are no mirrors, to discourage 'falsche Scham',[4] implying both a religious-inflected sexual prudery, and a wish to prevent individualistic vanity. Moreover, while the home's ethos of 'kamaradschaftliche[s] Zusammenleben' (G13) is encouraged by the absence of locks on the children's cupboards, frequent thefts mean that the children have secret hiding-places, so that ownership of private possessions becomes illicit, and the adults' aim of creating a trusting atmosphere fails. Perhaps the most extreme – and grotesque – physical metaphor for social cohesion, however, is the home's regulation concerning underwear: although each child is assigned his or her own set of clothing, clean underwear is distributed weekly from a central pool. Thus 'die Leibwäsche ist gleichsam die Wäsche für einen einzigen großen Kollektivleib' (G15).

The fantasy of a collective body appeals strongly to the protagonist, and is reflected in aspects of her own body, with its absorbency and lack of clearly defined boundaries, although, as I shall argue, this contributes – paradoxically – to her exclusion from the group. The collective body also reflects GDR ideology, which according to Julia Hell was partly built on the fantasy of the sublime Communist body, conceptualised as asexual.[5] In the GDR novels Hell analyses, 'sexuality is defined as that part of subjectivity which links the subject to its fascist past, and the new subject comes about as the result of the erasure of its material body, its sexual body'.[6] The post-fascist body, Hell argues, is based on identification with an idealised Communist father-figure, the leader. If the non-sexual Communist body belonged to the father, it is perhaps appropriate that in this post-*Wende* novella, the body in question becomes that of an orphaned child, whose asexual body now reacts with disgusted rejection to the pollution represented by Western capitalism. Whereas the sublime Communist body represented a new beginning in a post-fascist era, the post-GDR girl's attempt to stave off puberty is clearly doomed to failure, and her disgust of sexuality appears – in spite of the 'ganz neuen Anfang' (G13) the orphanage claims to offer – as self-deception and an anachronistic refusal to move on. I wish to explore the status of the protagonist's asexual body in *Geschichte vom alten Kind*, considering both the author's and the protagonist's own use of this body as a discursive tool.

The disgusting body as boundary

Physical disgust is one of the most prominent ways in which the protagonist expresses her need for clear social boundaries. Childhood, as represented by the confines of the home, provides security, and thus anything evoking the outside – adult – world must be rejected. The model of disgust used here is therefore one based on psychological and psychoanalytic accounts, in which disgust functions as a defence mechanism, safeguarding physical and psychic boundaries. In her anthropological study *Purity and Danger*, Mary Douglas argues that concepts of pollution arise from societies' need for order. Dirt is defined as anything that is perceived as out of place, since this threatens good order, but most threatening of all is dirt whose origins are still recognisable, such as bodily waste products: 'This is the stage at which they are dangerous; their half-identity still clings to them and the clarity of the scene in which they obtrude is impaired by their presence.'[7] This half-identity of the rejected object is a key characteristic of the disgusting, seen, for example, in bodily emissions which are neither part of the body nor entirely separate, and which therefore blur the boundaries between the categories of 'self' and 'other'. According to psychologist Susan B.

Miller, 'moments of sharp disgust reinforce the sense of self-other boundary, of inside and outside, of body under the protective watch of consciousness'.[8] Both Miller and Douglas thus imply that disgust of a particular object depends on its context; disgust is a complex emotion, rather than a simple physical impulse. However, disgust is considered to be more visceral than other emotions, such as love or contempt; it is triggered by either the actual or imagined presence of a *physical* object perceived as a contaminant, and is associated with nausea and spontaneous physical rejection.[9] Disgust therefore seems particularly appropriate as a motif in *Geschichte vom alten Kind*, since its physical expression of imagined contamination is paralleled by Erpenbeck's own use of the body as metaphor.

In line with the model outlined above, the protagonist of *Geschichte vom alten Kind* is obsessed with maintaining order, and perceives disorder as a disgust-inducing existential threat:

> Jegliche Unordnung ist feindlich, das fängt bei diesen Dingen an, welche, eben weil sie unordentlich in einem Schrank angehäuft sind, einem entgegenfallen, sobald man den Schrank öffnet, aber es endet in Fäulnis, Tod und Verwirrung. (G46)

However, her own body is characterised by elements of disorder, and may itself be perceived as disgusting. Before considering the girl's boundary-protecting reactions of disgust, I wish to explore the ways in which her body provokes disgust in other characters, and potentially also the reader. Her potential to disgust stems from her status as a marginal figure, one who cannot be assimilated into any familiar system of categorisation. She is presented from the outset as external, and unnecessary, to existing social systems, as the police are forced to the conclusion that 'das Mädchen war übrig' (G8). This lack of social belonging is reflected in her body, whose formlessness and nondescript quality prevent categorisation. Her hair is 'weder lang noch kurz […], und weder ist es braun, noch auch wirklich schwarz' (G9). Similarly, the girl's flesh refuses to fit itself into an acceptable shape; she is at various points likened to a shapeless 'Holzkloben' (G14), a 'bleiches Stück Teig mit Kopf' (G40), and a 'verkommene Masse', which seems 'zwar lebendig, weil ja ein Körper zwangsläufig lebendig ist, aber eben doch auch irgendwie tot' (G59).

This analogy of the dead body, which recurs when the girl perceives her own body as a 'riesigen atmenden Kadaver' (G118), suggests a further element of the disgusting. The significance of death in relation to disgust is widely accepted amongst theorists; indeed, Winfried Menninghaus even claims that 'jedes Buch über den Ekel ist nicht zuletzt ein Buch über den verwesenden Leichnam'.[10] Writing in the eighteenth century, Herder uses the analogy of death to describe the disgust provoked by protruding knuckles and veins, which for him resemble crawling worms: 'Gleichsam zu dem *Einen Stücke des Körpers* gehören sie nicht; sie sind außerwesentliche Zuwächse, oder Lostrennungen, die gleichsam [...] ein früher Tod sind.'[11] Recent theory in cognitive psychology and in psychoanalysis also suggests that disgust develops as a reaction against the inevitability of death and decay.[12] Susan Miller sees the primary function of disgust as being the protection of self-boundaries:

> Disgust toward the waxy-skinned corpse or the dry skeleton is the effort to refuse this monumental change of state, to reject it as a possibility. In this context, the idea of life outside normal boundary is expressed [...] through the sudden meaninglessness of the human body as a container for life.[13]

Thus Erpenbeck's protagonist can be related to the experience of disgust at death in two senses. In metaphorical terms, attached to and yet separate from the *social* body formed by her classmates, she might be described as an 'außerwesentlicher Zuwachs' like the protruding veins that reminded Herder of an early death. She also blurs the boundaries between life and death in a physical sense, as her formless, leaky body, which constantly drips snot, is perceived as having characteristics of both the living and the dead body. This ambiguous position on the borderline between life and death is particularly disturbing, as it threatens the boundaries which, according to Miller, the disgust reaction aims to protect.

The ambiguity with regard to boundaries also extends to gender, as the girl evades sexual as well as aesthetic categorisation. Referred to in grammatically neuter terms, her neutrality is also represented through the physical location she comes to occupy by about the middle of the story. While her fourteen-year-old classmates stand secretly smoking in gender-segregated groups in opposite corners of the playground, the protagonist plays with the younger children in the middle, thus occupying a space in between the gendered groups. It is at this point too that her increasing 'physische Neutralität' (G82) becomes apparent to her classmates. Whereas previously the girl had, due to her size, been the target of practical jokes, 'die [...] nie ganz unschuldig waren' (G81), such as a group of boys stealing her knickers, it now becomes evident to the boys in her class that such jokes are pointless:

> Dieser Körper ist gar keine Provokation, stellt sich heraus, und es hätte wenig Sinn, ihn hart anzufassen, weil er einem von innem her keinen Widerstand entgegensetzt, all das auf ihn gerichtete, mit Ekel vermischte Begehren versinkt in ihm wie in einem Filz, es wird einfach geschluckt, es versackt, es erstickt. (G82)

Thus for the adolescent boys, nascent sexuality, with its combined elements of disgust and desire, is swallowed up by the sexual neutrality of the girl's body. This neutrality is itself, however, described in terms which provoke disgust; rather than being neutral in a clinical, aseptic sense, this is a swampy, absorbent body in which the boys' feelings suffocate.

Indeed, although the children eventually come to accept the girl as part of their group, they never quite overcome feelings of ambivalence towards her. Thus, when she finally leaves the home due to illness, her classmates' main reaction is one of relief. Intending to visit the girl in the hospital, but continually putting it off, her room mate Nicole eventually realises, 'daß sie eine Abneigung, ja sogar eine heftige Abneigung dagegen empfand, das Mädchen zu besuchen' (G118-9), and for the class in general, 'eine ungeheure Hoffnung blüht, es möge nicht zurückkehren' (G119). Furthermore, the children's reluctance to ask after or even mention the girl following her departure testifies to a more fundamental rejection than one occasioned by mere dislike, suggesting, rather, the need to distance themselves from the girl's disturbing otherness and unwanted proximity.[14]

The girl's physical appearance and resistance to categorisation are also reflected in aspects of the narrative form. For example, Nobile draws parallels between the repetition of fairly cumbersome words and the protagonist's unchanging appearance, and between Erpenbeck's block-like, individually independent clauses and the girl's shape, that of a 'fleischerner Block, sehr hermetisch verschlossen'.[15] This analogy between specific elements of Erpenbeck's style and her protagonist may be extended even further, as more general stylistic aspects also reflect the subject-matter. Erpenbeck's deliberate use of obvious devices, such as the GDR allusions, is comparable to the girl's very definite physical presence. However, like the girl, the text nonetheless evades easy definition, due to strategies of understatement and concealment. For example, although the narrator provides often somewhat heavy-handed explanations of the girl's mode of reasoning, we are only offered partial glimpses of her background and underlying motivations.

Indeed, the narrator serves as a distancing barrier between the reader and the protagonist, preventing identification. The narrator's privileged knowledge and external, reflecting position are repeatedly underlined. Often the narrator provides interpretations of characters' behaviour they would not themselves be in a position to make:

> Ein wenig *erinnert* das Verhalten des Mädchens an die Art und Weise, mit welcher es immer das viele Essen in sich hineinfrißt, auch hier zeigt es diese stille Gefräßigkeit, die alles in sich aufnimmt, um es niemals wieder herauszurücken, *aber dieser Zusammenhang fällt den anderen nicht auf.* (G89, emphases: KJ)

Here, the verb 'erinnern' draws the reader's attention to the presence of the narrator, as the person being reminded cannot in this case be the other children, who do not make the connection. The reader is thus invited to observe the girl and analyse her behaviour, rather than sympathising with her. Erpenbeck's intention was to create 'ein Buch wie ein Block, wo man als Leser immer draußen bleibt'; the difficulty in identifying with the protagonist contributes to keeping the reader on the outside.[16] Indeed, the reader's attitude towards the girl is most likely to reflect the ambivalence of the children, who eventually befriend her, but are 'angewidert von [ihrer] Minderwertigkeit' (G36); whilst she and her story are compelling in their strangeness, the girl's manipulative behaviour and collusion with authority, which will be discussed in the following sections, make her simultaneously rather repellent.

'Body Language'

Communication between the protagonist and other characters often takes the form of 'body language'. The girl's attempts at verbal communication, appropriating the language of the other children, are relatively unsuccessful, and her weak, unconvincing voice proves more effective as part of the general impression of physical inferiority she projects. Mirroring the author's use of body metaphors, in particular the figure of the protagonist, to convey meaning, the girl makes use of her own body as a means of manipulation. The most obvious instance is her success in convincing others that she is a child, so that her body functions as a disguise, although the extent to which this is deliberate remains unclear. When questioned by the police about her background, we learn that the girl 'konnte sich einfach nicht daran erinnern' (G7) in the indicative, suggesting that the masquerade is not a conscious deception. However, shortly afterwards the narration suggests a more calculating attitude, as the girl deliberately avoids attracting the attention of potential adoptive parents, in order to stay in the home:

> So hat es sich gedacht. So wie andere danach streben, aus einem umzäunten Gebiet [...] auszubrechen, ist das Mädchen genau im Gegenteil in ein solches umzäuntes Gebiet, in ein Kinderheim eben, eingebrochen. (G11)

The physical deceptions the girl practises on her teachers are a less ambiguous, strategic display of helpless incapacity. For example, in a German lesson, she tricks her teacher into questioning her by adopting the posture of a student trying to evade attention, but exaggerating this posture to a suspicious degree: '[Das Mädchen] zwingt die Lehrerin geradezu, es aufzurufen, seine Demutshaltung ist wie ein Sog, der den bösen Willen der anderen, den der Lehrerin eingeschlossen, auf sich zieht' (G27). Having been tricked into humiliating the girl, the teacher is made to feel ashamed of her own cruelty, and subsequently leaves the girl in peace. A similar strategy is also practised on the more sympathetic English teacher, as the girl controls his attention and sympathy by raising her hand. The hierarchical positions of teacher and pupil are reversed, as the teacher falls victim to his own exaggerated feelings of guilt and pity at the girl's apparent stupidity:

> von Furcht und Mitleid geschüttelt sieht der Englischlehrer den Meldungen des Mädchens entgegen, und biegt sich dann dessen fleischiger Arm in die Höhe, wird er schleppenden Gangs an den Tisch des Mädchens treten (G30).

Although the teacher is in a position of authority, he is controlled by the girl's raised arm and his duty to respond to it. Furthermore, in both examples, the narrator insists on the coercive intention behind the girl's gestures and on both teachers' failure to notice it. Thus in the case of the unsympathetic female teacher, we learn: 'Daß das Mädchen selbst sie mittels eines Soges förmlich gezwungen hat, es zu traktieren, weiß die Lehrerin natürlich nicht' (G28), and the manipulation of the male teacher is also described in terms of force:

> So entgeht ihm der durchaus *zwingende* Charackter dieses in die Höhe gereckten Mädchenarmes, es entgeht ihm, daß er diesem Ruf nicht nur folgt, sondern folgen *muß*, daß er von dieser mit Recht an ihn gestellten Forderung, Hilfe zu leisten, und dem gleichzeitigen Unvermögen, diese Hilfe leisten zu können, ganz zerrissen, daß heißt also *beherrscht* ist. (G31, emphases: KJ)

The girl's use of her physical appearance to manipulate other people's perceptions of and behaviour towards her appears here at its most calculating, in stark contrast with the image of helplessness she projects to others. The exaggerated weakness she displays to authority figures enables her to retain her position at the bottom of the classroom hierarchy, as the teachers come to the conclusion that she is unteachable, and she is not expected to make progress. This voluntary assumption of a position of powerlessness also reflects the element of *Mitläufertum* on the part of ordinary people which helped to maintain the authoritarian regime of the GDR. Erpenbeck's insistence on her protagonist's deliberately deceptive behaviour may thus be seen as a scathing critique of this type of affected passivity, which, she suggests, aims at protecting the status quo.

Despite the girl's success in manipulating her teachers, however, she is less successful in her interactions with the other children. Listening to conversations between some of her classmates, she tries to integrate herself into the group by stealing words and phrases, which she can then repeat to other children. However, the ordinary phrases – observations about the cafeteria food – become unconvincing when spoken by the girl, and the children do not respond (G39). Although this is a failure in verbal, rather than physical communication, the girl's inability to speak in a way that convinces even herself still appears to be triggered by the inadequacy of her body. The words she speaks are described as though they were visible, physical objects: 'alles, was aus seinem Mund herauskommt, sieht immer wie eine Lüge aus, auch wenn es gar keine

Lüge ist' (G34). Furthermore, her body appears to exert a contaminating influence over the words and ideas that pass through it:

> als würde alles, was durch seine Person hindurch muß, von diesem Durchgang beschmutzt oder erschöpft. Als Beschmutztes oder Erschöpftes tritt es dann wieder hervor, und macht einen ganz fremden Eindruck (G34).

Abstract words and ideas are often described as though they were material objects, in line with the use of other physical images in the novella. The reference here to ideas passing through the girl's 'Person', which could refer to her whole body, rather than simply her head, evokes the image of a digestive process, with the contaminated ideas emerging as soiled waste products. But descriptions of eating and metaphors of digestion, prominent throughout *Geschichte vom alten Kind*, do initially also have a more positive meaning as communal eating together. Before the turning point, when the girl proves her usefulness to her classmates by guarding some stolen money, and begins to be accepted (G72), mealtimes represent one of the few occasions when she manages to integrate herself into the group of children. This success is demonstrated by the children's behaviour at the table; although they are disgusted by the way she eats – 'wie [das Mädchen] stumm das Essen in sich hineinschaufelt' (G63) – , they do not question her right to sit at their table:

> So erregt das Mädchen zwar den Unwillen und den Ekel derer, vor deren Blicken es so unmäßig viel ißt, hat aber auch teil an der allgemeinen Geselligkeit, und der Unwillen und der Ekel sind ganz gewöhnlicher Unwillen und Ekel, sind ganz alltäglich. (G64)

Although the children do also try to put the girl off her food by describing disgusting events, such as the dissection of pigs' eyes in biology classes, or showing her a festering cold sore, this teasing also implies a 'schwarze Variante der Anerkennung' (G64), and the girl appreciates it as such.

The girl also experiences a sense of integration on a more profound level, as sharing her classmates' food becomes spiritually significant:

> an manchen Tagen entblödet es sich nicht einmal zu fragen, ob es von ihren Tellern die Reste abessen dürfe, falls etwas übrigbleibe, die Knochen abnagen, die Soße ablecken, die Puddingnäpfe mit dem Finger ausputzen, aus abgestandenen Büchsen die letzten Tropfen saugen. Von äußerstem Verlangen gepeinigt, ergattert es an glücklichen Tagen solcherlei Überbleibsel der Achtkläßler, ißt, wovon diese gegessen haben, trinkt, wovon diese getrunken haben, das reinigt sein Blut. (G63)

Eating the children's leftovers is presented as degrading; the reference to gnawing on bones, in particular, suggests the behaviour of a pet dog, rather than a child on equal terms with the others. However, the girl experiences it as a ritual of purification: by eating the same food as the children, she will become like them. The shared food and drink, here explicitly linked to blood and the concept of purity, also evoke the Last Supper, with the girl's desire for everlasting childhood in place of the eternal life promised by Christ: 'Whoso eateth my flesh, and drinketh my blood, hath eternal life.' (John, 6:54) Her longing for physical integration into the group of children thus leads to a travesty of a religious communion, in which her behaviour both brings her closer – in her own eyes – to the children, and distances her from them as inferior.

This scene in the dining room is referred to in a later passage, in which the girl listens to her roommates' stories with the same 'stille Gefräßigkeit' with which she eats (G89). The children's verbal storytelling is here consumed by the protagonist as though it were food, in a manner reminiscent of her 'digestion' of the stolen phrases earlier in the story. This scene also has echoes of the earlier biblical theme, as the stories of the children's awakening sexuality are presented as 'Beichte'; this time, however, it is the protagonist's own regained sexual innocence and purity that she hopes will protect the others from the consequences of their impure, contaminating thoughts:

> In diesen Momenten vermag es seine Augen nicht länger vor der Tatsache zu verschließen, daß seine Gefährtinnen sich gerade aus der Kindheit verabschieden. Seine eigene Reinheit ist das einzige, was den Verfall jener noch eine kurze Zeit wird aufhalten können, darauf setzt es in blinder Hoffnung, und erteilt Absolution. (G91)

The girl's consumption is thus presented as a swallowing up and containment of the threatening sexual thoughts, comparable to the way she eats, in that the huge bulk of her body gives the impression that the food is simply piling up and being contained inside, rather than passing through her digestive system: 'als häufe dieser Körper ohne jeden Sinn und Verstand alles, was in ihn hineingegeben wird, einfach an, [wie] ein Materiallager' (G58). The metaphor of containment also applies to her wish to delay her roommates' 'Verfall', as this will lead to their departure from the idealised realm of childhood enclosed by the fence of the children's home.

Sexual and social boundary transgressions

In contrast to her classmates' developing interest in sex, the protagonist thus experiences anything sexual as an existential threat, as her continued existence as a child 'geradezu davon abhängt, derlei Verunreinigungen niemals in einen Zusammenhang mit sich selbst zu bringen' (G91). The sexual innocence with which she absorbs her roommates' confessions takes the form of a willed ignorance or repression of any sexual knowledge, an (iron) 'Vorhang, den das Mädchen selbst zugenäht hat (G91). However, when faced with visible or tangible evidence of adult sexuality, of whose nature she cannot simply remain ignorant, the girl reacts with spontaneous physical rejection of the contaminant. A first instance occurs towards the start of the girl's time at the orphanage, when she accidentally comes across a couple kissing, and experiences an attack of hysterical blindness:

> Da steht auf dem Treppenabsatz ein Paar, das sich küßt, ein Wust von Haaren, Händen und Hosen. Plötzlich sieht [das Mädchen] nichts mehr, es schaut hin, aber es kann nichts mehr sehen, nicht nur das Paar nicht, sondern auch sonst nichts, nicht das Treppenhaus, nicht die hölzernen Stufen, nichts vor sich, nichts hinter sich, nichts. Es reißt die Augen auf, aber es sieht nichts. (G29)

The blindness can also be seen as a physical symptom of the girl's desire for ignorance, and, by actively not seeing, of her wish to maintain her illusions regarding children's innocence. When standing guard for teenagers having sex in the dormitories, the girl does not react in the same way to the cries she hears, since, not actually being faced with incontrovertible evidence of sexual activity, she can choose not to understand them: 'es […] fragt nicht danach, was das für Schmerzen sein mögen' (G83).

Similarly, in two further passages, when, faced with evidence of adult sexual activity or potential, the girl is disgusted to the point of vomiting, an element of unavoidable understanding appears to be central to her reaction of disgust. The first such incident occurs when the girl is menstruating. Suffering initially only from the usual type of cramps and mild discomfort, it is only when her roommate Nicole asks 'was das eigentlich für ein Gefühl wäre, wenn das Blut unten so aus einem rausläuft, also, wenn man sozusagen eine richtige Frau sei' that the girl is suddenly overwhelmed by nausea and vomits into Nicole's lap (G93). This sudden physical reaction suggests that the definition of menstruation as evidence of being a 'real woman' has made it disgusting in a way that the menstrual blood itself would not otherwise have been, reflecting the idea that disgust depends on the cultural context of its object.

The second occasion on which the girl is moved to extreme physical disgust is more complex and occurs shortly before the paralysis that leads to her being removed from the home. On entering a storeroom used by her classmates as a meeting-place, the girl sees two boys, one of whom is masturbating the other, while pretending to be Nicole:

> Der Hockende reibt das Glied seines Freundes heftiger. Er lispelt: Ich zeige dir meine Brüste, Dennis, ich bin Nicole, deine Nicole, faß mich an, faß mir zwischen die Beine, ich bin schon ganz naß, Dennis, Dennis, ich will, daß du ihn mir reinsteckst, steck ihn mir rein, Dennis, steck ihn mir rein. (G105)

After Dennis ejaculates, the girl leaves the storeroom and 'übergibt sich gründlich' (G106). However, unlike her disgust of her own menstrual blood, with its unambiguous rejection of her female sexual potential, here it is unclear whether the trigger for the girl's vomiting is the sight of semen,[17] the homosexual element of the scene, the boy's fantasy of being Nicole, the encounter with any type of sexual activity, or a combination of these factors. It seems likely, though, that the increased complexity of the scene, especially when contrasted with her earlier reaction to the relatively innocent kissing couple, contributes to the girl's disgust, as well as her eventual paralysis, as it reflects her growing awareness of the complexity of social life within the home. The narration of the boys' activities in the storeroom is followed by an account of the girl's realisation that there is no common consensus upon which she can base her behaviour, so that she cannot escape making her own decisions: 'das Mädchen [...] will das, was alle wollen, aber das gibt es nicht. Und in dem Moment, da ihm das klar wird, wird ihm auch klar, daß seine Kräfte es verlassen' (G108).

As sex is associated with the adult world outside the home, and, by metaphorical extension, with the threat of Western capitalism and individualism, the teenagers' furtive sexual encounters in secluded corners and empty dormitories can be read as acts of subversion against the authoritarian order of the home perpetrated from within its boundaries. The allegorical representation of geo-political aspects of German history in terms of the physical spaces of the children's home thus suggests both the clear division provided by the fence and single guarded gate, and the fluidity of this apparently immutable boundary. The coldness of the city streets outside the home infiltrates certain areas of the orphanage, such as the storeroom and the women's rest room for menstruating girls, both sites of potentially contaminating adult behaviour. This may also be associated with the infiltration of Western culture and ideas into the GDR, for example the popularity of Western television and radio stations in some areas or the increase in Western-inspired consumerist culture from the 1970s on.[18] The physical disgust that the protagonist experiences at these violations of the physical boundaries between childhood and adulthood reflects her desire for the security of the existing social order. Yet the girl herself also represents marginality and blurred boundaries, as her body incorporates elements from both sides of several culturally established divisions: her body is both adult in its age and size, and childlike in form; it appears as both living and dead, as neither masculine nor feminine. Just as the girl experiences boundary violations as threatening and therefore disgusting, so the other characters, too, react to her unnerving presence with disgust, as she cannot be assimilated into their system of understanding. However, the failure of her project is ultimately attributable to the complex fluidity of the social order in the home, as the children go through puberty and experience a variety of unpredictable individual desires, bypassing the home's rules at will. In the light of this failure, the girl's disgusted rejection of anything associated with adulthood is an act of self-deception; change, and the breakdown of rigid boundaries, are inevitable, if not necessarily desirable.

However, in the city hospital where the girl's deception is discovered, the doctors react with an unspoken moral disapprobation.

Whether or not the masquerade was deliberate, the girl has offended against decency and the accepted order both by reversing the aging process, and by seeming to be something she was not:

> in dieser Haltung liegt, bei aller Bescheidenheit, die das Mädchen als Kind an den Tag gelegt hat und die es auch jetzt unverändert an den Tag legt, etwas Anstößiges, etwas Hochmütiges, den Lauf der Dinge Verachtendes, ja Gott Versuchendes (G124).

Thus although the girl's experience and her fluid, indefinable corporeality themselves represent the flexibility and uncontrollability of both social and individual bodies, through their disapproving rejection of her deviation from the norm, the city doctors reinstate the notion of bodies, and societies, as subject to inflexible and unchanging patterns of behaviour. The reader of *Geschichte vom alten Kind* may also become implicated in this new set of restrictive bodily norms. Within the confines of the home the children's sexual behaviour was appealingly subversive, in contrast to the girl's collusion with authority. Yet outside, in the adult world, their subversion becomes acceptable as part of normal sexual development. Thus the reader, rejecting the girl's behaviour in the home, suddenly finds him- or herself aligned with the doctors' repressive disapproval of the girl's transgression.

Furthermore, although Erpenbeck's portrayal of the girl's fluid, never entirely controllable body is extremely effective as an allegorical representation of complex social hierarchies and boundaries, this could be seen as reproducing misogynist stereotypes of the *female* body as inherently unruly and unreliable, especially as her choice of a female protagonist may perpetuate the idea that women are more closely linked to their bodies than men.[19] Although the girl is referred to in neuter terms, this is in itself rather conspicuous; in modern German it would be more conventional to switch to 'sie' when referring to a 'Mädchen'. Thus it is always clear that, despite her apparent gender neutrality, the gender identity which the girl conspicuously lacks is a female one, which is also implied by her blindness and paralysis, both stereotypical symptoms of womanly hysteria. Moreover, her desire to avoid the contamination of sexuality leads to a rejection of the adult, sexual, female body, which has long figured as a key disgust-object in misogynist thought. Her nauseated rejection of her own menstrual blood thus not only symbolises – extremely vividly – the rejection of an unfamiliar state of adulthood, it also resonates with a longstanding tradition of male disgust at female sexual potential, expressed for example by the elder Pliny's assertion that 'nothing in nature is more monstrous and disgusting than a woman's menstrual fluid'.[20] Furthermore, in spite of the radical corporeal potential implied by the girl's reversal of the aging process, by the end of the novella, bodily norms have been comfortably reinstated, and the protagonist is portrayed as a woman, at the mercy of female biology.

Notes

1 Monika Maron, *Stille Zeile Sechs*, Fischer: Frankfurt am Main, 1993; Thomas Brussig, *Helden wie wir*, Fischer: Frankfurt am Main, 1998.

2 Tobias Dennehy, 'Weise Einfältigkeit vom unteren Ende der Hierarchieleiter,' *Literaturkritik*, 2 (2000), www.literaturkritik.de/public/rezension.php?rez_id=835 [09/08/05]

3 Nancy Nobile, '"So morgen wie heut": Time and Context in Jenny Erpenbeck's Geschichte vom alten Kind,' in: Paul Michael Lützeler, ed., *Gegenwartsliteratur II*, Stauffenburg: Tübingen, 2003, pp. 283-310 (here: p. 284). Nobile considers some of the GDR metaphors, as well as the protagonist's suitability for her allegorical function; however, her main interest is in intertextual links between *Geschichte vom alten Kind* and Ludwig Tieck's *Der blonde Eckbert*, which offer an extremely illuminating approach.

4 Jenny Erpenbeck, *Geschichte vom alten Kind*, btb: Frankfurt am Main, 2. Auflage, 2001, p. 15. Subsequent references will be given as 'G' in the text.

5 Julia Hell, *Post-fascist Fantasies. Psychoanalysis, History, and the Literature of East Germany*, Duke University Press: Durham and London, 1997

6 Hell, *Post-fascist Fantasies*, p. 19.

7 Mary Douglas, *Purity and Danger. An Analysis of the Concepts of Pollution and Taboo*, Routledge: London & New York, 1991, p. 161. Although disgust is not the only or main focus of Douglas's book, her work provides the starting point for several later theorists of disgust.

8 Susan B. Miller, *Disgust. The Gatekeeper Emotion*, The Analytic Press: Hillsdale, N.J. & London, 2004, p. 6.

9 My definition of disgust for the purposes of this article is based on a number of sources, including those already cited. For a similar definition see Winfried Menninghaus, *Ekel. Theorie und Geschichte einer starken Empfindung*, suhrkamp taschenbuch: Frankfurt am Main, 2002, p. 7.

10 Menninghaus, *Ekel*, p. 7.

11 Johann Herder, cited in Menninghaus, *Ekel*, p. 80.

12 See S. Miller, *Disgust*, pp. 188-9; Martha Nussbaum, *Hiding From Humanity. Disgust, Shame, and the Law*, Princeton University Press: Princeton & Oxford, 2004, pp. 89-91.

13 S. Miller, *Disgust*, p. 189.

14 Menninghaus, *Ekel*, p. 7: ‘Das elementare Muster des Ekels ist die Erfahrung einer Nähe, die nicht gewollt wird’.

15 Nobile, ‘“So morgen wie heut”,’ p. 290; Erpenbeck, cited in Nobile, p. 291.

16 Erpenbeck, cited in Nobile, ‘“So morgen wie heut”,’ p. 283.

17 On the contaminating and disgust-inducing properties of semen, see William Ian Miller, *The Anatomy of Disgust*, Harvard University Press: Cambridge, Mass., 1997, pp. 105-7. In contrast to most other theorists of disgust, William Miller considers semen to be the most disgusting body fluid.

18 For a brief discussion of GDR ‘Konsumsozialismus’ in the 1970s and 80s see Wolfgang Emmerich, *Kleine Literaturgeschichte der DDR. Erweiterte Neuausgabe*, Kiepenheuer: Leipzig, 1996, pp. 243-6.

19 See Elizabeth Grosz, *Volatile Bodies. Toward a Corporeal Feminism*, Indiana University Press: Bloomington, 1994, pp. 13-15.

20 The elder Pliny, cited in: Nussbaum, *Hiding From Humanity*, p. 120.

Lyn Marven

'Nur manchmal mußten sie laut und unverhofft lachen': Kerstin Hensel's Use of Märchen

This article examines the changing perspectives of Kerstin Hensel's versions of Märchen. Three early texts from 1989-1990 parody traditional Märchen by the Brothers Grimm and Hans Christian Andersen; alluding to their GDR origins, these tales lend themselves to interpretations as political allegory. A more recent text is a modern fairy tale told in an ironic and feminist tone. Through close examination of the texts and their intertextual references, this article considers how Hensel's Märchen versions contain social criticism while interrogating the genre's conventions and function. Above all, the parodies highlight Hensel's interest in narrative and storytelling.

The Grimms' *Kinder- und Hausmärchen* have cast a long shadow in German literature. Their enduring popularity and wide-spread reception – Jack Zipes refers to them as an institution – has spawned numerous copies, revisions and parodies; as literary archetypes, the tales lend themselves to reinterpretations and modern rewritings which highlight contemporary socio-political issues.[1] Fairytales, particularly the Grimm's Märchen, constitute some of the most frequent intertexts for Kerstin Hensel's work, and the different ways she has treated these sources tie in with the wider trajectory of her prose work and its changing context since 1989. While the focus of her intertextual references, parodies and creative versions has shifted, her work remains in dialogue with these earlier tales, confirming both their vitality, and Hensel's interest in narrative forms and story-telling.

Images and quotations from fairytales recur in Hensel's work, from fragmentary passing references to full-length parodies, which are my interest here.[2] Literary parody is the imitation of a text (or genre) with an implied, usually critical, attitude towards that text (or genre); in this it functions as a particular literary form of irony, which also implies an evaluative attitude, and where the meaning of the whole (utterance or text) exceeds the literal meaning, and needs to be completed by the interpreter (the reader). Hensel writes alternative versions of 'Hänsel und Gretel' in 'Da ward gutes Essen aufgetragen' in *Hallimasch* (1989), and Hans Christian Andersen's 'The Emperor's New Clothes' in 'Des Kaisers Rad' in *Neunerlei* (1997); and she parodies the Grimms' Märchen as a genre in 'Ein Hausmärchen', a short piece published in a newspaper in 1990.[3] 'Das Licht von Zauche', written in 1995 and first published in 2002, draws on elements of the Grimms' narrative style, and alludes particularly to the dancing princesses of 'Die zertanzten Schuhe', but goes far beyond these references: this later text is less a parody than an ironic, modern version of a Märchen.[4] These parodies take on particular motifs, themes, form and language from their models; they are constructed through a range of narrative devices, such as exaggerating, reversing, foreshortening or omitting aspects of the source texts, or by adding incongruous new elements. Above all, parodies highlight their new context and are often used to criticise contemporary socio-political conditions. As well as incorporating critical distance both to individual texts and to the genre, Hensel's literary parodies also work as satire, implying critical comment of society through allegory or by using irony to engage with cultural norms. The specific, early parodies are clearly directed against the GDR state and people; moreover, the twist Hensel's texts give to this satirical or symbolic function also implies criticism of the relation between literature and politics particular to the GDR. The later text 'Das Licht von Zauche' is set in contemporary post-unification Germany and takes on a generic Western society, particularly the representation of women; Hensel's feminist stance is characterised by, and constituted through, irony. In this modern fairytale, the narrative style converges with her other prose writing, most notably *Im Spinnhaus* (2003), which employs a similar distanced, ironic perspective to relate fantastic occurrences.

Kerstin Hensel (b. 1961) belongs to the youngest generation to have begun writing under the GDR, and her first prose collection, *Hallimasch*, was published in 1989 in slightly different forms in East and West Germany. *Hallimasch* contains a parodic rewriting of part of the tale of 'Hänsel und Gretel', 'Da ward gutes Essen aufgetragen'.[5] The title quotes the Grimms' story, describing the feast that the witch offers the lost and starving brother and sister when she invites them into her house.[6] Hensel takes up the narrative just after the story shifts into the marvellous. Her tale consists of a single, breathless sentence which exaggerates the parataxis typical of the Grimms' style (the Mitteldeutscher version of Hensel's text does not even end with a full stop) and emphasises the oral storytelling on which the Grimms claimed to have based their texts. Hensel alters significant elements of the story: both children are imprisoned, whereas in the original it was only Hänsel. The children make no attempt to trick the old woman, whereas in the original the short-sighted woman, explicitly referred to as a witch, feels Hänsel's fingers to see if he needs more fattening, so Hänsel offers her bones to feel instead. Hensel's children scold the old woman for her bad food, and even when she dies, they do not immediately try to free themselves. The Grimms' timescale of approximately four weeks is expanded: years pass, and, rather than being killed by Gretel pushing her into the oven, the old woman eventually dies of old age. It transpires that the door had in fact been open all along, so the children, by now adults, open it,

> und da fragten sie sich, wohin sie jetzt gehen sollen, NACH HAUS, sprach der
> Junge, und da sah ihn das Mädchen zum erstenmal an, zum erstenmal nach
> den Jahren, und sagte, WIE FETT DU GEWORDEN BIST, HANS, und da
> sah es auch Hans und sprach, WIE DUMM DU GEWORDEN BIST,
> MARGARETE, und da gingen sie und wußten nicht, wohin. (H148)

The tale ends on this critical, uncertain note – with a further allusion to
'Rotkäppchen' – quite contrary to the Grimms' story, where the children
return home safely.

Far from illustrating the enterprise, patience and courage of the two
protagonists, it is greed which motivates the children in Hensel's version:
instead of using cunning to escape, they are complicit in their
imprisonment. The old woman is also driven by greed:

> die Alte befahl sich selbst, weiter zu warten, denn nichts sei schon fett genug,
> als daß es nicht besser werden könnte, und im Vorgeschmack ihres
> kommenden Genusses schob sie den Kindern weiter das Essen durch die
> Stäbe. (H147)

Striking too, is the shift in power relations between the old woman and
the children. Despite being imprisoned by the old woman, the children
nonetheless make demands which she fulfils: 'sie rührten abschätzend in
der Speise, so daß die Alte dazugab, was die Kinder verlangten'. (H147)
Rather than identifying with the protagonists, the reader is more likely to
be critical of their greediness and laziness. 'Da ward gutes Essen'
symbolises the process of repression: the children repress their
knowledge of their fate, and, since the story suggests that they are aware
of their predecessors in the Grimms' tale, they repress this knowledge
too. The Grimms state explicitly that the witch intends to kill the children,
and the witch tells Gretel that she will kill Hänsel. Though there are
repeated references to a cooking knife, in Hensel's version the threat
remains otherwise unvoiced and the children sleep 'in blütenweißen
Betten hinter kunterbunten Stäben, von denen sie bald wußten, wozu sie
gut waren und die sie hernach vergaßen' (H147). They repress their
knowledge, indeed collude in their fate, in order to indulge their greed.
The old woman also forgets why they are there: 'sie merkte es nicht, daß
sie kein Messer mehr hielt, denn die Jahre lassen vergessen [...] die Alte
hörte nichts mehr und vergaß sie, und eines Tages vergaß sie aufzustehen
aus ihrem Stuhl' (H148). Rather than dramatise a struggle between two
entities with competing interests, as Maria Tatar interprets the tale,[7] or
the class struggle, which was the reading of the Grimms' tales promoted
in the GDR,[8] Hensel's shows a co-existence of oppressor and oppressed,
based on the one hand on mutual exploitation, and on the other on the
children's repression and collusion, and the old woman's deferral of
pleasure, which results in her never even attempting to kill the children.

The tale is a self-conscious parody, which quotes its source text
directly and refers to 'die berühmte Speise, die fett machen sollte'

(H147), relying on and acknowledging the reader's familiarity with the original. Moreover, the children although aware of their predecessors, choose not to act accordingly: 'kein Gedanke kam mehr in ihnen auf, etwa ein solcher, wie ihn Gretel am Anfang ihrer Zeit gehabt hatte (die Alte müsse verbrannt werden), aber das war wie gesagt lange her.' (H147) Gretel's words, signalled by the subjunctive, indicate both their knowledge and its repression (into brackets). The aside 'wie gesagt' further imputes a contemporary, incongruous level of self-consciousness, and a distinctly oral style, to the narrative voice.

Hensel's version of 'Hansel and Gretel' invites a reading which refers to the GDR. The illusory 'Himmel' that the children believe they have found and the utopian, deferred 'Vorgeschmack [des] kommenden Genusses', as well as the tale's time span of years, all suggest a critical allegory directed against the self-deception and collusion of the population and the regime's violence and oppression. One might see the children as representing the 'Volk' and the old woman as the regime – a reading which thus also debunks the ideological interpretation of the original tales in the GDR which portrayed the protagonists as the lower classes who overcame oppression. The ending, extraordinarily prescient in 1989 when the 'Volk' of the GDR did end up on the street, seems to predict the downfall of the decrepit state, with the children finally freed, grown-up and self-aware, if somewhat uncertain. Such a reading would, however, if pursued, end up with a problematically extreme position in equating the communist utopia with a murderous state which swallowed its people. Perhaps one might instead think of their road, the door to which opens with a gentle push, as socialism, 'von der sie gekommen waren, irgendwann vor Jahren, und sie erkannten die Straße auch wieder' (H148) – here one thinks too of the many calls in 1989 and 1990 for a 'new' form of socialism. Whichever interpretation one follows, it is hardly a complimentary image – the heroes are unattractive, lazy, greedy and apathetic; the revolution is not brought about by their actions, and it leaves them directionless.

'Des Kaisers Rad' also provides an alternative ending for a familiar tale, 'The Emperor's New Clothes'.[9] Hensel's version does not feature the trickster tailors who supply the invisible 'cloth' in Andersen's original; rather than illustrating the individual's desire not to look stupid, Hensel demonstrates the collusion of the crowd in the Emperor's delusion. The tale begins with the cry 'Aber der Kaiser ist ja nackt', by a six year old child, which comes towards the end of Andersen's tale, and focuses on the reactions and repression, drawing on phrases ('was für Muster! Diese herrlichen Farben!' [N131]), ceremonial titles (the 'Oberzeremonienmeister') and specific motifs (the 'Thronhimmel') which evoke Andersen.[10] Instead of the child's revelation allowing the crowd to admit what they are all too aware of, the child's parents, the officials and the rest of the crowd try to suppress the child. Hensel's narrative is explicit about the Emperor's nakedness, which serves to emphasise that the mother and the rest of the crowd choose not to back up the child, despite the evidence of their own eyes:

> Die Mutter des Kindes rührten die dünnen, behaarten Beine des Herrschers. Sie erschrak vor dem faßförmigen Bauch, der sich auf diesen Beinchen hielt […]. Keiner stand dem Kind zur Seite und gab zu, daß er auch nicht mehr sah als den nackten Wanst des Herrschers, an dessen Unterseite ein winziges Klunkerchen Gemächt seine Männlichkeit zeigte. (N130-1)

The physical descriptions make the Emperor even more ridiculous than in Andersen's tale, which mocks his vanity, pride and fear of seeming ignorant.

In Hensel's tale, the mother calls her child 'die Stimme der Unvernunft' (N130): no longer is the ability to see the truth and speak it a sign of laudable and excusable innocence – in Andersen's version the child's is 'die Stimme der Unschuld' – but instead one of culpable and potentially dangerous stupidity. The child's father in turn reprimands the mother for drawing attention to them, 'Daß du so viel Aufhebens um unser dummes Kind machen mußt! […] Wir sind unser Leben lang nicht aufgefallen' (N130). The child keeps on talking, however, until, instructed that the child is 'nicht nur dumm, sondern auch gefährlich' (Andersen's tailors claim that only stupid people cannot see the cloth), the Emperor has him killed on the wheel. However, when the *Oberzeremonienmeister* exclaims jubilantly 'keiner wird jemals wieder sagen, der Kaiser sei nackt' (N132), the Emperor orders him, too, to be put to death – even in the ambiguous subjunctive the statement is dangerous. Someone else repeats the assertion, only to meet the same fate, and the cycle continues until only the Emperor himself is left and 'der letzte Mensch, den er noch lebend sehen konnte, ein sechsjähriger Knabe, folgte ihm und trug die Schleppe' (N133). At the end of Hensel's tale, a child confirms the Emperor in his delusion, rather than shattering it – Andersen's version has the Emperor's courtiers carrying 'die Schleppe, die gar nicht da war'.

Like 'Da ward gutes Essen', 'Des Kaisers Rad' focuses on the repression of knowledge – that the Emperor has no clothes on; ultimately death is necessary to uphold the delusion. Hensel's tale emphasises physicality and violence, as indicated by her title; it details the Emperor's nakedness, the brutal treatment of the child and the crowd's willing participation in the blood-bath. The Emperor seems both more ridiculous, and more tyrannous, not to mention more paranoid; he does not admit his error, and decides to carry on at the end in order to uphold the ritual and pomp, meaningless as this is: 'Nun muß ich die Prozession durchhalten' (N133), he comments. Compare Andersen's Emperor's more humble determination not to falter when he realises that he is in fact naked, 'das Volk schien ihm recht zu haben, aber er dachte bei sich: 'Nun muß ich aushalten'. Although Hensel's tale was first published in *Neunerlei* in 1997 it dates from around 1988, as the author has confirmed, and resembles 'Da ward gutes Essen' in its focus and the strategies which constitute the parody, of using familiar language while modifying the content in significant ways. The tale similarly lends itself to an interpretation as a representation of the GDR and the psychological processes of conformity and collusion: the crowd's unwillingness to speak out or to condemn fellow subjects, and the violent suppression of dissidence – the refusal to even admit it – are an exaggerated depiction of the socialist state.

'Ein Hausmärchen' refers to the 'Kinder- und Hausmärchen' collected by the Brothers Grimm and draws on elements and motifs from several tales, parodying the Grimms' style. The parody is constructed through exaggeration, foreshortening and incongruity, as well as by the confusion of references. The short narrative – given the lack of coherence and logical progression, narrative is perhaps a misnomer – starts *in medias res*, with a magical transformation: a 'Mädchen', Marie, is literally showered with gold, an image from the Grimms' 'Sterntaler', while her name further recalls Goldmarie in 'Frau Holle'. The 'Mädchen' regards this as just reward for her toils: she has worked for 'sechs mal sieben Jahre', making her substantially older than the conventional girl protagonist. Yet the gold comes from out of the blue, rather than as a result of a wish, a gift, or an adventure. Hensel also takes the magical occurrence literally: 'Marie aber konnte nicht antworten. Das Gold war ihr bis auf die Zunge gedrungen und wollte auch von da nicht wieder abgehen'; the gold sets hard, eventually killing the woman: 'Drei Tage lang hatte sie nichts gegessen und getrunken, ihre Haut war vom Gold verstopft und fiel zusammen'. The narrative piles on motif after motif, drawn from 'Tischchen deck dich, Zauberesel und Knüppel aus dem Sack' and 'Rumpelstilzchen'.[11] A 'Rumpelmüller' turns up, with a 'Zauberesel' who produces gold coins, and a magic stick which moves on its own (only two elements of the original). Taking the golden woman to his mill, he deposits her in the same room as the queen, who must spin the gold into straw; in the Grimms' tale, the miller's daughter is to spin straw into gold, and when she does this, with the help of Rumpelstilzchen, the king marries her, making her queen. The ending also travesties the Grimms' narratives: when all the gold is spun into straw, (by a 'Männlein' borne by the queen, here collapsing two aspects of 'Rumpelstilzchen'), all at once, the donkey dies, the stick refuses to work any more and '[d]ie Königin riß sich vor Freude mehrmals mitten durch'. The conventional ending, 'und wenn sie nicht gestorben sind, dann leben sie noch', is invoked and reversed: 'Das Land aber versank bis zur Hälfte in der Erde, und wenn es gestorben ist, stinkt es zum Himmel'.

Hensel uses motifs and language which place her tale clearly within the Grimms' Märchen tradition, emphasising her parodic intent. Time passing is structured in threes or in multiples; she uses the archaic form 'ward' ('Das Tor ward aufgetan'), paratactic structures and the demonstrative rather than relative pronoun ('Nach drei mal drei Monaten brachte die Königin ein Männlein zur Welt, das setzte sich sofort an das Spinnrad'), diminutives, repetitive structures, lists of three adjectives ('brav und reinlich und ohne Widerspruch'), and traditional folk terms such as 'der Graurock' for the donkey. The whole tale is consistent with the rapidly moving, plot-oriented *Kinder- und Hausmärchen* which avoid detailed presentation of characters' psychology (see the flat assertion that 'Marie freute sich bis zum Abend'). As with the proliferation of intertextual references, the sheer number of these stereotypical features signals the self-consciousness of parody.

Aside from exaggeration on the level of the plot and form, and comic reversal (spinning gold into straw is surely pointless), the narrative signals its parodic intent by including incongruous grotesque and sexual physical detail – in editing their tales, the Grimms excised sexual content.[12] Hensel replaces the Grimms' coy formulation that the donkey 'speit Gold [...] hinten und vorn' with unconventionally literal, bodily content.[13] Hensel's donkey produces coins by regurgitation, 'es würgte ihn erbärmlich. Meistens verklemmte sich die Münze auch noch zwischen Gaumen und Oberkiefer und der Esel mußte sie mit seiner Zunge zu guter Letzt aus dem Gespieenen befreien', or defecation: 'so kam die Münze aus dem Loch im Hintern, das aber, durch das scharfe Metall von vielerlei schmerzhaften Ragaden und Hämorrhoiden befallen war und dem armen Tier hirnzerreißende Klagelaute entlockte'. This graphic, grotesque content explains the magic words, which mimic the Grimms' instruction 'Tischchen, deck dich': 'Goldesel, reck dich!' and 'Goldesel, streck dich!'. Hensel also adds innuendo, taking the 'cudgel in the sack' as *double entendre*:

> Der Rumpelmüller trat sogleich auf Marie zu und befahl: 'Knüppel aus dem Sack!' Der Knüppel erschien und stand dem Herren zu Diensten. Nun versuchte der Rumpelmüller den Knüppel der Marie nahezubringen, allein, es wollte nicht gelingen, denn das Gold hatte ihren Leib kompakt umschlossen und nicht das winzigste Löchlein freigelassen.

This turns the miller's threat to the queen – that he'll come with the cudgel if she doesn't do the spinning – into a threat of rape; and the remark at the end that, once the queen had borne a 'child', 'der Knüppel verweigerte fortan den Dienst an seinem Herren', thus alludes to impotence. Further adult content is imputed in allusions to profanities: 'Der Rumpelmüller fluchte, daß es dem Esel die Ohren einrollte'.

Hensel's parody also departs from the Grimms' didactic intent, deliberately undermining the moral message in their tales. In this 'Hausmärchen', avarice, sexual violence, meaninglessness, stagnation and death are rife. As an explanation of the world, it presents a particularly negative view. It is not entirely lacking a message though: like the others, it can also be read as an allegory of the (collapse of the) GDR, a reading which seems all the more prominent in this 1990 text, published in the public forum of the *Deutsche Volkszeitung*, a left-wing newspaper. The 'Tor' which is opened in the first sentence, allowing gold to flow, is obviously the Brandenburg Gate; Marie's working life was forty two years, the lifespan of the GDR; the magic donkey which produces gold is a 'Zauberesel aus dem Nachbarland'. Even more directly, the final lines – 'das Land aber versank bis zur Hälfte in der Erde' – suggest the collapse of the rotten half of Germany ('und wenn es gestorben ist, stinkt es zum Himmel'). While these allusions to the greed and wastefulness of the corrupt state are clear enough, they remain relatively disparate, and the incongruous physicality and linguistic parody draw our attention back to the narrative as a literary text.

Jack Zipes characterises the Grimms' tales as offering a 'compensatory image of reconciliation', and providing a realm where transformations can be realised and the protagonists are integrated into society through their innate virtues and wits.[14] Hensel's tales are dystopian: all transformations are negative and brought about by the stupidity of the protagonists, although in some ways this might be seen as in keeping with, or even revealing, the darker elements which the Grimms attempted to suppress in their tales. Zipes also reads the Grimms' tales as a critique of their contemporary social and political conditions in the values they promote, and in their allegorical interpretations Hensel's tales, too, function as criticism of the conditions of the GDR. However, there are problems with these political readings, particularly in the weight of detail which cannot be assimilated into the allegories: the threat of being eaten, in 'Da ward gutes Essen', for example, or the orgy of violence in 'Des Kaisers Rad'. But this, I think, is precisely the point: Hensel deliberately disrupts the symbolic reading, even while seeming to encourage it. In this way, the parody also satirises the use of fairy-tales in East Germany both by the regime as pedagogical tools and by writers as a literary vehicle for criticism. The similarity between the names Hänsel and Hensel may point to a self-conscious interest in the role of literature. In the introduction to the 1996 edition of his *Kleine Literaturgeschichte der DDR*, Wolfgang Emmerich notes that 'die sogenannten kritischen DDR-Autoren, die man veröffentlichen ließ, hätten vielleicht an einer

"Verbesserung der Haftbedingungen" mitgewirkt, nicht aber die Haft selbst in Frage gestellt', exactly what the children do in Hensel's narrative.[15] Perhaps Hensel is criticising the collaboration of 'Geist und Macht' in this tale, and challenging the use of fairy-tales as a substitute social dialogue, both their conventional utopian function, as well as the specific function of 'Ersatzöffentlichkeit' which literature fulfilled in the GDR. She does this by disrupting the narrative's ability to function as allegory: the reader's expectation of meaning, especially political meaning, that the parody creates is frustrated.

These earlier texts draw on individual tales, assuming the reader's knowledge of the source text and using this for parodic effect and for a wider, critical comment on the GDR. 'Das Licht von Zauche', a satirical tale about women in pursuit of men to love, is less a parody than a fairy-tale in a modern idiom. Though set in a recognisable German landscape, this later text's social criticism is directed towards a generic capitalist society – particularly its perception and representation of women – and is located within a narrative characterised chiefly by irony, in part resulting from the use of the Märchen genre. In Hensel's tale, the single women of Zauche (twelve are mentioned), frustrated with their lives, spirit married men away from their beds to dance with them under the full moon; the men try to stop them, but the marauding women are not deterred by chains or doors nailed shut. The men consider asking an international space agency to stop the moon shining, but this meets with derision. The women eventually tire of their partners, although they carry on dancing with each other in silence: the tale ends, 'Nur manchmal, wenn der Mond vor Wolken unsichtbar war, mußten sie laut und unverhofft lachen' (LZ4). The central image of the tale invokes the Grimms' 'Die zertanzten Schuhe', where the twelve princesses steal away at night to dance with princes in a magical kingdom, giving a sleeping potion to the men sent to spy on them in order to escape; Hensel's men are returned to their beds 'nackt und zertanzt' (LZ3).[16]

The tale seems to qualify as a fairytale – albeit a modern, literary one – through a combination of content and style: the familiar magical occurrence is narrated in the third person, by a distanced, matter-of-fact voice. The tale is short and driven by plot, above description or psychological insight; it sets up a typical, non-realist situation to be resolved (although in Hensel's tale this resolution does not happen) and proceeds to unfold the action quickly, skipping over the passage of time to emphasise repetition – 'Nach diesem Erlebnis, was sich von nun an regelmäßig alle vier Wochen wiederholte' (LZ3). Hensel also uses the motif of three days passing, and formal story-telling language such as 'Es ergab sich' (LZ1), as well as a predominately nocturnal, moonlit and rural setting (with the landmark 'Lustigberg'), and type characters known only by their job title.

In updating the abduction motif, Hensel adds similar elements to those in her revisions of specific Märchen, particularly the concern with sexuality and group behaviour. Her dancing women, quite unlike the Grimms' chaste princesses, are predatory and aggressive, grabbing several men each: 'Die Frauen von Zauche ergriffen die Männer. Sie rissen ihnen Unterwäsche und Pyjama vom Leib und walzten mit ihnen durch Schlehendorn, Disteln und Brombeergestrüpp'. (LZ2) The women act as a group – they are referred to throughout simply as 'die Frauen von Zauche' – and succumb to a form of collective 'Rausch' influenced by the moon, 'sie vollführten einen stampfenden Reigen nach ihrer inneren gierigen Musik. Bis es Nacht wurde und das Mondlicht glitzernder Wahn.' (LZ2) In the interview in the same volume as the text, Hensel declares that 'Gruppenverhalten ist immer Machtverhalten'.[17] The women's behaviour here is not a sign of a reversal of power, however, although their actions are a form of revenge on the men who normally ignore them; rather it emphasises the fact that without magic they are powerless and invisible. The text embodies a fear of female sexuality in a grotesque but ultimately also pathetic display of desperation, and mocks this fear, deflating it through humour.

The dominant mode of 'Das Licht von Zauche' is not satire or allegory, but rather irony, which, as Linda Hutcheon states,

> operate[s] on a microcosmic (semantic) level in the same way that parody does on a macrocosmic (textual) level, because parody too is a marking of difference, also by means of superimposition (this time, of textual rather than semantic contexts).[18]

Irony in 'Das Licht von Zauche' thus marks its shift towards extra-textual, as opposed to specific intertextual, targets: it is directed at gender relations, particularly the treatment of women and sexuality, although it also ironises the fairytale narrative in general, suggesting that Hensel is concerned with gender roles in literary texts as well as society. The opening paragraphs illustrate both aspects:

> In Zauche, einem Landstrich im Märkischen, wurden, bei zunehmenden Mond, die Frauen gefährlich. Es waren jene, die nur ungern ihre Dörfer verließen und in die Stadt gingen. Wenn sie doch einmal in der Stadt auftauchten, im Supermarkt, vor dem Kino oder in der Sparkasse, verfolgten sie die Männer dort mit hochmütigen Blicken, oder, was noch schlimmer war: sie sahen sie gar nicht, als ob es sie nicht gäbe. Nur eine dieser Frauen hatte selbst einen Mann. Die einbeinige Sylphe aus Borkheide war mit einem Schäfer vermählt, der, wie man munkelte, einen Dachschaden besäße und sie mit zwei gesunden Beinen gewißt verschmäht hätte. Die anderen Frauen hatten wohl den Versuch unternommen, einen Mann aus der Gegend zu finden, aber diese hatten sich mit den Dorfschönsten oder mit hübschen Mädchen aus der Stadt zusammengetan, oder sie waren mit den Ledigen auf

> irgendeine Weise verwandt. Oft saßen die Frauen beieinander. An den
> Küchentischen mischten sie ihre Karten, teilten und spielten sie aus. Sie
> reizten, stachen und übertrumpften einander in den Hoffnungen, das Glück zu
> finden. 'Wir werden gewinnen', sagten sie.
> Es ergab sich, daß die einsamen Frauen von Zauche eines Abends in der Nähe
> des Lustigberges auf einer Wiese zusammentrafen. Sie hatten ihrer
> Tagesgeschäfte erledigt und waren alle gekommen: die Dünnhaarige, die
> Großköpfige, die Zweimeterfrau aus Oberjünne, die Rotäugige, die
> Schiefzahnige, die Grauhäutige, die dicke Margit, das Mädchen mit den
> Fadengliedern, die Mineralienforscherin, die Bücherleserin und natürlich die
> einbeinige Sylphe. Über ihnen stand der Mond drei Tage vor seiner
> Vollendung. (LZ1)

In this passage, as in the rest of the text, the irony draws on expectations
of genre, contrasting fairy-tale elements with comically banal, realist
touches, such as the description of 'die einbeinige Sylphe': the
connotations of 'Sylphe' – a mythical, ethereal, graceful, beautiful
creature – are entirely contradicted by the literal and unattractive
physicality of 'einbeinig'. The other women possess similarly grotesque,
abnormal and exaggerated features: they are excessively tall ('die
Zweimeterfrau'), thin ('das Mädchen mit den Fadengliedern') or fat ('die
dicke Margit'); they have odd proportions ('die Großköpfige') and
demonic aspects ('die Rotäugige', 'die Schiefzahnige'). The list itself is
ironic, initially defining the women by physical characteristics, but
suddenly changing topos with 'die Mineralienforscherin' and 'die
Bücherleserin'. The comic shift suggests that scientific jobs and a
predilection for reading are as abnormal as the physical aberrations, and
therefore account for the women's unmarried status. Here Hensel plays
on stereotypes of female scientists and blue-stockings, whilst at the same
time mocking such prejudice.

Irony derives from the expectations of genre – the fairytale or
supernatural is indicated in the first sentence by a reference to the moon.
Generic expectations are, however, disrupted in the use of modern
locations (the *Sparkasse*, the cinema) which do not exist in conventional
fairy-tale settings, and also in the naming of real places (Borkheide,
Oberjünne as well as the more recognisable Berlin and Mark
Brandenburg), whereas fairy-tales take place within the archetypal and
closed world of the marvellous. The modern intrudes even more later on
in the text, where the unnamed men include the 'Diskothekenburschen'
and the 'Makler, der im schönsten Haus der Stadt wohnte' (LZ2), and
most clearly in the references to the 'Internationale Raumfahrtsbehörde'
(LZ3).

Other linguistic techniques signal irony: the excessively correct
formulation of the first sentence, which leaves the most important
information – 'gefährlich' – until after several detailed qualifications, or
changes in register, as in the shift from this proper beginning to the casual

aside (indicating an oral narrative), 'was noch schlimmer war', and then to 'der, wie man munkelte, einen Dachschaden besäße', where the colloquial terms sit uncomfortably with the high use of the subjunctive, and again to the old-fashioned literary 'Es ergab sich'. Differing associations or contexts are evoked throughout the passage, creating a hybrid text – this reminiscent of Hensel's other parodies, *Ulriche und Kühleborn* in particular[19] – which veers from the bathetic to the ominous gothic of 'das Mondlicht glitzernder Wahn', or from the realistic to the awkward coincidence of the real and the symbolic in the card-game, '[sie] übertrumpften einander in den Hoffnungen, das Glück zu finden'.

The reader's relation to the text and the characters is also unstable. Where the descriptions of the women desperate for a husband will, in all probability, meet with amusement, the despair expressed by 'die Rotäugige' in her curses on the other hand, is treated seriously:

> Die Rotäugige war es, die plötzlich mit Fluchen begann. Sie fluchte auf die langen Tage und Nächte, auf die Arbeit im Haus; auf ihre kranke, kraftfressende Mutter, die bei ihr wohnte; auf alles, was ihr die Zeit vom Leben abriß und verschleuderte. (LZ1-2)

The last phrase here appears to be narrative comment, rather than reported speech, and alerts us to the narrative sympathy for the character. Hensel's women reject the long-suffering industriousness of the typical Grimms' heroine, whose uncomplaining hard work earns her the reward (Cinderella, for example), demonstrating a modern sensibility which is more likely to arouse sympathy.

The ending of the tale demonstrates Hensel's ironic take on the Märchen tradition in both content and in structure, which rejects the conventional marvellous resolutions in favour of realism. The men's plan to block the moon's light – 'man könne sich ein Abdunkeln, eine Sprengung oder eine Änderung der Umlaufbahn vorstellen' (LZ3-4) – is mocked. The university professor reminds both the men of Zauche and the readers of the principles of science, protesting, 'Die erklären uns für verrückt, außerdem liegt die Ursache des Mondlichtes nicht beim Mond selbst, sondern bei der Sonne' (LZ4), and ensuring that the high-tech fantasy does not simply function as a modern equivalent of the magical. His realism is clearly endorsed by the narrative voice and is justified by the ridicule with which the plan meets: 'Die Raumfahrtbehörde schickte niemals eine Antwort. Es war ein Jahrhundertgelächter, das durch das märkische Land lief'. (LZ4) In the end, the women simply lose interest in the men, preferring to dance with each other, although their laughter – 'laut und unverhofft' – remains a sign of defiance. The anti-climactic ending fails to resolve the situation, and is, moreover, notably negative. That the ending frustrates, demonstrates how the tale relies for its effect on the tradition which underlies the reader's expectations of resolution.

Hensel's text thus still remains in dialogue with the genre, even despite the modern interferences, bringing into question the Märchen's role and possible function within a modern world.

With increasing historical distance from the GDR, Hensel's versions of Märchen become less overtly political; the real, but generic setting of 'Das Licht von Zauche' replaces the allegorical references to the East German state. However, the later text, a modern creation rather than a parody, retains the element of social criticism and takes this seriously, despite its ironic narrative voice, and remains in dialogue with the tradition. The stylised, laconic narrative also resembles the voice in Hensel's recent prose text, *Im Spinnhaus* (2003), a novel of anecdotal and occasionally fantastic narratives, based around the symbol of weaving, or spinning tales. The text combines an assortment of incredible characters – from a 60-year old woman who is pregnant for ten years, to a bear which seems to pose for the photographer's camera – with grotesque episodes from German history. The continuing influence of the Grimms is confirmed by its frontispiece motto, 'Frau, schlag mir den Vogel im Munde tot!', a quote from the Grimms' tale 'Der Hund und der Sperling'. The Märchen, in all its forms, stands for Hensel's interest in the possibilities and potential of story-telling, the common thread in all her writing – not as a means of escape into a fantasy world, but rather as a form of engagement with the real world.

Notes

1 Jack Zipes, *The Brothers Grimm: From Enchanted Forests to the Modern World*, Routledge: London & NewYork, 1988, p. 81.
Thanks to Mererid Puw Davies for her helpful comments and suggestion.

2 These intertextual fragments deserve closer attention than I can give them here: the poem 'Fieberkurve' (in the collection *Gewitterfront*, 1991) incorporates references to 'Aschenputtel' (Cinderella); the limited art edition *Augenpfad* (1995) features the one-eyed giant Polyphem and three sisters with respectively one, two and three eyes, alluding to 'Einäuglein, Zweiäuglein und Dreiäuglein'; 'Lämmerdeern', in *Neunerlei* (1997), draws on an image of 'Das Mädchen ohne Hände'; and 'Vogelgreif', also in *Neunerlei*, refers to an otherwise unrelated Grimm tale, 'Der Vogel Greif', when a young girl is carried off by a bird (an owl, rather than a gryphon – 'greif' here derives from the verb, rather than the noun).

3 Kerstin Hensel, 'Hausmärchen', *Deutsche Volkszeitung*, 29.6.1990, p. 13.

4 Kerstin Hensel, 'Das Licht von Zauche' (hereafter 'LZ'), in: Beth Linklater and Birgit Dahlke, eds., *Kerstin Hensel*, University of Wales Press: Cardiff, 2002, pp. 1-4.

5 Page references will be to the more widely available West German edition, *Hallimasch*, Luchterhand: Frankfurt/Main, 1989 (hereafter 'H'), pp. 147-8 (compare

Hallimasch, Mitteldeutscher Verlag: Halle, 1989, pp. 6-8). The two editions differ slightly in typography.

6 Hensel quotes the sixth and final version of the Grimms' tale, which is the version referred to here, 'Hänsel und Gretel' in Brüder Grimm, *Kinder- und Hausmärchen* [Jubiläumsausgabe], Philipp Reclam: Stuttgart, 1980, 1984 (hereafter 'KHM'), vol. i, pp. 100-108. John Ellis, *One Fairy Story too Many: The Brothers Grimm and Their Tales*, University of Chicago Press: Chicago, 1983, pp. 154-94, gives the different versions of the tale. The title quotation in the Luchterhand version has only one slight grammatical difference from the Grimms', reading 'Milch und Pfannekuchen mit Zucker, Äpfeln und Nüssen', where the Grimms and the Mitteldeutscher version have 'Milch und Pfannekuchen mit Zucker, Äpfel und Nüsse', changing the apposition: in late twentieth-century West Germany apples and nuts were perhaps no longer considered special luxuries.

7 Maria Tatar, *The Hard Facts of the Grimms' Fairy Tales*, Princeton University Press: Princeton, NJ, 1987, p. 51.

8 See also Jack Zipes, 'The Struggle for the Grimms' Throne: The Legacy of the Grimms' tales in the FRG and GDR since 1945,' in: Donald Haase, ed., *The Reception of the Grimms' Fairy Tales: Responses, Reactions, Revisions*, Wayne State University Press: Detroit, 1993, pp. 167-206 (here: pp. 190-1).

9 Kerstin Hensel, *Neunerlei*, Kiepenheuer: Leipzig, 1997 (hereafter 'N'), pp. 130-3.

10 While it is difficult to establish whether Hensel is quoting a specific translation without having access to the same version, the precision of her phrasing suggests that this is the case. Very similar phrases are used in the otherwise unattributed translation on <http://gutenberg.spiegel.de/andersen/maerchen/kaisersn.htm> [accessed 29 March 2004], from which I therefore quote here.

11 ,Tischchen deck dich, Zauberesel und Knüppel aus dem Sack', and 'Rumpelstilzchen', KHM, vol. i, pp. 195-205 and 285-8 respectively.

12 See Ellis esp. pp. 53-93, and also Ruth B. Bottigheimer, *Grimms' Bad Girls and Bold Boys: the Moral and Social Vision of the 'Tales'*, Yale University Press: New Haven, 1987, esp. pp. 165-66.

13 KHM, vol. i, p. 200.

14 Zipes, *The Brothers Grimm*, p. 84.

15 Wolfgang Emmerich, *Kleine Literaturgeschichte der DDR* [Erweiterte Ausgabe], Kiepenheuer: Leipzig, 1996, p. 14.

16 'Die zertanzten Schuhe', KHM, vol. ii, pp. 217-21.

17 Beth Linklater and Birgit Dahlke, '"Mir reicht mein Leben nicht aus, um all die Geschichten zu erzählen, die ich in mir habe": Gespräch mit Kerstin Hensel,' in: Dahlke and Linklater, eds., *Kerstin Hensel*, pp. 10-24 (here: p. 19)

18 Linda Hutcheon, *A Theory of Parody: The Teachings of Twentieth-Century Art Forms*, London: Methuen, 1985, p. 54.

19 Mererid Puw Davies refers to the 'disconcerting generic hybridity' of the text: 'Fishy Tales: Kerstin Hensel, Ulriche und Kühleborn,' in: Dahlke and Linklater, eds., *Kertin Hensel*, pp. 51-66 (here: p. 57).

Petra M. Bagley

Granny Knows Best: The Voice of the Granddaughter in 'Grossmütterliteratur'

This article explores a recent trend in German literature, namely the portrayal of the grandmother by women writers. The term 'Grossmütterliteratur' will be used of the selected texts, published at the beginning of the twenty-first century, to highlight the link with the genre of 'Väter- und Mütterliteratur', which dominated the German literary scene during the 1970s and 1980s. Research into grandmotherhood is discussed as a further context to appreciate how Jenny Erpenbeck's *Tand* (2000) and Maike Wetzel's *Schlaf* (2003) exemplify the changing relationship between grandmothers and granddaughters in today's society.

This article will argue the case for a new term that may be applied to a number of recent German narratives, written by a new generation of female authors, stories which have the grandmother as the main character and/or the role of the grandmother as a central theme. The term 'Grossmütterliteratur' inevitably invites comparison with the literary sub-genre of autobiographical or semi-autobiographical texts, prevalent in the 1970s and 1980s and designated as either 'Väterliteratur' or 'Mütterliteratur'. I shall therefore consider to what extent similarities and differences exist between the established genres and this emergent trend. Some recent research into the shifting role of grandmothers in today's society will provide a further context. Writing in today's unified Germany, a new generation of authors is further removed in time from the Third Reich than their parents' generation, so that the accusatory exposure of guilt or bitter criticism of political faults expressed in the earlier father/mother memoirs may be less prevalent. Focus on intergenerational tensions in families has been one of the main ways in which German literature has reflected upon the past. Given the endless examples of prose narratives that explore the national or political past through generations in the family and the ever-growing distance from the Third Reich, the advent of a 'Grossväter-/Grosssmütterliteratur' should thus not be unexpected. Examples of such texts include Monika Maron's *Pavels Briefe* (1999) and Reinhard Jirgl's *Die Unvollendeten* (2003). But a further non-specifically German reason might explain the advent of such a genre, namely current demographic and social changes. Moreover, even within the 'Väter-/ Mütterliteratur', there is a tendency in women's writing towards a more intimate engagement with family relations in social and personal terms, which is rather different from the historical concern with a national past. In this article, I therefore note the continuing intermixing of familial and political history in some texts, but the main focus is to explore how some authors centre on the intimate relations of granddaughter and grandmother without a political agenda as such, though their texts may raise other social questions. I will begin by looking at examples of the earlier generational writing before turning to some reflections on changes evident not only in Germany in the role and nature of the grandmother as a further context within which to consider two main recent examples. Ultimately, I will suggest that this kind of writing is symptomatic of the passage of time in unified Germany and of the advent of a generation more at ease with itself.

Given the limits of space, I concentrate on two key texts, Jenny Erpenbeck's short story 'Tand' (2000) and Maike Wetzel's short story 'Schlaf' (2003). The year 2000 seemed a good starting point to make a choice, given the advent of a new generation of German women authors who attracted international critical acclaim. In particular, Volker Hage, made headlines with two articles in 1999 for *Spiegel* magazine. In the first he caused controversy by using the label 'ein literarisches Fräuleinwunder' to describe the phenomenon of the number of young German women writers.[1] Hage reduced the literary achievement of writers such as Judith Hermann, Zoë Jenny, and Karen Duve to just one dominant characteristic, namely their ability to write about love and eroticism without inhibition. The label was factually unsustainable as well as belittling, since 'Miss Miracle' covered writers whose ages ranged between twenty plus to forty plus and included women, like Birgit Vanderbeke, who had been publishing for over a decade. For publishers, however, Hage's new label became a useful marketing tool. New female writers could immediately be categorised and no allowance made for a variety of styles and themes. Later that year, a second article entitled 'Die Enkel kommen' coincided with the success of 'young' new German writers at the Frankfurt Book Fair.[2] Here, Hage referred to a new generation of writers, who were making an impact worldwide by dint of their ability to tell a good story, as the grandchildren of Günter Grass. Works by women included Birgit Vanderbeke's seventh novel *Ich sehe was, was du nicht siehst* (1999) and Jenny Erpenbeck's debut novel *Geschichte vom alten Kind* (1999).[3] In both articles Hage suggested that this third post-war generation of authors have come to terms with their German past, and are writing with a new and refreshing freedom, which the Austrian author, Josef Haslinger, also described as 'eine neue Unbekümmertheit'.[4] It will be worth considering these comments again in the conclusion.

As noted above, Jenny Erpenbeck (born 1967 in East Berlin) is one of the new generation of German writers, whose success is reflected in the award of literary prizes. In 2001 Erpenbeck was awarded second prize at the Klagenfurt literature festival for an excerpt from her short story 'Sibirien'.[5] The jury praised her adeptness at understatement, her economical style and her ability to write non-judgementally.[6] Like

Erpenbeck, Maike Wetzel (born 1974 in Nauheim) also has a penchant for the short story form. Her two publications to date, *Hochzeiten* (2000) and *Lange Tage* (2003) are both collections of short stories. Since 1995 she has received four prizes. Both Wetzel and Erpenbeck commented on Hage's 'Fräuleinwunder' label in 2001 in Wiebke Eden's *Keine Angst vor grossen Gefühlen* which contains interviews with eleven new women writers about their childhood, their experiences of writing and of success, as well as their opinion of the 'Fräuleinwunder' debate.[7] Erpenbeck was unconcerned by the label because she felt that her writing was being taken seriously. In contrast, Wetzel was concerned about its demeaning effect in reducing the author to an object to be marketed and felt the burden of expectations among interviewers more interested in the author than in the book: 'Die Forderung nach einem Image als Schriftstellerin macht es einem nicht leichter, natürlich authentisch zu bleiben'.[8] Clearly the reactions of the new generation of women writers to the 'Fräuleinwunder' debate do depend very much on the confidence and experience of the individual.

The grandmother figure appears in short stories by Erpenbeck and Wenzel and in both instances the first-person narrator is the granddaughter, making them an apt choice to illustrate the term 'Grossmütterliteratur'. It would be misleading, however, to define 'Grossmütterliteratur' purely in terms of first-person narratives. Recent third-person narratives figuring grandmothers include Helga Königdorf's *Die Entsorgung der Grossmutter* (1997) and Helene Flöss's *Löwen im Holz* (2003).[9] In a collection of international stories about female relationships published in 2000, Asta Scheib wrote from the perspective of the grandmother about the granddaughter/grandmother relationship in her short story, 'Jelena oder komm in die Nacktschneckendisco.'[10] Monika Maron uses a first-person narrator to reconstruct the lives of her grandparents in *Pawels Briefe* (1999).[11] (The letters of the title refer to those her grandfather sent to his family from a Polish ghetto before his tragic death in 1942.) And it is not just granddaughters: Reinhard Jirgl's, *Die Unvollendeten* (2003) is a three-generational saga narrated by the grandson about his grandmother and mother.[12] In Melitta Breznik's partly autobiographical novel, *Das Umstellformat* (2003), the first-person narrator, the granddaughter, never met her grandmother who died in 1943.[13] Rather than a grandmother-granddaughter relationship, this text explores family secrets surrounding the Nazi euthanasia programme, as the granddaughter attempts to establish the cause of her grandmother's death, her search partly driven by the fear that she may have inherited her grandmother's schizophrenia. Breznik, thereby, extends our definition of 'Grossmütterliteratur' and as a personal 'her'story lends further credence to our revisiting the terms 'Väterliteratur' and 'Mütterliteratur'.[14]

These two sub-genres of autobiographical writing emerged in the 1970s in conjunction with the phenomenon of 'Neue Subjektivität', as writers turned to personal themes and a confessional manner. The frequency of biographical works by writers, generally aged between thirty and forty, portraying their deceased fathers or mothers resulted in the terms 'Väterliteratur' and 'Mütterliteratur' being readily applied by reviewers and publishers.[15] Literature about fathers usually focused on the daughter's or son's struggle with the father's private and political power, linked to his activities or passivity during the Third Reich, and showed an often 'futile struggle to break away from paternal dominance and establish autonomous selfhood'.[16] Novels about mothers were mainly written from the daughter's perspective. These too explored a process of separation and individuation but centring the mother-daughter bond and any recrimination often being less historically or politically motivated.[17] Lack of communication, the inability to express oneself without inhibition or fear of reprisals, caused the greatest rift between child and parent. In most of these literary obituaries the narrator displayed a need, not only to understand the father or mother, but also to discover his/her own identity and worth.

Whereas many works portrayed painful parent-child relationships, more recent examples of the genre offer parental portraits less weighed down by guilt. The greater distance from the Third Reich is worth noting. In Margit Schreiner's memoir *Nackte Väter* (1999), for instance, which focuses on the father's deterioration and death, there is no suggestion that the daughter desires separation from her father.[18] At times physical closeness borders on the erotic, but remains innocent, unlike Alissa Walser's portrayal of a seemingly incestuous relationship between father and daughter in her short story 'Geschenkt' of 1992, which caused quite a sensation due to the author's father being Martin Walser.[19] Here was a young newcomer to the literary scene, who had the temerity to write tongue-in-cheek about a daughter-father relationship in an explicitly sexual way, whilst the father figure in the story as well as her own father, a highly acclaimed author, were still alive. Even more significantly this story, like Schreiner's novel, did not question the father's conduct under National Socialism and so marks a shift in focus in the genre.

In contrast, the older generation of established writers continue to this day to write bitterly, indeed almost spitefully about their parents. Back in 1980 at the height of 'Väterliteratur' as a trend, Christoph Meckel had written a critical account, entitled *Suchbild. Über meinen Vater,* a memoir of his father, the writer Eberhard Meckel, who died in 1969. The portrait had a documentary quality, since it included excerpts from his father's poetry and war diaries, which highlighted the professional activities of a man who was once loved but after the war hated by his children for his conformity. Whilst the portrayal is damning, there is a sense of regret for missed opportunities to understand one another. No such emotion is evident in Meckel's portrait of his mother, *Suchbild. Meine Mutter*, published in 2002, shortly after her death but written, until the last two pages, while she was alive.[20] Meckel charts the upbringing, marriage and middle-class lifestyle of his mother until her death in an old people's home at the age of 92. Having felt unloved by his mother from when he was a small boy, the narrator comments on the first page with a sense of relief and shock (for the reader as well): 'ich habe meine Mutter nicht geliebt'.[21] Perhaps because of his own age, the only emotional understanding of his mother's life the author shows is empathy with the ageing process (in June 2005 Meckel celebrated his 70th birthday):

> Es ist in der Art ihres Altseins etwas, das mich berührt. Ich sehe eine Frau, die um ihr Selbstbild kämpft, mit allen Ausflüchten, Listen und Täuschungen, die ihr verfügbar sind. Ich sehe sie in der Bitternis ihres Alters.[22]

A positive aspect of the mother's old age to which Meckel devotes just one paragraph is that she becomes a grandmother, which brings her untold joy and gives her a new lease of life in her last years. Psychologists highlight the birth of a grandchild as 'a defining moment – a grand passage', whereby the grandmother is given another chance; she is no longer on the front line, she 'can just watch the show'.[23] Meckel's mother figure acquires a new role as grandmother, which, because of the physical distance between her and her grandchildren, involves no responsibility, but brings a new meaning into her life. As a child, the narrator had had little to do with his maternal grandmother, apart from obligatory thank-you letters for Christmas and birthday presents, and occasional visits. The adult narrator can only recall a friendly, old matron-figure with soft skin, her grey hair tied in a bun, wearing dark clothes and grey glasses. These brief references encapsulate the essence of the stereotypical image of the grandmother.

Such images are being assigned to history as a new generation of young German women writers portray modern grandmothers in their fiction. Their depictions accord with what sociologists tell us of grandmothers in contemporary Western society. Research into grandmotherhood is still in its infancy, especially in Europe, which is surprising, when estimates suggest that the average life expectancy of women in industrialised countries could reach ninety.[24] By the middle of this century, it is predicted that more than half of the population of Europe will be over 65.[25] Furthermore, adults used to be grandparents for an average of ten years; nowadays the range is between 20-40 years and for the next generation the role of grandparenting is likely to extend to half of their life. In all cultures the term 'grandmother' has been historically associated with older women, but in the twentieth century and even more so now the definition of 'older' shifted with changes in life expectancy. Longevity and lower birth rates have also transformed social roles grandmothers play and the cultural images.[26] Long gone is the image of the kindly old woman with her silver hair in a bun, as Meckel depicted, dressed in bonnets, shawls and aprons, baking in the kitchen or knitting by the fireside. Of course, as the novelist Shena Mackay points out, 'societies have always shown ambivalence towards and a tendency to stereotype the granny figure, who appears variously as matriarch or monster, wise woman, fairy godmother or wicked witch.'[27] Although not an actual grandmother, Frau Oktober, the 72-year-old woman in Karen Duve's story 'Im tiefen Schnee ein stilles Heim' (1999) does initially embody the good grandmotherly traits of sweetness and kindness but then horribly metamorphoses into a monstrous creature, reminiscent of the witch in Grimms' 'Hansel and Gretel' fairy tale.[28] In contrast to Duve's horrific witch, the sentimental stereotype is glorified in children's storybooks, in greeting cards, in advertising, even in knitting patterns. Dominant cultural stereotypes of old women and grandmothers long evoked their difference and otherness, whether in the figure of the witch or the sweet old lady, which Duve satirises by eerily combining them. But grandmothers are now losing their difference as they become more integrated into 'normal' working life, whether they work themselves or care for the children so that the parents may work. In a recent survey it was discovered that the average twenty-first century grandmother was 69 years old, but only felt 48.[29]

Research on grandparents is more developed in America than in Europe and offers a useful analysis of styles of grandparenting.[30] In the early sixties Neugarten and Weinstein already listed five: the formal, with clear divisions between parenting and grandparenting; the informal and playful; the distant grandparents, who rarely see their grandchildren; the surrogate parents, who take on responsibility for the grandchildren; and the wise grandparents, who share skills and knowledge with the new generation.[31] Of course a mixture of styles is more than likely to be the norm. In her 2004 study of maternal relationships Miller-Day notes that 'for many women, using mother and grandmother as referents is actually part of the process of carving out a unique identity.'[32] In the 1970s and 1980s when father and mother memoirs dominated the German book market, theory focused on the need for separation from the parental figure to achieve individuation as an autonomous individual, especially in the case of the mother/daughter relationship.[33] Over the past decade, however, identity theorists have begun to acknowledge the development of individuality within relationships, and, as Miller-Day notes, are moving 'towards a paradigm of the embedded self, or self in relation.'[34]

This latter position helps to explain why in the genre of 'Mütterliteratur' so many daughters were even as adults still struggling to differentiate themselves from their mothers but staying emotionally connected to her.[35] By contrast, the grandmother/granddaughter relation is usually freer from such power struggles and sense of ambivalence.[36] Compared to the 1970s and 1980s there is also less of a cultural gap between the generations.[37] The young are less radical and the old less reactionary, so that generation conflict is less likely, while in Germany, as the distance from the Third Reich grows, some family narratives appear to be less burdened by all the guilt associated with this particular period of history. As we shall see, this is true of the grandmother portrayals by Erpenbeck and Wetzel, whose stories also underscore the belief of many child experts that the grandparent/grandchild relationship is second in emotional importance only to the parent/child relationship.

In Erpenbeck's collection of short stories, *Tand*, the figure of the grandmother appears not only in the title story, but twice more, firstly, in 'Sibirien', for which, as noted earlier, Erpenbeck had won the Jury Prize in 2001 at the Klagenfurt literary festival.[38] In 'Sibirien' the adult daughter learns about the strong and passionate character of her grandmother second hand from her father. In particular he recalls the day his mother returned from three years captivity in Siberia and on finding her husband in the arms of another woman, literally dragged the woman by her hair out of the house. This reversal of the usual gender roles evidenced in 'Heimkehrer-Literatur' does also have a comic effect. Then there is the final story of the collection, 'Anzünden oder Abreisen', which is just five pages long and reads like a summary of the granddaughter's life, who is, as in the 'Tand' story, the narrator. Here the theme of decay and death pervades the story, and reminds us of the seven ages of man, or rather of woman, as each of the seven paragraphs highlights a different role played by the narrator up until what appears to be her death.[39] One moment she is a child, then a young woman, who as she grows older becomes more like her mother.[40] Finally, like the grandmother in 'Tand', she too becomes weak and infirm, and spends all her time sitting and waiting for visitors. Worth noting is that exactly the same image of the grandmother and even the same words as in 'Tand' are repeated in the paragraph devoted to the granddaughter-grandmother relationship. Such repetition suggests that the author places great importance on both the person and her role as grandmother. All three grandmother-figures allude to Jenny Erpenbeck's grandmother in real life, Hedda Zinner, who had herself been an established GDR dramatist and novelist in the fifties and sixties and had lived in exile in Vienna, Hungary and the Soviet Union during the Nazi dictatorship and war years. The idea for Erpenbeck's debut novel *Geschichte vom alten Kind* had come from her grandmother, who had been corresponding with a 14 year-old hospital patient, who turned out to be a 30 year-old woman.

In the title story 'Tand' the narrator describes in a series of snapshots the effects, both physical and mental, of the ageing process on her grandmother, a famous recitalist, with whom as a child she used to spend her summer holidays.[41] The predominant use of the present tense allows the reader to grow up with the granddaughter and grow old with the grandmother until the final farewell. The young granddaughter's curiosity about her elderly grandmother's appearance and her activities awaken the readers' senses.[42] We too feel the papery thin skin of her hand as it shimmers like mother of pearl in the summer sunshine; we see the grandmother dressed in a hand-knitted bikini, on her head a striped bathing-hat, on her feet rubber bathing shoes decorated with flowers; and we see her floating on her back in the lake, her nose sticking out of the water like the tail fin of a shark; Erpenbeck uses the colloquial phrase of 'den Toten Mann schwimmen' for 'to float on one's back', for the German reader the first premonition of the demise of the grandmother.[43] We too hear her practising her recitals behind closed doors and hear her putting on different voices, sometimes a young girl, sometimes a man. The child-narrator is only able to watch and listen from a distance. The relationship changes as she becomes an adult and her grandmother becomes increasingly dependent on her help. The bond becomes one of give and take: the grandmother teaches her granddaughter to recite in public to the extent that she takes over this role from her professionally; on the domestic front she learns to run the household in as orderly a way as her grandmother. The adult granddaughter sleeps in the bed next to the now confused old woman, who has become forgetful and no longer recognises her own home, and who calls out 'Tand' in her sleep. On stage she had recited 'Tand, Tand, ist das Gebilde von Menschenhand!' from Fontane's 1879 poem 'Die Brücke am Tay'. For the narrator (and by association, for the reader) the reference is an ominous one, a portent of an event which is prophesised by the three evil witches, reminiscent of the witches in Shakespeare's *Macbeth*, the first line of which introduces the poem: 'When shall we three meet again?'[44] As a child, the narrator had compared the outline of the grandmother's face to that of a witch on account of her sharp features, especially her nose like a shark's fin as she swims. In contrast to Duve's over-kindly old woman turning into a witch, here the witch is a beloved grandmother, but one who is never over-sweet.

Fontane's poem was based on the actual collapse of the railway bridge over the Tay during a storm in 1879, when more than a hundred train passengers drowned. In Erpenbeck's story the battle for survival by the grandmother is similarly one with nature and imminent death to the extent that she is afraid to go to sleep because time is slipping away. For the narrator her grandmother's last role is that of a mummy, 'die sich bei ihrer Entdeckung in Staub verwandelt und auffliegt.'[45] By the close of the story the grandmother is asleep in hospital with her arms outstretched towards her granddaughter, who has just embraced her for the first time. In having written this story, Erpenbeck has undertaken an act of literary mummification by ensuring that the grandmother is preserved in her words, just as she once took over the words her grandmother made her learn. The notion of the soul flying away also ties in with the grandmother's belief, one, which is repeated in 'Anzünden oder Abreisen', that she is on her way to the Golden Fleece. In Christian terms the Golden Fleece is symbolic of Christ.[46] At no point does the narrator refer directly to death by using the word 'Tod' or the verb 'sterben'. Likewise, there is no mention of love or hatred for grandmother or granddaughter. Instead the matter-of-fact tone, the innocent and amusing thoughts of a child (maybe her grandmother's many voices are due to the fact that she eats calves brains?), the uncompromising depiction of the effects of old age poignantly illustrates a relationship founded on mutual respect. With reference to Neugarten's and Weinstein's list of grandparenting styles, this story clearly illustrates the wise grandmother, who shares her knowledge and skills with her grandchild. Here Erpenbeck's use of the motif of mummification, the way in which she plays with the idea of creativity being linked to death rather than birth and her transmuting of the grandmother's body into the body of literature, lends an extra poignancy to the genre of 'Grossmutterliteratur'.

As in 'Tand', the narrator of Wetzel's story 'Schlaf' is the granddaughter, who as a child also spends most of her time with her grandmother, so much so that the grandmother becomes her legal guardian for six months, thereby taking on the role of surrogate mother.[47] Written in the simple past tense, this is a story without reflective commentary. The child narrator uses predominantly sentences with just main clauses to record everyday life with her grandmother. Through this minimalist approach to language, the author reduces the content to the bare essentials. In essence, the reader adopts the perspective of the child and only knows as little or as much as she does, for instance, that the mother suffers from some mental illness and often leaves her daughter with her mother, while she is in a clinic. For the granddaughter this means a move from town to village, a new school and a new freedom: her grandmother lets her sleep as long as she likes to the extent that she even encourages her to skip school in the belief that she can learn more from staying at home and reading the classics. This does change, however, after a court visit and the legal adoption by the grandmother because she is questioned about the child's absence from school. It is at this point too that we note how the grandmother's style of grandparenting is forced to alter according to her new role as surrogate mother: for her the boundaries become blurred because she takes on longer term care of her granddaughter. Her desire to keep her granddaughter permanently is the cause of conflict between herself and her daughter and clearly causes stress for the child. At the close of the story the young narrator is torn between the two adults. Yet, as in Erpenbeck's story, there is no expression by either the granddaughter or grandmother of love or hatred. Both stories focus on the strong-willed, independent, working grandmother. Neither granddaughter is resentful about spending significant amounts of time with her respective grandmother. Both authors depict the grandmother as having the most influential role in the life of her granddaughter. In neither story is there any mention of a grandfather.

The majority of father and mother memoirs were, and still are, written in the first person so that the narrator appears to voice the thoughts of the author. The aim of this study has been to hear the voice of the granddaughter. It was therefore logical to select prose texts written from the perspective of the granddaughter-cum-narrator in our discussion of the term 'Grossmütterliteratur'. Moreover, the figure of the grandmother had to be the protagonist, just as the parents had been in 'Väterliteratur' and 'Mütterliteratur'. What is particularly striking in these recent works by younger German writers is their ability to portray a close family bond in a matter-of-fact manner and to do so without any hidden agenda. As noted earlier, this third generation of writers is less weighed down by any historical burden, thus there are no recriminations evident in their stories. The affirmative tone and perspective is underscored by the decision to portray the grandmother, which in contrast to the mother/father portrayals, is also less likely to be burdened by familial tensions. The shift in focus to the grandmother is therefore quite liberating for the writer, as is partly evidenced by the return to comic images often found in fairy tales, and supports the earlier reference in Hage's second article about the more relaxed approach of this new generation of writers, their 'Unbekümmertheit'. With the advent of 'Grossmütterliteratur' there appears to be a trend away from the post-war literary tradition of family narratives as a direct testimony about the Third Reich. The majority of Germans today are not directly influenced by National Socialism, whereas the years 1989/90 have made their mark and resulted in the search for a new political and cultural identity in a new Berlin Republic. Erpenbeck and Wetzel have in common the German language but they write from an individual perspective and in their own style with scarcely any mention of their homeland and no reference to a collective past within the analysed texts, because these stories are not about being German. In an age of globalisation such narratives are less likely to be rooted in a specific country and/or a historical period of time. Instead, the past is held on to via the grandparent and the comfort of the old and familiar. When political themes do emerge, as in Erpenbeck's 'Sibirien', they are treated with a confidence and lack of guilt which judging by the volume of stories as a whole may appear as an inheritance from the grandmother as well as signify a generational shift towards a new self-understanding among younger German writers in general.

Both of the authors featured write with confidence which may come in part because they have successful jobs and/or experience in other areas of the arts: Jenny Erpenbeck stages her own operas and musicals, Maike Wetzel has worked in journalism and is currently studying at the 'Hochschule für Fernsehen und Film' in Munich. Unlike the earlier authors of father and mother memoirs, these granddaughters appear to have benefited from the wisdom of their grandmothers and have expressed their appreciation in these affectionate portrayals. They are comfortable with what they do and confident about who they are and, above all, they refuse to be pigeon-holed.

Notes

1 Volker Hage, 'Ganz schön abgedreht,' *Der Spiegel*, 12, 22 March 1999, pp. 244-246 (here: p. 244).

2 Volker Hage, 'Die Enkel kommen', *Der Spiegel*, 41, 11 Oct. 1999, pp. 244-254.

3 In 2005 Erpenbeck published her second novel *Wörterbuch*, dedicated to her father, John Erpenbeck, also a writer as well as a philosopher, psychologist and physicist. The narrator is a young woman, who turns out to be adopted, reflecting on her childhood in an unnamed South American country. With the realisation that her protected childhood was not what she thought comes an overwhelming sense of no longer being able to trust a memory, feeling or word.

4 Hage, 'Die Enkel kommen', p. 248.

5 'Sibirien' appears in Erpenbeck's second publication, a collection of short stories, entitled *Tand*, Eichborn: Frankfurt am Main, 2003, pp 97-112.

6 For a positive reception by reviewers, see for example, Hilde Malcomess, 'Frau mit Röntgenblick,' *Rheinischer Merkur*, 26 Oct. 2001, p. 25.

7 Wiebke Eden, *Keine Angst vor grossen Gefühlen*, edition Ebersbach: Berlin, 2001.

8 Wiebke Eden, 'Maike Wetzel: "Wenn der Knoten platzt, wird Schreiben toll",' in: Eden, *Keine Angst vor grossen Gefühlen*, pp. 198-212 (here: p. 211).

9 Helga Königsdorf, *Die Entsorgung der Grossmutter*, Aufbau-Verlag: Berlin, 1997; Helen Flöss, *Löwen im Holz*, Haymon: Innsbruck, 2003.

10 Petra Oelker, ed., *Eine starke Verbindung: Mütter, Töchter und andere Weibergeschichten*, Rowohlt: Reinbek bei Hamburg, 2000, pp. 167-179.

11 Monika Maron, *Pawels Briefe*, Fischer: Frankfurt am Main, 1999.

12 Reinhard Jirgl, *Die Unvollendeten*, Hanser: München, 2003.

13 Melitta Breznik's name is not associated with the 'Miss Miracle' group, yet born in 1961 she is a newcomer who fits the age group.

14 Breznik's first novel *Nachtdienst* (1995) similarly extended our understanding of father memoirs in centring not on the daughter's searching for a sense of identity but on the father's need for his family. For a detailed discussion of the (ir)relevance of the term 'Väterliteratur' in the 1990s, see Petra M Bagley, 'Exposing our Fathers: Alzheimer's and Alcoholism in an Austrian Setting,' in: Gisela Holfter et al., eds, *Beziehungen und Identitäten: Österreich, Irland und die Schweiz*, Peter Lang: Bern, 2004, pp. 241-254.

15 Recent studies include Emily Jeremiah, *Troubling Maternity: Mothering, Agency, and Ethics in Women's Writing in German of the 1970s and 1980s*, Maney Publishing: Leeds, 2003; Ernestine Schlant, *The Language of Silence: West German Literature and the Holocaust*, Routledge: New York, 1999.

16 Gisela Moffit, *Bonds and Bondage: Daughter-Father Relationships in the Father Memoirs of German-speaking Women Writers of the 1970s*, Peter Lang: New York, 1993, p. 48.

17 Amongst others, Gabriele Wohmann's *Ausflug mit der Mutter* (1976) and Anna Mitgutsch's *Die Züchtigung* (1985). There are of course always significant exceptions, such as Christa Wolf's *Kindheitsmuster* (1976), which does intimately relate family and political history.

18 *Nackte Väter* was Schreiner's fourth novel since she began publishing in 1989. Born 1953 in Linz she is just three years older than Birgit Vanderbeke, who is often grouped together with the younger newcomers.

19 In 1992 Alissa Walser (born 1961) was awarded the Ingeborg Bachmann prize for her reading of 'Geschenkt', which was first printed in *Spiegel* in 1992 (6 July 1992, pp. 182-185) and then later appeared as the first story in a collection, entitled *Dies ist nicht meine ganze Geschichte*, Rowohlt: Reinbek bei Hamburg, 1994.

20 Another author, who first wrote a father memoir, *Der Vater*, in 1980 and later published an autobiographical novel about the death of her mother, entitled *Der Tod meiner Mutter* (1997), is Julian (formerly Jutta) Schutting.

21 Christoph Meckel, *Suchbild. Meine Mutter*, Hanser: München, 2002, p. 7.

22 Meckel, *Suchbild*, p. 115.

23 Gail Sheehy, 'It's about pure love,' *Parade Magazine*, 12 May 2002, pp. 6-7 (here: p. 7).

24 Tessa Blackstone, 'On being a Grandmother,' in: Geoff Dench, ed., *Grandmothers: The Changing Culture*, Transaction: New Brunswick, London, 2002, pp. 83-92 (here: p. 91). Research in Germany on the role of the grandmother has tended to be embedded in larger studies of the family. See, for example, 'Das Online-Familienhandbuch' at:
http://familienhandbuch.de/cmain/f_Aktuelles/a_Elternschaft/s_903.html (accessed on 6.7.05).

25 Paul Henley, 'Population earthquake hits Germany,' *Crossing Continents*, BBC Radio 4, 21 July 2004,
http://news.bbc.co.uk/go/pr/fr//2/hi/programmes/crossing_continents/3910821.stm (accessed on 4.2.05).

26 Most of the social research is to be found in America, where there are numerous support groups for grandparents, data is collected at a national level and there are strong lobbying groups. See, for example, Carole Roy, *The Raging Grannies: Wild Hats, Cheeky Songs and Witty Actions for a Better World*, Black Rose Books: Montreal, 2004. Since 1987 the Raging Grannies have become a Canadian institution of protest with more than 50 groups across Canada, America, Australia and Greece, where the Greek Grannies call themselves the Furies! These grandmothers claim their space on the political scene, challenging the stereotypes of older women. In 1994 the American comic book series, *Defiant Comics*, launched a new super-person, a 55 year-old grey-haired grandmother named 'Glory', who conquers monsters from outer space. In the same year the *New York Sunday Times* published photos of image-conscious men and women in their nineties in the fashion section. Almost a decade earlier, Scottish TV ran 30 episodes of 'Supergran', a children's series based on the books of Forrest Wilson, in which Granny Smith, blessed with superhuman powers, defends her village against villains. These few examples show how perception of grandmothers is being re-shaped by socio-cultural messages as well as personal experience.

27 Shena Mackay, 'Going down my nan's,' in: Geoff Dench, ed., *Grandmothers: The Changing Culture*, Transaction: New Brunswick, London, 2002, pp. 123-132 (here: p. 123.

28 Karen Duve, 'Im tiefen Schnee ein stilles Heim,' in: *Keine Ahnung*, Suhrkamp: Frankfurt am Main, 1999, pp. 109-165.

29 Susannah Cullinane, 'Supergrans – the new girl power,' *BBC News Online*, 1.6.2004, http://news.bbc.co.uk/go/pr/fr/-/2/hi/uk_news/3855823.stm (accessed on 4.2.05).

30 See, for example, Arthur Kornhaber, *Contemporary Grandparenting*, Sage: Thosand Oaks, 1996. More recently sociologists, Reitzes and Mutran, have explored the overlapping meanings and experiences of being a parent and grandparent: Donald Reitzes and Elizabeth Mutran, 'Grandparent Identity, Intergenerational Family Identity, and Well-Being,' *Journals of Gerontology Series B: Psychological Sciences and Social Sciences*, 59 (2004), 213-222.

31 B. Neugarten and K.Weinstein, 'The changing American grandparent,' *Journal of Marriage and the Family*, vol.xxvi, part 2, 1964, as quoted by Jan Pahl, 'Our changing lives,' in: Dench, *Grandmothers*, p. 110.

32 Michelle A Miller-Day, *Communication among Grandmothers, Mothers and Adult Daughters: A Qualitative Study of Maternal Relationships*, Lawrence Erlbaum: New Jersey, 2004, p. 99.

33 Amongst others, Adrienne Rich, *Of Woman Born: Motherhood as Experience and Institution*, Norton: New York, 1976.

34 Michelle A Miller-Day, *Communication among Grandmothers, Mothers and Adult Daughters: A Qualitative Study of Maternal Relationships*, Lawrence Erlbaum: New Jersey, 2004, p. 100.

35 See, for example, William W. Wilmot, *Relational Communication*, McGraw-Hill: New York, 1994.

36 Susan V. Bosak, *How to Build the Grandma Connection*, Communication Project: Whitchurch-Stouffville, 2000.

37 The focus is here on the mainstream or majority population; the situation is rather different in immigrant or ethnic-minority communities.

38 Erpenbeck 'Sibirien', in: *Tand*.

39 This story was first published in the *Frankfurter Allgemeine Zeitung*, 5 June 2001.

40 In this story Erpenbeck's narrator hates the fact that she looks and sounds increasingly like mother, as if her own identity were slipping away as she grows older: 'Ich bin alt geworden, damit meine Mutter wieder eine Haut bekommt, in der sie sich breitmachen kann' ('Anzünden oder Abreisen', in: *Tand*, pp. 119-124 (here: p. 123). The emotions expressed here are reminiscent of Anna Mitgutsch's narrator in *Die Züchtigung*: 'Sie hat sich in mich verwandelt, sie hat mich geschaffen und ist in mich hineingeschlüpft...'. Waltraud Anna Mitgutsch, *Die Züchtigung*, dtv: München, 1985, p. 246.

41 'Tand' first appeared in a international collection of stories which highlighted the strong bond between mother and daughter as well as other females, including grandmothers, aunts, teachers, even neighbours. See: Petra Oelker, ed., *Eine starke Verbindung: Mütter, Töchter und andere Weibergeschichten*, Rowohlt: Reinbek bei Hamburg, 2000 (for 'Tand' pp. 51-63).

42 In an interview in 2001 Erpenbeck commented on how attractive she found old people: 'Alte Leute findet Jenny Erpenbeck spannend. Weil sie Abstand zum Leben haben. Sie können es von außen betrachten, sagt sie, haben Distanz dazu.' Jörg Petrasch, 'Abstand zum Leben,' *taz*, 25 Oct. 2001, p. 27.

43 Jenny Erpenbeck, 'Tand,' in: *Tand*, pp. 35-51 (here: p. 37)

44 Act 1, scene 1 of Shakespeare's *Macbeth*.

45 Erpenbeck, 'Tand,', p. 50; and 'Anzünden oder Abreisen,' in: *Tand*, pp. 119-124 (here: p. 120).

46 'Christian symbolism considered the Golden Fleece an image of Christ who rescued the children, helping them to soar above the darkness of the pagan world as long as they clung to his fleece (teachings),' Suzetta Tucker, 'Christ Story, Ram Page,' *Christ Story, Christian Bestiary*, 1998, available at http://ww2.netnitco.net/users/legend01/ram.htm (accessed on 43.05).

47 Maike Wetzel, 'Schlaf' in: *Lange Tage*, Fischer: Frankfurt am Main, 2003, pp. 115-135.

Franziska Meyer

‚und dabei heißt es immer *aufbruchstimmung'*. Das Verschwinden einer Metropole in ihren Texten

This article looks at a number of recently published novels and stories set in Berlin. It analyses common patterns in how these different texts map the city and its eastern and western districts. The essay argues that the construction of local and socially derelict city spaces in these texts not only challenges notions of a 'Neue Metropole' and its neoliberal 'Generation Berlin', but also depicts Berlin as a backdrop for self-obsessed, alienated characters who seek to avoid disturbing encounters with alien others. In their celebration of disengagement, these texts tend to turn the 'New Berlin' into an empty, anti-civic space, without difference or variety, an urban desert full of people, but empty of citizens.

> Ich selbst befinde mich im Zentrum, ungefähr zwischen N12 und T7, und dieses Zentrum löst sich langsam auf. Am Tiergarten, abgegriffen vom vielen Blättern, kleben Krümel einstigen Grüns. Siegessäule und Brandenburger Tor sind völlig in Knickfurchen verschwunden. Am schlimmsten aber ist es um die Gegend rund um das nördliche Neukölln bestellt, denn dort ist ein Loch. Ich weiß, daß ich auf das Loch zurutsche [...] und in die dahinterliegende Dunkelheit stürzen werde. [...] Langsam rutsche ich mit bis aufs äußerste in Fluchtrichtung geneigtem Hals [...] in Richtung Moritzplatz. [...] Es gelingt mir, [...] zum Kanal zu rollen [...]. Vor mir ist jetzt nur noch das Wasser. [...] Kopfüber [...] tauche ich in ein Blau [...] eine schönwetterhimmelfarbene Druckschicht, die mich nach Osten trägt.[1]

Die Mitte ein Knick, verwischt sind die bedeutungsmächtigen Symbole Berliner Geschichte; an den schlimmsten Rändern Neuköllns entgeht Inka Pareis Schattenboxerin in diesem Stadtplantraum dem Absturz in ein schwarzes Loch, um im Kreuzberger Landwehrkanal in den Osten zu treiben.

Ein Ich allein und doch im Zentrum, Auflösungserscheinungen einer imaginierten Mitte, Kontrollverlust, Flucht und Selbstbehauptung: der Alptraum von Pareis Schattenboxerin soll hier den Ausgangspunkt einer kursorischen Tour durch jüngere Berlin-Texte markieren, die in unterschiedlichen, vornehmlich realistischen Erzählmodi ihre meist jüngeren Protagonistinnen mit der Hauptstadt konfrontieren. Besichtigt werden neben Pareis preisgekrönter *Schattenboxerin* (1999; abgekürzt: Sch) folgende Texte anderer westdeutscher Autorinnen: Anke Stellings gesammelte Berliner Unglücke (*Glückliche Fügung*, 2004; GF), Unda Hörners Umzugs-Roman *Unter Nachbarn* (2000), Judith Hermanns Inszenierungen Berliner Abwesenheiten (*Nichts als Gespenster*, 2003), der Stadthaß-Roman der Popliteratin Sibylle Berg (*Sex II*, 1998; S) sowie die Szenebeschreibungen der Poptexte Tanja Dückers' (*Spielzone*, 1999; Sp. *Café Brazil*, 2001; CB) und Alexa Hennig von Langes (mit Daniel Haaksman und Till Müller-Klug) im Tagebuchroman *Mai 3D* (2000).

Ostdeutsche Blicke auf die vereinigte Stadt öffnen Antje Rávic Strubels hochgelobtes Debüt, der New-York-Roman *Offene Blende* (2001), und der fingierte Kriminalroman *Fremd Gehen. Ein Nachtstück* (2002; FG). Provokante Berlin-Perspektiven inszenieren schließlich die Texte der mehrfach preisgekrönten Österreicherin Kathrin Röggla (*Abrauschen*, 1997; A. *Irres Wetter*, 2000; IW).

Nicht die durchaus disparaten Themen und Schreibweisen dieser Berlin-Texte, sondern Gemeinsamkeiten in den Strategien der Lesbar-machung der Stadt stehen hier im Vordergrund. Welche topographischen Muster strukturieren die Wahrnehmung der Stadt? Wie verschränken sich diese mit den imaginierten Landkarten des vereinigten Berlin?[2] Und wie verhalten sich schließlich gegenwärtige Texte von Autorinnen zu dem Ruf der Medien nach einer Berliner Republik und der zu ihr passenden Generation? „Der Trend hat immer Recht", weiß *Die Welt*: „Eine ganze Generation junger Autoren faßt den Hauptstadt-Kult in Worte".[3]

In hegemoniale Diskurse der Gegenwartsliteratur hat sich die Trope der ‚Generation', „a deeply national concept", fest eingeschrieben.[4] „Muß man eine Generation haben? Im Moment scheint es so, sind es unsere großen 15 Minuten. Wieviele 15 Minuten ist ein Schriftsteller-leben?", fragt provokativ Terézia Mora.[5] Wenn Richard Herzinger von „‚Generation' als kulturelle[m] Kampfbegriff" spricht und staunt, daß der Osten „in den neuesten Generationsdebatten verblüffenderweise so gut wie gar nicht vor [kommt]",[6] so wird erstaunlicherweise übersehen, daß eben diese absentia der ‚Generation Berlin' aufs deutlichste einge-schrieben ist. Denn das Paradigma der Generation – diese „mythisch-narrative Form der Zeitrechnung jenseits von Kalender und Historio-graphie" –, das jetzt von kollektiven biologischen Identitäten spricht, insistiert gerade auf historische und politische Zäsuren.[7] Eine „Berliner Republik jenseits vergangenheitspolitischer Alarmreflexe zu begründen", diese „Aufgabe" formulierte der Erfinder des Begriffs, der Soziologe Heinz Bude, für die „Generation Berlin",[8] um auf den Nullpunkt, eine historische tabula rasa, zu orientieren, ohne den Osten: „Schon meldet sich eine ‚junge Generation' ohne Erinnerung an 1945 oder 1968, aber mit eigenen Erfahrungen in den neuen Erregungssphären von Wissen, Macht und Geld. Die Zukunft großer Erwartungen dürfte für sie wichtiger sein als die Vergangenheit großer Zäsuren."[9] Und schon ist auch die Er-innerung an 1989 und das davor in Phantasmagorien täglich neu zu erfin-dender urbaner Jetztzeiten verschwunden. Dies erlaubt nun auch neue Kanonisierungen der Gegenwartsliteratur. Nicht zuletzt, wenn es heißt, die „Gattung der Wendeliteratur" sei „buchstäblich vom Stadtthema auf-gesogen" worden, und „der Stadtmensch" sei „eine ungleich schillerndere Figur als das zoon politicon".[10] Solche Juxtapositionen beanspruchen nicht nur eine westliche Deutungshoheit über einen Textkörper, der vor allem von Pluralität gekennzeichnet ist; zugleich etabliert das Lob neuer „Berlinunbefangenheiten"[11] – ,Wir kennen nur noch Berliner!' – Geschichtsvergessenheit als neues Gattungsmerkmal: „Vergangenheitspolitik eignet sich weder zur Bestimmung außenpolitischer Orientierungen noch zur Reaktion auf gefährliche Bewegungen von rechts", verkündet Bude: „Vor der Zukunft stehen wir im freien Feld."[12] Und dieses Feld ist tatsächlich umkämpft.

Allein in der Wahl ihres Handlungsortes bedienen die hier besichtigten Texte einen florierenden literarischen Markt. Die Zahl der allein zwischen 1989 und 1999 publizierten Berlin-Prosa-Texte umfaßt mehr als 220 Titel.[13] Doch zeigen uns viele der hier besichtigten Texte nicht nur geographisch ein relativ kleines Neues Berlin in deutlich lokalisierbaren Ausschnitten, wenn sich die gesuchten Stadterfahrungen immer wieder auf den Ostberliner Bezirk Prenzlauer Berg oder das westliche Neukölln und Kreuzberg konzentrieren. Den ikonisierten Räumen der neuen Mitte, einer Hauptstadt, in der „jeder zweite" „Salsa tanzt",[14] weichen die meisten Texte programmatisch aus. Potsdamer Platz, Hackescher Markt und Friedrichstraße oder gar der Kurfürstendamm werden vermieden. Stattdessen führen sie uns an der Seite unbehauster und singularisierter Bewohnerinnen in außen wie innen verwahrloste Stadträume. Auf „den Straßen der normale Großstadtscheiß. Baulärm, Verkehrslärm, Menschenlärm", dies das Szenario in Sibylle Bergs *Sex II*, der ein Inferno ruinierter Großstadttypen vorführt, zentriert um ein illusionsloses Ich, das schon auf der ersten Seite nichts als Ablenkung von „der großen Stadt" sucht: „ein Haufen Mist, den niemand bestellt hat [...]. Niemand braucht die Stadt".[15]

Anke Stellings Berlin-Erzählungen der *Glücklichen Fügung*, Inka Pareis *Schattenboxerin* und auch Tanja Dückers' poppige *Spielzone* situieren ihre Figuren inmitten „vergammelnder städtischer Substanzen", in „mit Schutt und Müll übersäten", „verrümpelten" Hinterhöfen noch nicht sanierter Mietshäuser des Ostens.[16] Strubels Kreuzberger Protagonistin in *Fremd Gehen* imaginiert die gesamte Stadt als Müllhaufen, wenn die nächtliche Straße zur Prärie triumphaler Selbstbehauptung wird:

> Ich fuhr auf meinem Rad durch die Straßen, kippte unterwegs Mülleimer um, berauscht von der Eintönigkeit, in der sie hinter mir auf den Asphalt knallten und dann all das alte, abgegriffene, ausgelaugte, entleerte, das zerschredderte, zerfetzte, zerdengelte, das nutzlos übriggebliebene, unbrauchbare [...] zerstörte Material vergangener Reize in der gesamten Stadt auf die gleiche Weise auf den Gehweg rutschte. Oder ich fuhr nur so, das Gesicht in die Nacht gelegt, bis mir ein Fußgänger vors Vorderrad lief und ich ihn gerade fest genug streifte, daß es ihn umwarf, ich jedoch nicht mal strauchelte.[17]

Der einzige deutlich markierte Ostberliner Bezirk der großen vereinigten Stadt, auf dem der Blick westdeutscher Autorinnen ausführlicher verweilt, ist der nach der Wende rapide gentrifizierte Prenzlauer Berg: ein

„Transitbezirk", dessen Bevölkerung zwischen 1991 und 1996 zur Hälfte „ausgetauscht" wurde und der einen „Bevölkerungsumbruch" sah, der „sonst nur aus Kriegszeiten bekannt ist".[18] Umgekehrt begeben sich die Romane der Potsdamerin Strubel (die beide von einer ost-westdeutschen Frauenbeziehung erzählen) an den Kreuzberger Landwehrkanal, in einen Bezirk, dessen Gegenwart von der Mehrheit der hier besichtigten Texte westdeutscher Autorinnen abgeschrieben wird; oder richten aus dem distanzierten Abstand des New Yorks der Jahre 1995-97 den weiter schweifenden Blick auf die Vielfalt disparater östlicher und westlicher Stadtgegenden.[19]

Das Äußere eines als ramponiert wahrgenommenen Stadtkörpers spiegelt sich in seinen Innenräumen. Durch Strubels Kreuzberger Wohnung pfeift „nachts der Wind durch die undichten Fenster [...] und der Küchenboden schimmelte" (FG99). Stellings Figuren leben in Wohnungen mit „faustgroßen" Löchern im „Küchenfenster", wegen „der unbenutzten Außenklos roch es im ganzen Treppenhaus nach Kaninchenstall";[20] fasziniert von den „muffelnde[n] Außenklos"[21] dieser Stadt sind auch Unda Hörner und Parei. Illegal lebt die Schattenboxerin mit ihrer „Außenklo-Partnerin" im jetzt privatisierten Hinterhaus des Prenzlauer Bergs: „umzingelt [...] von Asseln, Schaben und kleinen Ratten", mit „regelmäßig[en]" Rohrbrüchen, „die dafür sorgen, daß Scheiße und Spülwasser der Nachbarn von unten ins Waschbecken hochkriechen"; die Farbe im Hausflur „ähnelt [...] dem Kot, den die Schäferhunde hier aufs Pflaster werfen" (Sch8-10, 58, 7). Nur der immer wieder evozierte Geruch erfüllt zeitlose Erwartungen an Berlin-Prosa der Nachkriegszeit: „meine Schuhe sind voller Hundekot [...] ich weiß, daß ich die Schuhe voller Scheiße habe, weil ich sie rieche. Und ich weiß, daß ich mit diesem Dreck eine Prüfung bestehen muß." (S33) So Bergs wortreicher Haßgesang auf die hier nicht mehr benannte Großstadt, die (nicht nur) in diesem Bild existentialistischer Konfrontationen als die deutsche Hauptstadt zu identifizieren ist.

Doch verspricht der Rückzug in Innenräume weder ein Versteck, noch einen Reflexionsraum, aus dem das Ich als ein anderes wieder vor die Tür treten könnte. Diese Berliner Wohnungen sind Fluchtorte, allenfalls Schutz vor infektuösen Berührungen einer „ungeschützte[n] Hohlheit" auf der Straße: Fern der Uni und dem „aufdringlichen Rasierwasser" der „Erstsemester" bleibt Strubels Student „in diesem Zimmer über der Stadt" sitzen, „während sie da unten der blöden Individualitätsnorm hinterherrasten" (FG146, 79); von der Stadt abgehängt sitzt auch Kathrin Rögglas 39jähriger Karl „in seiner kreuzberger wohnung [...] und drohte [...] verlorenzugehen, im emaillächeln der jüngeren" und der „männer im betrieblook".[22] Eingepfercht in „[s]chleichende Verwahrlosung" treffen wir Stellings Sonja:

> Die Temperatur vom Backofen ist nicht mehr kontrollierbar. Die Heizkörper
> werden nur zur Hälfte warm. Irreparabler Diskettenfehler im Laufwerk A.
> Klebriger Film auf der Unterseite des Bügeleisens. [...] Sonja wünschte sich
> ein Heim. Wie es genau aussehen sollte, wußte sie nicht. [...] Die Wege durch
> die Wohnung waren hoffnungslos ausgetreten. (GF22, 30)[23]

Und auch Rögglas junge Protagonistin flieht in eine häusliche
‚Gefangenschaft': „vorbei an der katzenmusik an häusern, zurück in die
wohnung im hinterhaus 2. stock, schließt die tür ab und atmet auf" (A12).

Der Blick aus dem Fenster – zu sehen war „nur das billigleben der
tauben im gegenüberhaus" (A11) – oder das Gewühl der Straße, diese für
die literarische Stadt einmal so ergiebigen Perspektiven, sind in diesen
Texten des Neuen Berlin obsolet geworden. Unüberbrückbar scheinen die
Grenzen zwischen Ich und Stadt, ausgeschlossen ehemals genußvoll ein-
genomme Beobachterpositionen gegenüber den anderen. Beobachtungs-
scharf, doch sich abwendend, sitzt Pareis Schattenboxerin in den neuen
Cafés des Prenzlauer Bergs, wo nur noch verblichene Schriftzüge von
einer Ostberliner Vergangenheit sprechen:

> Früher war hier ein Schuhladen. [...] Mondäne Freiberufler sitzen ruhelos und
> übersättigt vor den Resten ihrer Sektfrühstücke. Drei Handwerker gießen sich
> gegenseitig Schnaps in den Kaffee. [...] Ich [...] nehme mir [...] eine Zeitung
> aus dem ledernen Wandgestell. (Sch43-44)

Auch das ästhetische Material vergangener Reize der Stadt ist un-
brauchbar geworden, dies führen zahlreiche Texte immer wieder vor.
Hier heißt es Abstand zu wahren, und es wird ostentativ weggeschaut –
nicht ohne das Spiel mit falschen Erwartungen auszustellen: „In Berlin
angekommen, stellte sie sich zu der Gruppe von Menschen, die in der
Ankunftshalle auf die Videowand schauten." (GF184)

Draußen treiben die Texte verletzte und gehetzte Figuren durch
Stadtlandschaften, in denen sie jeglicher Begegnung mit anderen auszu-
weichen suchen. „Wie eine Fremde" läuft Pareis Schattenboxerin durch
ihre Geburtsstadt (Sch76). Der öffentliche Raum ist Ort des Anstoß-
nehmens, die Wege führen bestens in den Dönerladen, die U-Bahn oder
ins Kaufhaus. Der urbanen ‚Kakophonie',[24] der Präsenz anderer BewohnerInnen auf der Straße, begegnen diese Neuen (durchaus selbständigen)
Berlinerinnen mit Abwehr, Angst, Mißtrauen oder „Abscheu" (Sch42),
und nicht selten in einer vorwurfsvollen Opferhaltung. Bergs verhohlene
Identitätssuchen, die im Gestus totaler Negation nicht zuletzt das vorge-
stellte Elend ihrer Figuren kolonisieren, räumen mit jedwedem urbanem
Individualitätsversprechen auf: „zum Töten taugt die Stadt, denn was soll
wachsen inmitten von Dreck. [...] Millionen Menschen, dicht, sich
riechend, sich schauend" (S9); mit „verheulte[m] Gesicht" taxiert das
namenlose Ich eine „wirklich moderne Familie" auf der Straße: Vater,
Mutter, Kind, mit „Hosen, die auf der Hälfte des fastfoodfetten Arsches
hängen. [...] Sie wollen [...] glauben, daß das Leben eine geile Sache ist.

[...] Ich habe niemanden. [...] warum laufe ich hier rum, zwischen tausend anderen, ich will doch individuell sein" (S69).

In ihrer Faszination am ärmsten Westberliner Bezirk Neukölln, den programmatischen Revisionen von Zentrum und Peripherie, schreiben sich die Texte von Parei und Dückers nun vom Rande in ein neues allegorisches Zentrum, mit spiegelbildlich verkehrten Repräsentationsfunktionen.[25] „„Null Hauptstadtstreß"", freut sich Dückers' 14jährige Laura (Sp73), in ein „von Tagespolitik unberührtes Neukölln" entweicht Pareis Schattenboxerin (Sch66). Das imaginierte Neukölln der so unterschiedlichen Texte Parei und Dückers, dieser von krasser sozialer Verelendung gezeichnete Bezirk mit der höchsten MigrantInnenpopulation, fungiert als pars pro toto ungemütlicher Stadterfahrungen: „Ihre Nachbarn, das ganze Viertel, die ganze Stadt kotzt sie an", weiß Dückers' freischaffende, die Wohnung kaum verlassende Übersetzerin Elke (Sp81): „Berlin ist offener Vollzug" (Sp55). Die Struktur der *Spielzone* baut auf die plakativen Kontraste des Prenzlauer Bergs – „„Klassenfahrtsstimmung da im Osten"" (Sp58-59) – und ‚unhipper' Kulissen der Armut auf der (lumpen)proletarischen Trashmeile der Hermannstraße, die das hergibt, was der Text braucht: „nichts außer Billigmärkten, Friedhöfen und Pitbulls" (Sp38) oder „im Mülleimer wühlend[e] Penner" (Sp74).

Pareis durchtrainierte junge Schattenboxerin und Dückers' Rentnerin Roswitha begegnen der sozialen Häßlichkeit des Hermannplatzes mit ähnlichen Perspektiven: Überfallen vom Menschenlärm „brüllende[r] Marktfrauen" und „brüllende[r]" Karstadt-Kassiererinnen (Sp44, 43), inmitten „sich Allgemeinplätze zuschreiend[er]" Alter (Sch81). Bedroht von „bettelnden Kindern" beim Gang über den „chaotischen Billigmarkt", wo man angerempelt wird und Angst um seine Handtasche haben muß", unter „Penner[n] mit glasigen Augen", die „Bier auf ihre Schuhe" verschütten, führt Roswithas Fluchtweg „schnurstracks auf Karstadt zu" (Sp39). Vom Bus „ausgespuckt", nach einer „Karussellfahrt der Invaliden" (Sch79), flieht auch die Schattenboxerin über den gleichen „schlechtsortierte[n] Wochenmarkt" (Sch82):

> Mit seitlich ausscherenden Bewegungen entkomme ich den Ausgestiegenen und gerate an die Bordsteinkante [...]. Schnell bin ich [...] eingekeilt und gerate in das typische Sammelsurium unnützer und häßlicher Dinge, die den hiesigen Kaufrausch ausmachen [...]. [...] auf den wenigen Bänken, neben übervollen, mit Senf und alten Kaugummis beschmierten Abfallbehältern sammeln sich Männer [...], um Mädchen anzusprechen, windige Deals einzufädeln oder jemandem gegenüber so zu tun, als ob. Sonst bleibt hier niemand stehen. (Sch81-2)

Hier wird niemand „überspielt von der Eile der anderen" hier nimmt keiner „ein Bad in der Brandung" und sucht schon gar nicht „den ersten Blick".[26] Wo der flanierende Blick die Subjekte der Kontrolle bemächtigt, erfahren diese Städterinnen Kontrollverlust.[27] Pareis indirekte Antwort auf Franz Hessel räumt auf mit Traditionen, aber auch Moden ästhetischer Stadtwahrnehmung, die sich – wie Heinrich Wefings treffende Kritik Berliner Stadtplanung gezeigt hat – in der „Renaissance des Flaneurs"[28] auf historische Muster der Stadtbetrachtung verlassen wollen. Wenn den Figuren etwas fehlt, dann sind es „gegenseitige Reserve und Indifferenz", die psychischen Dispositionen für die „Unabhängigkeit des Individuums", die Georg Simmel (der mit dem Neuen Berlin nicht rechnen konnte) einst als wesentliche Unterscheidungsmerkmale des Groß- vom Kleinstädter identifiziert hatte.[29] Abhängigkeit und tiefe Verstörung von den Eindrücken der großen Stadt, die das Ich ins Zentrum unberechenbarer Anfechtungen versetzt, kennzeichnet die Perspektiven der Neuen Berlinerinnen. In ihrer Abwehr sind diese Figuren zutiefst involviert. Die Straße ist nicht (mehr) tote oder leere Durchgangpassage einer postmodernen Nowhere City, sondern Fluchtmeile und Kriegszone. Hier wäre man am liebsten allein oder haut ganz ab: „Draußen geht also der Wahnsinn weiter", heißt es bei Berg, „[a]ber bald ohne uns. Morgen früh verschwinden wir aus der Stadt. Wir […] versuchen ein Auto anzuhalten, vielleicht eines stehlen. Im Krieg ist alles erlaubt. Hauptsache weg" (S162).[30]

Es sind die Romane der Österreicherin Röggla, die hauptstädtische Ideologeme kontinuierlich als Stimmspuren mitführen und hierin am eindrücklichsten herausfordern. Im unnachgiebigen gehetzten Gehämmere dieser mit Berlin konfrontierten weiblichen Ich-Stimmen fallen Rögglas Texte der immer schon besprochenen Stadt provokativ ins Wort. Rögglas reflektiver sprachkritischer Gestus sticht in die „affirmationsblasen" des Hauptstadttextes, ja, haut ihn den LeserInnen um die Ohren.

> alle reden von berlin, doch was soll das sein. ich meine, wo gibt's noch so was. ich für meinen teil behaupte, es gibt kein berlin, es gibt nur neukölln. […] immer fand ich mich in neukölln wieder. […] und draußen lag dann die stadt da […], eine eins-zu-eins-stadt, wie es immer heißt, nicht kleinzukriegen, immer einen schritt weiter, immer schon auf und davon, da kommt man einfach nicht nach. (A10-11)

Rögglas ‚Neukölln' zielt nicht auf das Milieu von Genrebildern und räumt auf mit der Allegorisierung der ‚Stadt als Stadt'. In seiner Wachheit für geteilte Perspektiven antwortet *Irres Wetter* auf die redselige „vollversion" einer Stadt, die an der „realo-welt" ihrer BewohnerInnen vorbeirauscht:

> in neukölln jedenfalls kann man jetzt in ruhe seine kriegstagebücher führen, nein, für den *spiegel* nicht, […] so ganz für sich […], denn auch hier ist die realo-welt geladen [...]. man sieht: auch hier, wo die menschen stattfinden, die „kein glück hatten", gibt es stellen aus krieg und nichtkrieg, aber nicht das volle programm, weiß er schon wieder, nur shareware! „die vollversion, hörst du", schreit er, „kostet ein vermögen, die kriegst du niemals!"[31]

Lokale Lektüren der Stadt zeugen auch von einer ‚Nostalgie urbaner Lesbarkeit'.[32] Doch wird nicht zuletzt in der kognitiven Verschränkung von

Stadtbezirken und ihnen angehafteten sozialen Mentalitäten, die den Bezirken homogene erzählerische Funktionen zuschreibt, die ‚city in flux' gezähmt und ausgebremst.[33] Berlins Bezirke verschwinden hinter ihren Kulissen und erhalten keine Chance – mit Roland Barthes – „zu Signi-fikanten von *etwas anderem* zu werden".[34]

Und jede Zentrierung bedarf der Peripherie; an dieser, da draußen, finden wir die Ostberliner, deren Stadthälfte auf so wenige Planquadrate zusammengeschrumpft ist. Stefan Neuhaus' Beobachtung der Adaption einer Stadt-Land-Dichtomie auf das neue Deutschland trifft Perspektiven auf die vereinte Hauptstadt nicht minder:[35] Dückers' Benno aus dem Prenzlauer Berg verläßt „unbelehrbare Wessis" auf „Ost-Hinterhöfe[n]", der Text schickt ihn in den Tiergarten: „Er ist dort sehr gerne […]. Ein Park ist doch viel schöner!" (Sp165-166) Auch Pareis entmietete Ostler räumen die Innenstadt: sie sind weggezogen „in Plattenbau, mit Zentral-heizung und Müllschlucker, draußen in Marzahn oder Hellersdorf" (Sch7).

Im Westen verlaufen andere Grenzen, am südlichen Rande Neuköllns, unter „Buckower Analphabeten" (Sp81) oder in Erfindungen eines „Schicki-Micki-Mehringdamm[s]" in Kreuzberg (Sp199).

> Gerade fahre ich im Taxi über die Jannowitzbrücke nach Kreuzberg. [...] Draußen huschen die achtziger Jahre vorbei […]. Wie kann man heute noch in Kreuzberg wohnen, ohne zu verwesen? […] Ich sage nein zu Retro und ja zum Leben […],

tönt es poppig aus Hennig von Langes *Mai 3D*.[36] Abwesend ist das Vor-wendeberlin des Ostens, anwesend eine spezifische Vergangenheit des Westens, meist im metaphorischen Bezug auf Kreuzberg; dieser Bezirk (ein Westberliner Brennpunkt der neuen sozialen Bewegungen der 70er und 80er Jahre) wird zur vergangenheitspolitischen Projektionsfläche neuer politischer Mythen über die alte Bundesrepublik: An symbolischem Ort und Datum, am Rande der Straßenschlachten des Kreuzberger 1. Mais 1989,[37] gerät das Leben der politisch unbeteiligten Schattenboxerin, die am Görlitzer Bahnhof von einem Franzosen vergewaltigt wird, „aus den Fugen" (Sch31). In Rückblicken konfrontiert Pareis Text die Jetztzeit der Heldin mit dem „alten, jetzt völlig unwirklichen Leben an der west-lichen Achse der Stadt", einem Leben der „Täuschung", „riskant und sorglos" (Sch15). Romantisch imaginiert Unda Hörners *Unter Nachbarn* das von der Mauer ummantelte Westberlin der „Achtziger": „eine um-friedete Stadt [...], ein Schutzraum, ein geschlossenes Ganzes. […] Wir wurden ins Exil geschickt".[38] Sentimentale Erfindungen eines ehemaligen politischen Schonraums auf der einen, Konstruktionen eines „West-berliner Biotop[s]" oder einer „Mulitkulti-Oase"[39] auf der anderen Seite, dominieren Post-Wende-Erinnerungen an Westberlin. Als Kehrseiten einer Medaille ziehen sie im Bilde Kreuzbergs den Schlußstrich unter

Politik- und Lebensformen jenseits des Marktes und dort verwertbarer Individualitätsnormen. Vom „definitive[n] Verlust aller [...] Utopien" des 20. Jahrhunderts, vom Ersatz der „Kritik" durch „Definition" zum Zwecke „transzendentale[r] Nüchternheit", spricht der Verfechter neuer historischer Nullpunkte Heinz Bude.[40]

Andere historische Räume öffnen Rögglas polyphone Texte; in steter Insistenz auf die Gleichzeitigkeit städtischer und historischer Differenz zeigen sie auch im Rückblick viele Berlins. Karl hat „vom vormauerfallberlin erzählt, vom wehrdienstfluchtberlin, rolfdieterbrinkmann, bakuninberlin, otto sander-, bloß nicht ostenberlin, camus- ‚der fremde'-berlin, und marx ohne filter-, ‚es atmet, wärmt, ißt. es scheißt, es fickt'-berlin, durch die köpfe schießt italien-berlin" (A25). Die Einbrüche der Vergangenheit in die übrige Zeit schießen bei Röggla als Stachel in die Jetztzeit. Im historischen Zitat der populistischen Hetze gegen die Studentenbewegung – acht Wochen vor dem Attentat auf Rudi Dutschke – stellt Rögglas hintergründige Verkehrung der Generationsperspektive gerade die Ideologeme der Geschichtsvergessenheit, aber auch politischer Universalisierungen zur Schau, an denen nicht nur die eskapistischen Poptexte mitschreiben: „deine generation, pflegt karl [...] zu sagen, sunlicht live, schau sie dir doch an, die gestalten, wie sie unbeweglich dastehen in den kneipen mit nichts im kopf" (A24-25).[41]

Während die Erregungssphäre des Geldes allein die Popliteraten von Geldautomat zu Geldautomat treibt – „Das Leben ohne EC-karte ist umständlich. Entweder schleppst du immer einen Sack Bargeld mit dir rum, oder du fährst öfter nach Hause, nur um Geld zu holen. Vorhin habe ich bei *Saturn* einen Ghettoblaster aufs Kassenband gehievt und konnte nicht zahlen"[42] – halten die Texte Pareis, Stellings und Bergs der Verwandlung von Bürgern in Konsumenten, dem neoliberalen Credo der Individualität, einen Zerrspiegel vor: „das Ende des modernen Menschen ist es, vor dem Geldautomaten zu stehen und nichts kommt raus", weiß Bergs Protagonistin (S112), „eh keinen dispo und groß rauskommen wollen, das motto der neunziger! ha" (A45), tönt es unbeindruckt aus Rögglas fragmentiertem Sprachteppich: „klarheit muß man kriegen, klarheit, wo vorne und hinten ist in einem leben, fehlt nur das geld. man braucht eben geld, um loszuheizen quer durch die selbstprärie." (A22)

Rögglas *Abrauschen* stichelt im Generations-Gerede herum und öffnet nun in Anspielung auf die biologischen Generationszüchtungen Alfred Mendels Ausblicke, die nicht vorgesehen sind:

> doch sind wir nicht die erbengeneration, fiel mir plötzlich ein, [...] so sagen sie doch alle immer, die erbsengeneration und nichts anderes, [...] nur die eltern sind steinreich und wissen noch am rädchen zu drehen, während den jungen nichts übrigbleibt, als des weges zu kollern. (A14)

Irres Wetter belauscht den Dialog zwischen der „messehosteß" und einem „wochenendbesucher":

> [...] ob sie denn das glaube? und sie weiß schon wieder nicht, was.
> - na das mit „generation berlin".
> - und?
> [...]
> - mensch, das steht doch überall.
> - und?
> an generationen hängt man heute alles auf, weiß auch er längst bescheid. doch während sie ihm noch so king-vokabeln der 90er vorbetet, ist er schon umsetzbereit: „jetzt aber los!" (IW100)

Rögglas sarkastische Berlin-Fratzen intervenieren in Kulte der Jugend, ohne es auszulassen, Berlin als literarischen Markenartikel bloßzustellen:

> oder sind das etwa schon wieder so germanistikstudentinnen, die [...] von nichts anderem als ihren berlin-anthologien reden? richtig! „unter 35" nennen sie die dann: „feste pop schreiben wir auch noch drauf." – [...] und: „liest sich in der u-bahn", werden sie [...] im klappentext schreiben, [...]. und wie schnell diese stadt sei, wird darin auch noch zugesagt. (IW105-6)

Der Stadt enteignete, in „Tatschwäche"[43] festgestellte Figuren kollern durch Stellings Erzählungen und halten Berlin, im überlegen-befremdeten Außenblick der Zugereisten, einen trostlosen Spiegel vor:

> Du stehst auf der Brücke und starrst nach Osten. Friedrichshain, Lichtenberg. Du hättest gern was zu diesen Orten zu sagen, aber mach dir da nichts vor. Sie haben nichts mit dir zu tun. Dir gehört weder die bröckelnde Altbauwohnung in der Thaerstraße, noch der Sitzplatz in der S-Bahn nach Strausberg. Deine schäbige kleine Möchtegernfigur gehört in ein mit erbsgrünen Asbestplatten verkleidetes Zweifamilienhaus am Autobahnzubringer von Vaihingen.[44]

Stellings kühle Blicke auf neue östliche Investitionsbrachen sprechen jeglicher Aufbruchsstimmung einer „Neo-Erlebnisstadt"[45] Hohn:

> Er [der ungarische Freund, F.M.] hat dir die Stadt weggenommen, also was willst du noch hier. Stell dich auf die Warschauer Brücke und spuck auf die Gleise [...], wo er [...] rausfährt aus der Stadt, die ihm gehört [...]. Spuck auf die Gleise und sieh rüber zu den Narva-Werken, die jetzt auch eine neue Aufgabe kriegen als Oberbaumcity: Wiesbadener Immobilienmakler beherbergen, warum solltest du weniger flexibel sein? Geh einfach nach Wiesbaden und verteil dort Handzettel für ein Steakhaus, in dem man essen darf, so viel man will.[46]

Wie durch eine mattierte Scheibe starren diese Figuren, uninvolviert, auf eine Stadt, die nichts mit ihnen zu tun hat. Auch Stellings Texte isolieren ein Ich, abseits der anderen, an dem die Metropole abprallt: „Anders als Sonja hatten sich die Berliner Freunde an den Zustand ihrer Stadt gewöhnt." (GF146) Im Gestus sind Stellings Texte der zelebrierten Erfahrungsleere Judith Hermanns nicht unähnlich. Doch wo Stelling ihre regressiven Figuren im unbestimmten Heimweh aus Berlin wegschreibt – „Und hier wollte sie auch nicht mehr sein. Nach Bangkok vielleicht, oder zurück zu den Eltern" (GF150) – rückt Hermann die Hauptstadt der Deutschen aus der Ferne hintergründig ins (europäische) Zentrum: vorwurfsvoll bleiben die Figuren in ausländischen Hotelbetten liegen, mit „gekränktem Heimweh" nach Berlin.[47]

So wenig Vergangenheit und zu viel Zukunft fordern in diesem literarischen Berlin ihren Preis. In die unmögliche Startposition einer kontinuierlichen Gegenwart[48] versetzt – „Daß jeden Tag etwas Spannendes und Lustiges passieren sollte, [...] ließ Sandra nervös werden" (GF54) – , wollen die Neuen Berlinerinnen im freien Feld der Zukunft keinen Boden unter die Füße bekommen: „nur ich sitze hier und überlege mir, was nun machen?", provoziert Röggla,

> und dabei heißt es immer *aufbruchstimmung*, heute soll ja jeder in aufbruchstimmung sein, doch zeigte man früher noch filme über so junge menschen, die fröhlich durch die großstadt irren, so haben sie seit einiger zeit schon bissige gesichter. (A23)

Weniger bissige, als die Passivität zelebrierende Menschen, die unbeweglich daliegen, treffen wir in Bergs und Dückers' Berliner Betten: „Wenn ich keine Lust zum Arbeiten habe, liege ich auf meinem Bett und warte, daß die Zeit rumgeht" (S12); ich „lege mich aufs Bett und warte. [...] Ich lächele mich im Spiegel an. Hier ist niemand außer mir" (Sp158). Und auch Dückers' junge Frau vom Kurfürstendamm liegt auf ihrer Kissenburg und ‚warte[t] auf nichts als den Rauch. Abends steigt die Sonne blutrot hinter der Gedächtniskirche auf, ich sehe die ungleichmäßigen Zacken und denke, daß nichts gut ist, und dann fühle ich mich einigermaßen wohl.' (CB82) Berlin, ein Wartezimmer, in dem die mit sich beschäftigten Figuren sich um den Aufruf schon gar nicht mehr scheren. „nicht vor noch zurück, das ist eben die situation", so der spitze Kommentar Rögglas (IW73).

Wie ein schwarzes Loch scheinen diese Berlinerinnen in privatistischen Haltungen eines (un)zufriedenen Uninvolviertseins die Neue Metropole zu umkreisen. Die Attraktion solch eines gelähmten Erfahrungsunmuts – evoziert von Behauptungen einer Stadt, sie sei immer schon viel weiter – mag nicht zuletzt den kommerziellen Erfolg von Judith Hermanns Texten zu erklären, die ja irgendwie, irgendwo, irgendwas Wahres im Falschen berühren:

> Sie erzählte von dem Leben in Berlin, sie versuchte es zu beschreiben, [...] ihr kam alles etwas verwirrend vor, durcheinander und ziellos, „Wir machen dies und wir machen jenes", sie hatte das Gefühl, es nicht richtig beschreiben zu können. Geld verdienen, mal so und mal so.[49]

Wenn vielen der besichtigten Texte etwas gemeinsam ist, dann sind es die Blicke auf die fremden Anderen. Und hier rutschen sie vom Rande widerständiger Verwahrlosung, den Haltungen der Verweigerung und des Sich-Raushaltens, die den kommerzialisierten Erregungssphären der Berliner Republik einen trotzigen Spiegel vorhalten, auf schiefer Bahn in ein voll besetztes Zentrum, das implizit beruhigende Gemeinsamkeiten eines (nationalen) Aufgehobensein suggeriert.

Goutiert deuten die Berliner Einheimischen auf „sich abknallende" Araber deren „Bauchrolle[n]" aus „schmutziggelben T-Shirt[s] heraus [quellen]", „Pulk[s] türkischer Frauen", immer in Gruppen, diese „weißen und schwarzen Kopftücher"; wir sehen schon wieder sich „in den Schritt fassende", die „Augen verdrehende" Schwarze oder werden von „glühenden Augenpaaren" „irakischer Männer" mit „kehligen arabischen Stimmen" „angestarrt".[50] Und wo Stellings Ungar die Figur der ganzen Stadt beraubt, haben Strubels „Rastamänner aus der bolivianischen Provinz" bei Lidl gleich „den gesamten Kassenbereich übernommen" (FG81). Umgekehrt bedarf es in Judith Hermanns Paris der Begegnung mit einem Franzosen, den der Text als „Schwarzafrikaner" markiert, um die Reisende „nach Hause" zu treiben: „er hielt noch immer seine Hand auf und sah mich an, als müsse ich eigentlich für etwas ganz anderes bezahlen. [...] ich wußte plötzlich, daß ich abreisen mußte, daß ich nicht mehr geschützt war." „Zigeunerfrauen" an der Gare du Nord und die sie „anstarrende" „asiatische Fahrkartenverkäuferin" geben der Figur schließlich den Rest: „Ich dachte ‚Fahr weiter, [...] fahr weg, so weit wie möglich', [...] ‚Berlin', sagte ich, ‚eine Fahrkarte nach Berlin bitte', und das Gefühl in meinem Magen war jetzt eindeutig Angst".[51]

Kaum will es gelingen, in den hier gesichteten Texten hinter dem so oft verspeisten Döner ein Gesicht zu identifizieren: „Andächtig guckt er die Fliegen an, die über das süße Gebäck im Döner-Laden krabbeln" (Sp46); die türkischen BerlinerInnen, aber auch Afrikaner oder Araber, sind in den Kontaktzonen des Essens eingehegt, hinter „ein[em] mit Fett vollgesogene[n] Fladenmaul, gestopft mit Kalbfleischraspeln und Strähnen aus lila Krautsalat" (Sch86); oder der Dönermann evoziert wilde Urängste:

> Wenn sie in ihrer Wohnung saß, vergaß sie schnell, daß es die Stadt gab. Gab es die Stadt, gab es einen Zusammenhang. [...] Zwischen Sonjas dritter Kanne Fencheltee und dem Dönermann, der Bonbons an kleine Kinder verschenkte. Er ist trotzdem der schwarze Mann, dachte Sonja. (GF25)

Ja, die Westberliner Eingeborenen blieben am liebsten unter sich. Pareis zutiefst verunsicherte Protagonistin sieht sich bei der Maueröffnung mit einer gesichtslosen, gierigen Masse konfrontiert. Phantasien des Mundraubs, der Kolonisierung und Vertreibung überfallen die Schattenboxerin, und die Straße wird zur Partisanenzone:

> Und dann kommen sie. Plötzlich, an einem Tag im November, kommen sie. [...] In der Hand halte ich den offenen Einkaufskorb. Von der grenznahen Sackgasse her kommen sie in kleinen Gruppen auf mich zugelaufen. [...] Die ersten [...] umringen mich [...]. Sie starren auf meinen Korb. Ich bin umzingelt von fremden Leuten [...]. Ich lasse meinen Einkauf fallen und renne die Straße hinunter. [...] Die Vorstellung, mir meine Vorräte zurückzuholen, mich [...] in die teilnahmslos starrende Menge zu verstricken, [...] ist mir unerträglich. (Sch121-122)

Die „Fluchtrichtung" führt in den Untergrund, und die Schattenboxerin schließt, bevor sie in den „Tunnel gleite[t], die Augen" (Sch123). Augen zu und durch? Den imaginierten Angriffen der Außenwelt begegnen Pareis, Bergs und auch Stellings städtische Perspektiven mit monadischen Ich-Behauptungsversuchen, wenn nicht mit Gesten der tabula rasa, der Stadtzertrümmerung, die jetzt bei Gründungsmythen der alten Bundesrepublik Zuflucht suchen: „Wenn doch nur mal wieder Krieg wäre mit Bomben, die das hier ratzfatz wegknallen würden. Dann könntest du dir Strickjacke und Gummistiefel anziehen und anfangen aufzuräumen."[52]

Manche Befunde sind beunruhigend. Die Haltungen der Purifizierung und des Zumachens, der Abgrenzung von den störenden anderen, korrespondieren mit den Zeichnungen intimer und instrumentaler, ‚single-minded', städtischer Landkarten.[53] Es sollte anders sein, rufen viele Texte ins Neue Berlin, erlauben den BerlinerInnen aber nicht zurückzurufen. Und wenn denn Urbanität nichts anderes als Differenz, Ungleichzeitigkeiten und fortwährende Herausforderung der Begegnung mit Fremden meint, dann kapitulieren viele der hier besichtigten Texte vor dem Städtischen – und zeichnen eine Stadt ohne BürgerInnen. „Nur was uns anschaut sehen wir", hieß es einmal bei Franz Hessel.[54]

Goodbye to Berlin – von niemandem bestellt? Und „warum nicht", mit Kathrin Röggla, „einfach eine plastikplane über das ganze werfen, sich dann umdrehen und weggehen", ja sogar „auch wenn kein historischer moment" (A13)? Mit anderen Beleuchtungen der Stadt und verschiedenen Zeiten experimentieren Antje Rávic Strubel und ihre Fotografin Leah: In einer „Ästhetik des Verschwindens" inszeniert die *Offene Blende* das vereinigte Berlin als historischen Tatort, der Indizien wegen.[55] Die ostdeutsche Jo bricht aus New York zur Rückreise auf. Strubels skeptische Ausblicke sollen hier eine Tendenz des Neuen literarischen Berlin summieren, in der die Stadt verloren geht. Denn je näher Berlin in den Fokus rückt, desto weniger ist zu entdecken.

> So hätte sie Jo aufnehmen müssen. Im Vorübergehen und mit einer Belichtungszeit, die sie […] letztendlich auf dem Foto unsichtbar gemacht hätte. […] Das Foto hätte die Straße ohne sie gezeigt. Nur so hätte sie Jo aufnehmen dürfen, weil es das sein wird, was Jo sieht, wenn sie nach zehn Jahren zurückkommt: Berlin auf einem lange belichteten Foto, mit bekannter Architektur, aber entleert von allem Lebendigen.[56]

Anmerkungen

1 Inka Parei, *Die Schattenboxerin. Roman*, Fischer: Frankfurt am Main, 2003 (1999), S. 106-107. Im folgenden abgekürzt mit ‚Sch'. Ich danke Nina Helm für zahlreiche Anregungen und produktive Gespräche.

2 Zu den diversen Strategien des ‚mappings' ihrer Stadt seitens der BewohnerInnen vergl. Kevin Lynch, *The Image of the City*, M.I.T. Press: Cambridge MA, London, 1960.

3 ‚Berliner Szene zwischen Buchdeckeln,' *Die Welt*, 27. März 2003.

4 Andreas Huyssen, Werner Jung, Peter M. McIsaac, ‚Introduction,' *New German Critique* 88/2003; Special Issue: Contemporary German Literature, 7.

5 Terézia Mora, ‚Das Große Verschwinden – die Große Wiederkehr. Gibt es eine neue Generation deutschsprachiger Literatur?,' *neue deutsche literatur* 48/2000, H. 537, 165-73 (hier: 173). Vergl. hier die Dokumentation: ‚*Literatur und Generation. Vom Jungsein und Älterwerden der Dichter'. Symposion der Deutschen Literaturkonferenz Leipzig*, 25. März 2000. Siehe allein die jüngst erfundenen ‚Generationen' ‚X', ‚@com', ‚Ally', ‚Golf', ‚XTC' ‚Ich', ‚Dazwischen', oder die Spaß-, Millenniums- und No-Label-Generation. Auch kritische Diskurse, die, wie Christoph Dieckmann, von einer „system-kompatible[n] Spätlingsgeneration" sprechen, möchten nicht auf dieses Paradigma verzichten. Zitiert nach Phil C. Langer, *Kein Ort. Überall. Die Einschreibung von Berlin in die deutsche Literatur der neunziger Jahre*, Weidler: Berlin, 2002, S. 156-57.

6 Richard Herzinger, ‚Mythos, Stil und Simulation. „Generation" als kultureller Kampfbegriff und literarische Selbsterfindung,' *neue deutsche literatur* 48/2000, H. 537, 144-64 (hier: 152).

7 Sigrid Weigel, ‚Generation, Genealogie, Geschlecht. Zur Geschichte des Generationskonzepts und seiner wissenschaftlichen Konzeptualisierung seit dem Ende des 18. Jahrhunderts,' in: Lutz Musner, Gotthart Wunberg, Hgg., *Kulturwissenschaften. Forschung – Praxis – Positionen*, Rombach: Wien, 2002, S. 161-208 (hier: S. 179).

8 Heinz Bude, ‚Das „übertriebene Wir" der Generation,' *neue deutsche literatur* 48/2000, H. 537, 136-43 (hier: 142).

9 Heinz Bude, ‚Der Anspruch der Generationen,' in: *Generation Berlin*, Merve: Berlin, 2001, S. 66. Vergl. ähnlich: „Für die Generationengeschichte der Bundesrepublik ist die gesellschaftliche Nullstellung von 1945 der entscheidende Bezugspunkt." ‚Das „übertriebene Wir" der Generation,' S. 138.

10 Susanne Ledanff, ‚„Metropolisierung" der deutschen Literatur? Welche Möglichkeiten eröffnet das vereinigte Berlin und die neue Berliner Urbanität?,' in: Gerhard Fischer, David Roberts, Hgg., *Schreiben nach der Wende. Ein Jahrzehnt deutscher Literatur 1989-1999*, Stauffenburg: Tübingen, 2001, S. 275-89 (hier: S. 286, 285).

11 Ledanff, ‚„Metropolisierung" der deutschen Literatur?, S. 280.

12 Bude, ‚Generation Berlin,' in: *Generation Berlin*, S. 13-14.

13 Regine Jaszinski, ‚Bibliographie „Berlin in Prosa" 1989-1999,' in: Erhard Schütz, Jörg Döring, Hgg., *Text der Stadt - Reden von Berlin. Literatur und Metropole seit 1989*, Weidler: Berlin, 1999, S. 186-96.

14 Tanja Dückers, ‚Café Brazil,' in: *Café Brazil. Erzählungen*, Aufbau: Berlin, 2002 (2001), S. 57. Im folgenden abgekürzt mit ‚CB'. Jugend und Hauptstadtkult feiern die Popliteraten; hier posen die „jungen Berliner Wilden", bei „Fotoshootings" für das GEO-Spezial „„Berlin – die neue Metropole'": „Im Hintergrund: Friedrichstraße, der Blick über das Neue Berlin. Höhenangst." Alexa Hennig von Lange, Daniel Haaksman, Till Müller-Klug: *MAI 3D. Ein Tagebuchroman*, List: München, 2001 (2000), S. 83-4.

15 Sibylle Berg, *Sex II. Roman*, Reclam: Leipzig, 1998, S. 9. Im folgenden abgekürzt mit ‚S'.

16 Vergl. Parei, *Die Schattenboxerin* (Sch39); Tanja Dückers, *Spielzone. Roman*, Aufbau: Berlin, 1999, S. 138. Im folgenden abgekürzt mit ‚Sp'. Anke Stelling, ‚Amazing Grace,' in: *Glückliche Fügung. Erzählungen*, Fischer: Frankfurt am Main, 2004, S. 17. Im folgenden abgekürzt mit ‚GF'.

17 Antje Rávic Strubel, *Fremd Gehen. Ein Nachtstück*, dtv: München, 2002, S. 101-02. Im folgenden abgekürzt mit ‚FG'.

18 Annett Gröschner, Hg., *Jeder hat sein Stück Berlin gekriegt: Geschichten vom Prenzlauer Berg*, Rowohlt: Reinbek bei Hamburg, 1998, S. 11.

19 Strubel, *Fremd Gehen*; Dies., *Offene Blende. Roman*, dtv: München, 2001, siehe u.a. S. 307.

20 Stelling, ‚Amazing Grace,' in: GF, S. 9.

21 Unda Hörner, *Unter Nachbarn. Roman*, Suhrkamp: Frankfurt am Main, 2000, S. 45.

22 Kathrin Röggla, *Abrauschen. Roman*, Fischer: Frankfurt am Main, 2001 (1997), S. 23. Im folgenden abgekürzt mit ‚A'.

23 Vergl. die poppige Variation ähnlicher Muster: „Was fang ich nun mit meinen freien Wänden an? Ich hab's: das Radio-Eins-Plakat! Das Ding ist von der Stadtreklame und 3x5 Meter groß. Darauf zu sehen bin ich selbst [...]. Jedenfalls sieht das Plakat in meiner Wohnung riesig aus. Weil es eigentlich für draußen ist, macht es aus meiner Wohnung sozusagen die Straße." Hennig von Lange, Haaksman, Müller-Klug, *MAI 3D*, S. 79.

24 Diesen Begriff benutzt Burton Pike, *The Image of the City in Modern Literature*, Princeton University Press: Princeton, N.J., 1981.

25 Vergl. auch *das Neuköllnbuch*, Verbrecherverlag: Berlin, 2003. Darin Tanja Dückers: „Das ist Neukölln, fern der neuen Lifestylezentren der Friedrichstraße und der Hackeschen Höfe". ‚Der Zauberkönig,' S. 167-169 (S. 169). Für diesen Hinweis danke ich Johanna Peitsch.

26 Franz Hessel, ‚Der Verdächtige.' in: *Ein Flaneur in Berlin*, Das Arsenal: Berlin, 1984, S. 7.

27 Zu den Einbildungen des Flaneurs, „Regisseur zu sein", vergl. u.a. Zygmunt Bauman, ‚Vom Pilger zum Touristen'. Aus dem Engl. von Michael Haupt u. Nora Räthzel. *Das Argument* 36/1994, H. 5, 389-408 (hier: 399). [‚From Pilgrim to Tourist – or a Short History of Identity,' in: Stuart Hall, Paul du Gay, Hgg., *Questions of Cultural Identity*, London, Sage 1996, S. 18-36.]; ebenso ders., ‚Desert spectacular,' in: Keith Tester, Hg., *The Flâneur*, Routledge: London, 1994, S. 138-57.

28 Vergl. Heinrich Wefing, ‚Die neue Sehnsucht nach der Alten Stadt. Was ist Urbanität?' *Neue Rundschau* 109/1998, H. 2, 82-98 (hier: 96). Zu „modernen Apologien des Flaneurwesens" vergl. die konzise Kritik Heidrun Suhrs: ‚Die fremde Stadt. Über Geschichten von Aufstieg und Untergang in der Metropole,' in: Thomas Steinfeld, dies., Hgg., *In der großen Stadt: die Metropole als kulturtheoretische Kategorie*, Anton Hain: Frankfurt am Main, 1990, S. 23-40 (hier: S. 35).

29 Georg Simmel, ‚Die Großstädte und das Geistesleben,' in: *Soziologische Ästhetik*. Hg. u. eingeleitet von Klaus Lichtblau. Wissenschaftliche Buchgesellschaft: Darmstadt, 1998, S. 119-33 (hier: S. 128).

30 Zum Wandel der Straße vergl. u.a. Bauman, ‚Desert spectacular,' bes. S. 149.

31 Kathrin Röggla, *Irres Wetter*, Fischer: Frankfurt am Main, 2002 (2000), S. 131. Im folgenden abgekürzt mit ‚IW'.

32 Vergl. William Sharpe und Leonard Wallock, ‚From „Great Town" to „Nonplace Urban Realm": Reading the Modern City,' in: Diess., Hgg., *Visions of the Modern City*, Johns Hopkins University Press: Baltimore, 1987, S. 1-50 (hier: S. 36).

33 Vergl. hierzu grundlegend Pike, *The Image of the City*.

34 Roland Barthes, *Das semiologische Abenteuer*, Suhrkamp: Frankfurt am Main, 1988, S. 204-05.

35 „In principle the former GDR is associated with ‚country', the Federal Republic with ‚town'". Stefan Neuhaus, „„Stadt-Land-Frust": on the Metamorphoses of a Literary Dichotomy,' in: Julian Preece, Osman Durrani, Hgg., *Cityscapes and Countryside in Contemporary German Literature*, Peter Lang: Oxford, Bern et al., 2004, S. 13-28 (hier: S. 24).

36 Hennig von Lange, Haaksman, Müller-Klug, *MAI 3D*, S. 107, 119.

37 Seit den 80er Jahren wird die Gegend um das Kottbusser Tor und den Görlitzer Bahnhof am 1. Mai regelmäßig zum Schauplatz schärfster, mittlerweile ritualisierter, Zusammenstöße zwischen Mitgliedern der linken Autonomen Szene (bzw. der ehemaligen Hausbesetzerszene) und der Polizei.

38 Hörner, *Unter Nachbarn*, S. 53.

39 Ledanff, „„Metropolisierung" der deutschen Literatur?,' S. 282, 283. Der Kontrast zu Westberliner Stadttexten der 80er Jahre und ihren Bildern der Kälte und Härte könnte kaum größer sein. Vergl. Helmut Peitsch, ‚Wenn wir, bei Rot. Ampelszenen in der Berlin-Literatur 1945-1990,' *literatur für leser* (1993), H. 1, 1-17.

40 Bude, ,Unterscheidungen und Haltungen,' in: *Generation Berlin*, S. 49.

41 ,Schaut euch diese Typen an', so Berlins Regierender Bürgermeister Klaus Schütz und die Springer-Presse über die protestierenden StudentInnen. Auch Rögglas urbane Kurzskizzen, die ,mental maps' in *Irres Wetter* führen an Kreuzberger Orte, wo „Leute aufeinandertreffen […]: Wir sind nicht das neue Berlin. Wir sind nicht die neue Mitte. Wir müssen aufpassen, damit wir nicht weiter an den Rand gedrängt werden." Vergl. die Autorin 2000 in einem Interview. http://www.luise-berlin.de/Lesezei/Blz00_10/text2.htm. Zur Karikierung ,der' 68er vergl. u.a. Dückers' Spielzone, Sp20, 23.

42 Hennig von Lange, Haaksman, Müller-Klug, *Mai 3D*, S. 63. Vergl. auch *Spielzone*: hier schmeißt Dückers' 18jährige Ada vom Rad mit Geldstücken auf parkende Autos, „[w]ozu sich abrackern? Es gibt doch H&M und Burger King. Teuer ist out" (Sp204).

43 Ijoma Mangold identifiziert in dieser Haltung wieder die „Zeitstimmung" einer ganzen Generation. ,In Aspik. Anke Stellings Erzählungen „Glückliche Fügung"', *Süddeutsche Zeitung*, 2. März 2004.

44 Stelling, ,All you can eat,' in GF104.

45 Ledanff, „„Metropolisierung" der deutschen Literatur?,' S. 280.

46 Stelling, ,All you can eat,' in: GF103; vergl. ähnliche Stilspiele Bergs (S23), die Martin Hielscher als „Splatter-Bachmann" vorstellt (Martin Hielscher, ,Kritik der Krise in der jüngsten Literatur,' in: Keith Bullivant, Bernhard Spies, Hgg., *Literarisches Krisenbewusstsein: ein Perzeptions- und Produktionsmuster im 20. Jahrhundert*, Iudicium: München, 2001, S. 314-34 (hier: S. 332).

47 In verschiedenen Städten erfahren Hermanns Figuren immer das Gleiche (*Nichts als Gespenster*, Fischer: Frankfurt am Main, 2004 (2003)): „ich hatte zu lange in diesem Zimmer auf dem Bett herumgelegen, ich hatte ein gekränktes Heimweh […]. […] es hätte Tromsø sein können, es hätte aber auch irgeneine andere Stadt sein können, ich wollte es gar nicht wissen" (,Die Liebe zu Ari Oskarsson,' S. 293, 298); „unsinnigerweise ist mir, als hätte ich alles schon gesehen. […] ich würde am liebsten im Hotelzimmer sitzen bleiben" (,Acqua Alta,' S. 135); „Ich wußte, daß wir nicht in die Stadt gehen würden. [...] Es spielte keine Rolle, daß wir in Prag waren" (,Wohin des Wegs,' S. 252).

48 Vergl. Zygmunt Bauman zum „Spiel der Verantwortungslosigkeit": „Der Vergangenheit verbieten, auf die Gegenwart Einfluß zu nehmen. Kurz die Gegenwart an beiden Enden abzuschneiden, die Gegenwart aus der Geschichte herauszulösen. Die Zeit nur noch als geglättete Zusammenstellung oder als zufällige Folge gegenwärtiger Momente zu konzipieren: als kontinuierliche Gegenwart." ,Vom Pilger zum Touristen', S. 395.

49 Hermann, ,Nichts als Gespenster,' in: *Nichts als Gespenster*, S. 221.

50 Sp175, 54, 110, 44, 175; Hörner, *Unter Nachbarn*, S. 182, 183.

51 Hermann, ‚Freundinnen,' in: *Nichts als Gespenster*, S. 35, 36.

52 So der programmatische Schlußsatz in Stellings ‚All you can eat,' in: GF109.

53 Vergl. Kevin Robins, ‚Prisoners of the City: Whatever could a Postmodern City be?,' in: Erica Carter, James Donald u. Judith Squires, Hgg., *Space and Place. Theories of Identity and Location*, Lawrence & Wishart: London, 1993, S. 303-30 (hier: S. 314).

54 Vergl. das Ausstellungsbuch Franz Hessel, *Nur was uns anschaut sehen wir*. Erarbeitet von Ernest Wichner und Herbert Wiesner, Literaturhaus: Berlin, 1998.

55 Vergl. Christopher Isherwood: „I am a camera with its shutter open". Goodbye to Berlin, in: *The Berlin Novels*, Vintage: London, 1999, S. 243.

56 Strubel, *Offene Blende*, S. 314. Vergl. Walter Benjamin: „Atget, der die Pariser Straßen um 1900 in menschenleeren Aspekten festhielt. Sehr mit Recht hat man von ihm gesagt, daß er sie aufnahm wie einen Tatort. Auch der Tatort ist menschenleer. Seine Aufnahme geschieht der Indizien wegen. Die photographischen Aufnahmen beginnen bei Atget Beweistücke im historischen Prozeß zu werden. Das macht ihre verborgene politische Bedeutung aus." Walter Benjamin, *Gesammelte Schriften*. Hg. von Rolf Tiedemann u. Hermann Schweppenhäuser. Suhrkamp: Frankfurt am Main, 1991, Bd. i, 2, S. 445.

Notes on Contributors

Heike Bartel is Senior Lecturer in German at the University of Nottingham. She has worked and published on Friedrich Hölderlin, Goethe, Anne Duden, Paul Celan and Mythology. She is the author of *'Centaurengesänge': Friedrich Hölderlins Pindarfragmente* (2000) and *Mythos in der Literatur* (2004) and co-editor (with Elizabeth Boa) of *Anne Duden: A Revolution of Words. Approaches to her Fiction, Poetry and Essays* (German Monitor 56, 2003). She is currently working on the reception of the myth of Medea in literature, art and culture.

Petra M. Bagley is Senior Lecturer in German in the Department of Languages and International Studies at the University of Central Lancashire. Her research focuses on modern women's writing from German-speaking countries. She is the author of *Somebody's Daughter: The Portrayal of Daughter-Parent Relationships by Contemporary Women Writers from German-speaking Countries* (1996). Other publications include papers on the Catholic upbringing of women writers, daughter-father relationships, confessional literature and immigrant writing. She is currently working on a monograph with the working title of *Living the Good Life: Anglo-German Literary Perspectives of Provence.*

Anthea Bell is a freelance translator from German and French. Her translations include works of non-fiction, literary and popular fiction, and books for young people. She has received a number of translation awards, including the 2002 Schlegel-Tieck award (UK), Independent Foreign Fiction Prize (UK), and the Helen and Kurt Wolff Prize (USA), all three for the translation of W.G. Sebald's *Austerlitz*; the 2003 Schlegel-Tieck award for the translation of Karen Duve's *Rain* (Bloomsbury); and the 2003 Austrian State Prize for Literary Translation.

Elizabeth Boa is Emeritus Professor of German at the University of Nottingham. She has published books on Wedekind and Kafka, as well as a study of Heimat discourse between 1890-1990 (co-author Rachel Palfreyman) and numerous articles on German literature from the eighteenth century to the present. She was co-editor (with Janet Wharton) of *Women and the Wende* (German Monitor 31, 1994) and co-editor (with Heike Bartel) of *Anne Duden: A Revolution of Words* (German Monitor 56, 2003).

Peter Graves is Senior Lecturer and Head of German at the University of Leicester. He has written extensively on post-war German writers from both East and West, particularly Christa Wolf and Reiner Kunze. His current research interests are mainly in the German novel since unification. He is a regular reviewer for the *Times Literary Supplement*, with to date more than fifty contributions principally on contemporary German fiction.

Katie Jones is a research student at the University of Nottingham. She is currently writing a comparative doctoral thesis on disgust in contemporary women's writing in German and French, including works by Jenny Erpenbeck, Elfriede Jelinek, Karen Duve and Amélie Nothomb.

Teresa Ludden is Lecturer in German at the University of Newcastle upon Tyne. She has worked and published on cultural and critical theory, contemporary German literature, and New German Cinema. Her research interests include aesthetic theory, European philosophy and contemporary German literature and film.

Lucy Macnab is Literature Education Officer at the South Bank Centre, London. She has worked on corporeality in contemporary German writing by women, recently completing a Masters by Research at the University of Leeds. Her research interests include body theory, feminism and new writing.

Lyn Marven holds a Leverhulme Early Careers Fellowship at the University of Liverpool. She is the author of *Body and Narrative in Contemporary Literatures in German: Herta Müller, Libuše Moníková and Kerstin Hensel* and co-editor (with Brigid Haines) of *Libuše Moníková: In Memoriam* (German Monitor 62, 2005). She has published on contemporary literature and women's writing, and is currently working on images of Berlin in contemporary narrative.

Franziska Meyer is Senior Lecturer in German at the University of Nottingham, and author of *Avantgarde im Hinterland. Caroline Schlegel-Schelling in der DDR-Literatur* (1999). She has published on post-war women's writing , genre and gender, 18th-century epistolary friendship, cold war literary politics and the Holocaust in literature and film. She is co-editor (with Dirk Göttsche) of *Writing Against War: Ingeborg Bachmann and German-Language Literature since 1945* (2006), *Argonautenschiff. Jahrbuch der Anna-Seghers-Gesellschaft* (2004) and *Eine Kulturmetropole wird geteilt. Literarisches Leben in Berlin (West) 1945-1961* (1987). Her research interests include gender, 20th century women's writing and the city in literature.

Elisa Müller-Adams is DAAD-Lektorin for German at the University of Sheffield. She has worked on Caroline de la Motte Fouque and on the literary motif of the mermaid. Her research interests include: the public and the private in women's literature of the 19th century, gender and nationality and the so-called 'Fräuleinwunder' in German literature.

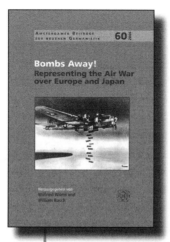